# THE PEOPLE OF ASIA

# THE PEOPLE OF ASIA

## Their History Ethnology, Manners and Customs

***With Many Illustrations***

**G.T. Bettany**

Publications

**KALPAZ PUBLICATIONS**

DELHI-110052

The People of Asia

Rs. 720

ISBN: 81-7835-



Published in 2005 in India by
Kalpaz Publications
C-30, Satyawati Nagar, Delhi-110052
E-mail : kalpaz@hotmail.com

*Laser Typesetting at* : Global Printer
*Printed at* : Salasar Imaging System

# INTRODUCTION.

BEYOND all other continents, Asia is full of varied interest to the inquiring and reflective mind. By its vast extent, its diversity of climates and physical features, its variety of population, its scattered tribes, its mighty empires and their wonderful history, its strange superstitions, its profound moral teachers, and its powerful religions, the Orient continent appeals in succession or in combination to the most far-reaching of our faculties and sympathies. Its historic records go back farther than those of any continent, unless perhaps Egyptian records may claim something like equality in this respect, and Egypt may almost be regarded as an annex of Asia. The prehistoric remains of Asia are as yet little known, but from what we already know of them early man in Asia passed through the same stages of using rough and polished stone implements for long ages as in Europe; and it may be inferred from the great age of historic records in Asia that the first men lived in Asia at an earlier period even than in Europe.

Instead of displaying the almost exclusive sway and progress of a single group of peoples, like Europe, Asia has been the theatre in which the Semite. the Aryan, and the Mongol have developed, have varied, have struggled with one another, and have thrown off branches which, as peaceful emigrants or conquering hordes, have invaded more or less all the other continents and islands. What the ancestors of the American Indians, the Polynesians, the Malays, and the Finns probably did long ages ago, the Turks, the Jews, the Arabs, the Hindus, and the Chinese are doing in various ways in our own day. The last three in particular are so prolific and hardy, that they seem capable of supplying a population for the entire globe, and their spread in many regions has excited keen hostility.

As Asia has been the cradle of peoples, so it has been the cradle of religions. In many respects the Asiatic is more religious than the European, and profoundly believes in the existence of superior and invisible powers. We are compelled to allow that nearly all great religions have arisen in Asia. Ancestor-worship and reverence for the spirits of the dead, combined with nature worship, are at the bottom of the varied developments of Confucianism, Taoism, Shintoism, Vedism, and Hinduism, while on them profound philosophers have grafted many of the most important moral teachings known to mankind. Buddhism and Zoroastrianism are extremes of divergence from primitive Aryan beliefs. It is remarkable that in Asia there have arisen the three great religions which have spread far beyond the confines of the race which gave them birth. Buddhism, a Hindu product, has made its home among such divergent people as the Japanese and the Tibetans. Christianity, at first purely Semitic, is professed by multitudes of Aryans, besides large numbers of Negroes, Polynesians, Melanesians, and a considerable number of Asiatics. Mahometanism, equally Semitic in origin, is the religion of Turks, Persians, many Negroes and North Africans, Hindus, and Malays. It is evident, therefore, that nothing is more interesting and indeed necessary for the intelligent mind than a study of Asia and its peoples.

To add to all this, there is the vast subject of extinct civilisations. Greatly as Greece and Rome predominate with many minds, it can at least be said that Nineveh and Babylon and other sites in Asia present almost as remarkable results of human skill, energy, and invention, and show that peoples who were great long before Greece and Rome have left monuments as enduring as any. The full value of these remains cannot be gathered so long as the Turk blocks the way; but what is already known makes us marvel at the engineering and architectural skill, the astronomical knowledge, and the governing power displayed by early races in Persia and Syria. Their libraries, only partially exhumed and deciphered, have afforded us history and legend of first-rate value, and have shown that a primitive record on baked clay can outlast any manuscript; whether our books will endure as long may be questioned. The historical student can never be satisfied until everything possible has been ascertained about those mighty races of bygone days.

Then, too, we find in scattered localities, as in Cambodia and Japan, remnants of races still living, who by their Aryan and Caucasian features startle the traveller, and seem to indicate that the Aryans once pervaded Asia as they have since conquered all Europe. Survivors of a still earlier time are multitudes of tribes in the hill countries of India, Further India, China, and on the inhospitable steppes of Siberia. While, on the one hand, they excite melancholy when we think of their low organisation, their superstitious beliefs, their brutish habits; on the other they may inspire us with cheerfulness when we reflect how far other portions of the human race have risen above them, and how much possibility there is for mankind. Why more people have not risen higher, why so many remain degraded, we must leave to the moral philosopher to determine if he can.

What is the future outlook for Asia, is a more practical subject for consideration. In modern times Russia has spread with marvellous energy over the whole north and much of the west of the continent, and has shown great colonising ability. With an energy and determination equal to that of British and American pioneers, her soldiers have traversed deserts and overcome obstacles which the proud and fierce natives of Turkestan and other lands deemed impregnable; her travellers have by their voyages and travels raised their country to a high rank in scientific exploration; her engineers have carried a railway from the Caspian to Bokhara and Samarcand, once sealed to all but Moslems. The British power has steadily extended throughout and beyond Hindustan, dominating Afghanistan and Beluchistan, and conquering Assam and Burmah. The French have begun to control and develop Tonkin, Cochin-China, Annam, and Cambodia. The spread of these nations and the decay of the Persian and Turkish powers suggest that at no distant date much of south-western Asia may fall under European influence, if not direct administration. Only the Arab appears to have sufficient energy, independence and resolution, aided by the nature of his domain, with its heat and frequent deserts, to successfully withstand the foreigner.

But in Eastern Asia matters are very different. Both China and Japan appear very unlikely to fall under the control of foreign powers, however much they may in time yield to foreign influence. Their old and tenacious civilisations are so firmly established in some things, that they present the utmost contrast to Europe. In others they are so far similar or superior to Europe, that they have nothing to gain by adopting Western methods. In intelligence and flexibility of power the Japanese are unlike any people who have come in contact with Europeans. They have shown a celerity in adopting new ideas only paralleled by the United States. They have plunged at once from aristocratic and monarchical rule into constitutional government, from Orientalism into the life of western Europe. Whether the pace is not too rapid to last, or whether originality will survive when imitation has done its utmost, is what may be feared as to Japan. China presents a different problem. The most rooted of all nations in ancient observances and mental attitudes, this people by its extraordinary multitude seems to defy outsiders to make an impression. The money of the outsiders however has come to be exceedingly valuable to the Chinese, and ultimately no doubt will prove to them the value of railways and telegrams. But we may expect that whatever the Chinese do will be marked by that originality of impress which stamps their language, their literature, their examination system, and their general procedure.

If Europeans will be content to regard Asiatics as fellow human beings, with a history behind them which accounts for their peculiarities, and will remember that the Asiatic has as good grounds for surveying with astonishment or scorn the special features which characterise Europeans in face, mode of thought, and conduct as they have for so regarding the Asiatic; if they will believe that they may have as much to learn from the Oriental as he from them,—the greatest benefits may flow from their intercourse. Already Europe has conferred the blessings of peace and increased numbers and wealth on vast regions of Asia, and has progressed to an appreciable extent in the path towards understanding and sympathising with Asiatic needs and feelings. Thus it is hoped that a cordial welcome may be given to this volume dealing with so large a portion of "the World's Inhabitants."

# CONTENTS.

# THE

# TEEMING MILLIONS OF THE EAST.

## CHAPTER I.

### The Early Inhabitants and History of India.

**India a museum of races—Prehistoric races—Arrival of the Aryans—The aborigines they found there—Faculties and possessions of the Aryans—Progress of the Aryans—The Aryan organisation and beliefs—Their view of a future state—Callings and castes—Influence of the priests—Rise of castes—Supremacy of the Brahmans—Code of Manu—Rights and duties defined—Adaptation to lower classes—Rise of Buddhism—Story of Gautama—Mission of Gautama—Spread of Buddhism—Asoka's council—Buddhist fluctuations—Decline of Buddhism in India—Alexander the Great and India—Alexander's retirement—Seleucus and Chandra Gupta—Megasthenes—Western influence on India—Mongolian conquerors—The Jats—First Mahometan invasion—Sultan Mahmoud—Mohammed Ghori—Allah-ud-din-Khilji—Tamerlane—Baber—Kingdom of Madura—Empire of Vijayanaga—Conquests of Baber—Reign of Akbar—Akbar's civil and religious policy—Shah Jahan—The Taj Mahal—Conquests of Aurungzebe—Rise of the Mahrattas—Nadir Shah—The Nawabs and Maharajahs.**

HINDU.

**India a museum of races.**

"INDIA," says Sir W. W. Hunter, "forms a great museum of races, in which we can study man from his lowest to his highest stages of culture." So, also, the history of India is like an epitome of history, for it has successively passed through nearly all stages, and come in contact with nearly all great conquering powers. The Russian is still held back, but who can say how near the attack may be?

**Prehistoric races.**

When we first discern anything of human life in India, we find remains of a palæolithic people in the Nerbuddah valley, where their agate knives and rough flint implements have been unearthed, together with remains of extinct species of elephant and hippopotamus. Neolithic tribes, using polished flint implements, succeeded them, destitute of all metals. Then later, approaching the historic period, there are rude stone circles, upright slabs, and mounds, all of them sepulchral, the remains in which show that the makers had iron weapons and earthenware vessels, and wore ornaments both of copper and gold. Some of the later of these burial-places have yielded Roman coins. These peoples have left no other sign of their existence; and it is impossible now to be certain to which of the now remaining aborigines of India they were related.

**Arrival of the Aryans.**

The earliest traces of India in history or literature indicate to us the arrival in India of the Aryan fair-skinned races from Central Asia, entering by the north-west. Then arose a fierce and long-continued struggle, animated by strong race-antagonism; for the new comers represented the stock which has proved itself highest throughout the world, the comparatively fair-skinned, constructive, poetic Aryans. They were proud of their finely-shaped features and fair complexion, so much so that their Sanscrit word for colour (varna) came to mean race, or caste. Their epic, the Rig Veda, terms the Indian aborigines Dasyas (enemies), and Dasas (slaves). They evidently could not endure the ugly features of their predecessors, whom they termed noseless or flat-nosed, and whom they contemned as gross feeders on flesh, raw-eaters, without gods and without rites. Yet notwithstanding such contempt, the aboriginal peoples were numerous enough and persistent enough to remain in large numbers, to mingle extensively with the conquerors,—so much so that five-sixths of the present population are of

**The aborigines they found there.**

mixed origin,—to ultimately form alliances in some cases with the Aryan invaders, and even to furnish rulers for powerful Indian kingdoms. But many of them have never put on even a superficial civilisation. They have been driven into the hills, forests, and jungles, and have successfully resisted all attempts to civilise them. They form the most interesting and varied collection of primitive races, perhaps, which can be found on the globe. But they have little part in history, and must be described after the general history of India has been reviewed.

**Faculties and possessions of the Aryans.**

The Aryans brought to India a more powerful physique, nurtured on the lofty table-lands of Central Asia, and much greater intellectual attainments than were possessed by those whom they conquered. They had many cattle, cultivated grains, were acquainted with cooking, and preferred cooked food to raw, wore clothes, which they wove and sewed themselves, and had some metals and metallic implements. The extent of their affinity to modern Europeans may be partly indicated by the fact that the important words "father," "mother," "brother," "sister," "widow," and several numerals are essentially the same in Sanscrit and in most European languages.

**Progress of the Aryans.**

The immigration of the Aryans into India was a gradual process, to be measured by centuries, long before the Christian era. They conquered, settled, and multiplied; and as their numbers or their enterprise increased, they pressed onwards, in time mastering the Punjab, the base of the Himalayas, and then extending to the Ganges valley. The Rig Veda, their ancient hymnal, in its successive portions, exhibits the stages of their settlements, from their first entry into India to their arrival, before 300 B.C., at the delta of the Ganges. By the second century A.D. they were established at the extreme south of India.

At the period of the Vedas, caste in its modern sense was unknown. The father of each family was its priest; and the chieftain was the priest of his tribe, only on special occasions calling in some one specially skilled to conduct the sacrifice. Marriage was sacred, and women were honoured; widows were not burned on their husbands' funeral piles. They believed in divinities which represented the great powers of nature, such as the Father-heaven (Dyaush-pitar), equivalent to Zeus and Jupiter; as well as Mother-earth; the Encompassing Sky (Varuna); and Indra, the aqueous vapour bringing fertilising rains; Agni, the god of fire; the storm gods, and many others. A conspicuous feature of these gods was their friendly propitious nature. The fierce gods of the later Brahmanism were unknown in the Rig Veda. The Aryans introduced cremation on the funeral pile, as their mode not merely of getting rid of a decaying body, but as accomplishing the liberation of man's immortal part from the body. "As for his unborn part," they sang, "do thou, Agni, quicken it with thy heat; let thy flame and thy brightness quicken it; convey it to the world of the righteous." In believing in the soul's immediate passage to a state of blessedness and reunion with those loved ones who had preceded it, they anticipated the widely prevalent belief and aspiration of their kin in Europe.

**The Aryan organisation and beliefs.**

**Their view of a future state.**

The Veda represents to us the Aryans as divided into numerous callings: husbandmen, carpenters, blacksmiths, coppersmiths, goldsmiths even. Cattle formed their principal wealth, and they ate beef and drank fermented liquor, offering also the same to their gods. Although skilled in the use of the plough, and already forming villages and towns rather than encampments, the taste for wandering was still on them, and impelled them to travel. As they went on conquering, they became changed from groups of loosely-connected tribes into nations under kings and priests; and the great system of caste was developed.

**Callings and castes.**

Some castes no doubt owed their origin to the priests. The great sacrifices being conducted by those specially skilled, families of such priests arose, among whom the hymns and sacrificial rites were transmitted from father to son, and they became of

**Influence of the priests.**

special importance to the tribes. "That king," says the Veda, "before whom marches the priest, he alone dwells well-established in his own house; to him the people bow down. The king who gives wealth to the priest, he will conquer; him the gods will protect." The potent prayer was termed "brahma," and he who offered it, "brahman." It is easy to understand that the brahmans magnified their office, developed their ritual, and acquired varied assistants, who, from their functions becoming stereotyped and their offices hereditary, formed castes.

**Rise of castes.**

But other castes simultaneously grew up. The superior warriors, who were Kshattriyas, "companions of the king," and have now come to be called "Rajput," or of royal descent, became markedly distinct from the husbandmen, or Vaisyas; and the two classes ceased to intermarry. But both these were far superior to the Dasas, or black slaves, whom they contemned as "once-born," whereas they themselves were "twice-born," and alone might attend the religious festivals.

**Supremacy of the Brahmans.**

As time went on, there was a remarkable struggle for supremacy between the warrior caste and the Brahmans, who claimed that only members of their families could be priests, and taught that they were divinely appointed priests from the beginning, having come forth from the mouth of God. In some tribes the Brahmans gained undisputed supremacy, especially in the land of the great river valleys of the Ganges and Jumna, and were regarded as divinely inspired; and when a king or ruler gained admission to their fraternity, they explained it as the reward of penances or as a mark of special divine favour. They developed a remarkable literature, and concentrated in their hands all religion and philosophy, with the principal arts and sciences as subsidiary spheres of activity. By their ability and skill they succeeded in elevating themselves to the positions of highest influence, and impressed their language, their religion, and their laws throughout India. That the Brahman system had in it a wonderful suitability to the people it controlled, is evident from the fact that it has lasted in various forms for three thousand years, and now exhibits no signs of speedy downfall. It has survived the assaults of Buddhism, of Greek, Mongolian, Mahometan, and British conquests, and it still supplies advisers to Hindu princes and teachers to the people.

The Brahmans early saw the importance of codes of law, and of ascribing to them a divine origin; and in the

**Code of Manu.**

code of Manu, dating from about the fifth century B.C., though portions are probably much older, and in the Yajna-Valkya, dating from the early times of Buddhism, they laid down rules to guide almost the whole of the circumstances of life. No opportunity was lost of inculcating mental cultivation on Brahmans, and of insisting on the reverence, obedience, and honour to be shown to all educated Brahmans. No slight amount of skill was evinced in the way in which the usages of the Aryans were thus gathered into fixed codes. Domestic and civil rights and duties were defined, the adminis-

**Rights and duties defined.**

tration of justice regulated, and systems of purification and penance laid down. The permissible employments of the various castes were distinctly presented, and strict rules laid down about non-intermixture of the castes, the higher being forbidden to eat, drink, or hold social intercourse with the lower, who were punished heavily for even touching those of higher caste. Yet even at this early period a vast multitude of people of mixed origin had arisen, who had to be assigned to special castes; and this has continued to the present day, when there are at least three hundred distinct castes.

While thus founded on intellectual power sanctioned by supposed divine authority, the Brahman system really

**Adaptation to lower classes.**

appealed intensely to individual prejudices and exclusiveness, while yet capable of recognising changes in time and space. The Brahman legislators believed in preserving local and tribal laws and customs. The higher castes established and preserved themselves as peoples within peoples, by obeying laws addressed to higher intelligence, while they carefully conciliated people in lower stages of civilisation.

Nevertheless Brahman exclusiveness and severity became too oppressive to retain undisputed sway; and the occurrence of able religious and social teachers in other castes than theirs was at last most conspicuously signalised in the person of the great originator of Buddhism. We can only briefly refer here to the marvellous career of Gautama, born about 560 B.C., the son of the ruler or rajah of the tribe called Sakya, in the district of Gorakhpur (Oude). At the age of twenty-nine he went into a seven years' retirement, which became known as "The great renunciation." He first studied under able Brahmans and then went into the jungle on the north of the Vindhya range, and with five companions, practised the severest asceticism for seven years. At last he learnt, as he believed, the true way to secure a pure heart, through overcoming impurity, envy, and hatred. Self-righteousness was the last enemy to be conquered, and universal charity was to crown the whole. Gautama, thus charged with truth, felt that he had become the Buddha, the Enlightened One; and he issued forth to proclaim this truth to a world largely dissatisfied with the Brahmans, and ready to be elevated. His commanding presence, noble countenance, and deep, thrilling voice were in his favour; and his earnestness gained multitudes of converts. He was able to call to his side multitudes of women, by offering to the young widow, the neglected wife, and the cast-off mistress an honourable career as nuns. We cannot detail here the resulting doctrines of Buddhism, but simply trace their general and political influence on the Indian peoples. It is well known that Buddha, after his death, in 481 B.C., was deified, and his birth was alleged to be a voluntary incarnation. The Hindus now regard him as an incarnation of Vishnu; and the Roman and Greek Churches have admitted him as a saint to their calendars. At present Buddhism is professed by one-third of the human race.

**Rise of Buddhism.**

**Story of Gautama.**

**Mission of Gautama.**

During the two hundred years following his death, Buddhism spread widely over Northern India. About 244 B.C., Asoka, king of Maghada, or Behar, adopted

Buddhism as a state religion, supported 64,000 Buddhist priests, founded many monasteries, and sent out many missionaries. He held a great council to settle the doctrines of Buddhism, and form an authoritative collection of the sacred books. Multitudes of his edicts, engraved on rocks or pillars, were spread throughout India. Thus Buddhism became a great system. Asoka was almost its second founder, and to him its greatest missions were due. Here it must suffice to say that Buddhism never entirely superseded Brahmanism in any large district of India; rather, the two existed side by side, Buddhism having the greater number of followers, for at least a thousand years. Certain kings—such as Kanishka (about A.D. 40), who reigned over North-western India and adjoining countries, from Yarkand and Khokand to Agra and Sind; Siladitya, in the seventh century, who reigned from the Punjab to North-eastern Bengal, and from the Himalayas to the Nerbudda—were especially Buddhistic; while, at times, reaction or stagnation occurred. A predominant feature of Buddhism—its spread by peaceful persuasion only—may have led to its ultimate decline in India, when we consider how Mahometanism was introduced and spread by the sword; but it is more likely that corruptions of practice and decline of faith were the causes. Yet again and again we hear of monarchs giving up their treasures and their royal garments for general distribution, by way of fulfilling the Buddhist injunctions to almsgiving. But from the seventh to the ninth centuries, Brahmanism again became predominant.

**Spread of Buddhism.**

**Asoka's council.**

**Buddhist fluctuations.**

**Decline of Buddhism in India.**

Europeans did not early learn much about India. Homer knew tin by an Indian name (Greek, *kassiteros;* Sanscrit, *kastira*); Herodotus knew something of the Indus; but the first authentic information was obtained by the learned companions of Alexander the Great (327 B.C.), and some portion of it is repeated by Strabo, Pliny, and Arrian. Alexander, it is well known, penetrated into India, reaching the Hydaspes (now the Jhelum), finding the Punjab divided

**Alexander the Great and India.**

into petty kingdoms. Porus, the most warlike of the kings, opposed him at a bend of the Jhelum, fourteen miles west of Chilianwallah, but was defeated and reduced to submission. Later, Alexander marched to the Hyphasis (now the Beas), not far from Sobraon, where he halted, finding his troops worn out and their spirits

WOMEN OF VARIOUS CASTES: MADRAS.

broken. He had to give up his idea of reaching the Ganges, and retrace his steps, having subjugated no province, although he had founded several cities, some of which, as Patala, the modern Hyderabad, the capital of Sind, remain to this day. But he left garrisons and satraps behind him; and the alliances he **Alexander's retirement.**

had made, and the rulers he had set up in various states and towns, preserved his influence; so that, from this time, the West always had influence in India

Soon after Alexander's departure, Chandra Gupta, an adventurer exiled from the Ganges valley, managed to found a kingdom in Magadha, or Behar, with its capital at Pataliputra (now Patna), and ultimately extended his sway to the North-west. Seleucus, Alexander's successor in Syria, having consolidated his power, aimed at subduing Chandra Gupta, and recovering the Punjab. But after a fruitless war, he made peace, for five hundred elephants resigning his Indian claims, and giving his daughter in marriage to Chandra Gupta, and sending an ambassador, Megasthenes, to the court of Patna (B.C. 306–298). To him we are indebted for the best account of the Indians of his time. The castes, the large number of kingdoms; the village system, with its almost republican features, producing peace and order; the valour, industry, honesty, truthfulness of the people; the chastity of the women; the absence of slavery; all these the Greek,—not hereditarily disposed to speak well of foreigners,—describes with admiration.

**Seleucus and Chandra Gupta.**

**Megasthenes.**

In succeeding centuries the Syrian and Bactrian monarchs continued to exert considerable influence upon North-western India, either sending expeditions or making treaties with local rulers. Not the least important effects were those exercised upon Indian science and the arts; Brahman astronomy and sculpture owing much to Greek teaching and examples. But, before the Christian era, a new influence was brought to bear on India from the North. The doubtful, but probably Mongolian, Scythian, began to advance southwards, and established a kingdom in the Punjab in the second century B.C. These Scythians became prominent disciples of Buddha; and their king, Kanishka, held the fourth Buddhist council, about A.D. 40; and a tradition developed that Buddha himself was of Scythian origin. He ruled from Yarkand to Agra. Numerous other Scythian conquerors

**Western influence on India.**

**Mongolian conquerors.**

are related to have arisen; and there seems to be no doubt that their influence extended down to the central provinces. It is even believed by many that the Jats, who constitute nearly one-half of the inhabitants of the Punjab, are the same as the Getas, a well-known division of the Scythians. The invaders, however, suffered numerous reverses, and were never accepted with cordiality by the Aryan or the aboriginal inhabitants. The unsettled condition of things, however, gave occasion to the aborigines in various localities to recover lost ground, and to set up again kingdoms which the Aryan invaders had destroyed. In fact, throughout vast territories, they were never displaced *en masse*, any more than the English were displaced by the Norman invaders.

**The Jats.**

Before any nations professing Christianity could influence India, the later religion of Mahometanism was destined to act most powerfully on the country. Mahomet only died in A.D. 632, and already in 664 the first Mahometan invasion of the Punjab took place. Sind was conquered in 711 by an Arab army owing allegiance to the Caliph of Damascus; but their power did not last at this time longer than 750, when the Hindus drove them out.

**First Mahometan invasion.**

Sultan Mahmoud was the first great Mahometan conqueror of India. He succeeded as ruler of Afghanistan and Khorassan, at Ghuznee, in 997; and in successive campaigns he led his armies seventeen times into the plains of India. The great battle of Peshawur rendered the Punjab a Mussulman province for nearly 800 years. In 1024, he marched into Gujerat, and plundered the celebrated temple of Siva at Somnath, himself destroying the idol. In the twelfth century, the last of his descendants was overthrown by an Afghan Mussulman leader, Allah-ud-din, whose nephew, Mohammed Ghori, was the second great Mahometan conqueror in India. He extended his sway from the Indus to the Brahmaputra, driving the Rajputs into the modern Rajputana. His viceroy, Kutab-ud-din, established himself as the first Sultan of Delhi. In 1294,

**Sultan Mahmoud.**

**Mohammed Ghori.**

Allah-ud-din Khilji, the third great Mahometan conqueror, raised himself to the throne of Delhi, and carried his conquests throughout India. He gained many victories in Rajputana, and thoroughly subdued the Deccan and Gujerat.

Allah-ud-din Khilji.

At the end of the next century, the Mongolian, or Mogul, empire—still Mahometan—was preluded by the advent of the famous invader Timor, or Tamerlane. The Afghan rulers had worn out their power by misgovernment, and Timor found India

Tamerlane.

HINDUS.

comparatively an easy conquest. Yet he did not remain, being probably too restless. It was not till 1525 that Baber, the fifth Mahometan conqueror, invaded India, and founded the Mogul empire, which endured, though only in partial vigour, till 1857.

Baber.

Referring briefly to the condition of Southern India during the Mahometan invasions of the North, we find the powerful kingdom of Pandya seated at Madura, not far from Cape Comorin, and maintaining an uninterrupted succession of sovereigns for nearly a thousand years. The numerous Dravidian

Kingdom of Madura.

peoples, speaking Tamil or allied languages, were long little troubled by Mahometan invasions. The Hindu empire of Vijayanagar held general sway over the south Deccan from the twelfth to the sixteenth centuries; but the capital city of that name was at last captured and destroyed, in 1565, by the united Mahometans of the Deccan, who had founded several kingdoms within it. Vast ruins still exist at Vijayanagar of temples, fortifications, and bridges, showing how great it once was. The Mahometan sultans of the Deccan did not acknowledge the sovereignty of the Afghan line seated at Agra and Delhi, and remained independent till conquered by Aurungzebe, in the seventeenth century.

**Empire of Vijayanagar.**

In referring to the empire of Timor, Baber, Akbar, etc., it is best to use the term Mogul,* or Moghul, by which it is so widely known, although we do not insist on the special Mongolian origin of these conquerors. Baber was born in 1482, at Farghana (Khokand), on the Jaxartes, and at the age of twelve became, by his father's death, successor to his share of Abu Said's dominions in Turkestan. At fifteen, he had already taken Samarcand, only

* The "Cyclopædia of India" (by Surgeon-General Edward Balfour), third edition, 1885, states that the term Moghul, derived from Mongol, was especially applied to the sovereigns of Delhi of the house of Timor, although they were equally at least of Turk descent, and presented in their appearance entirely Turkish characteristics. But Hindus apply this term, as also "Turk," to all Mahometans except the Afghans, whom they designate Pathans; and Moghulai is used to distinguish Mahometan laws and territories from those of the Hindus and the British. Each of the successive Emperors of Hindostan was known to Europe as the Grand Moghul; nevertheless, the father of Baber was a Chagtai Turk, who spoke and wrote in Chagtai Turki, and never alluded to the Moghuls but with contempt and aversion. His mother is said to have been a Moghul woman; but he said that the horde of Moghuls had uniformly been the authors of every kind of mischief and devastation. Moghul, in India, is at present applied to, and is indifferently used by, persons of Persian or Turk descent, though the former race assume also the title of Mirza, while the descendants of the civilians and soldiery from High Asia, whom Baber and others brought into India, have the tribal title of Beg, also that of Agha or Aga

to lose it again in one hundred days. After a most adventurous career, and many reverses, in 1504 he took Cabul; but in 1514 he had lost all his possessions but Bactria, and began to turn his attention to India, claiming the Punjab as part of the conquests of his ancestor Timor. In 1526 he totally defeated the army of the last Afghan Sultan of Agra, at Panipat, soon taking Delhi, Agra, and Gwalior. He extended his empire considerably over Northern and Central India, but died in 1530. In spite of his predominantly warlike character, Baber found time to keep a diary, and to compose many poems. He also largely occupied himself in making roads, reservoirs, and aqueducts, and paid much attention to the introduction of new fruits.

**Conquests of Baber.**

Akbar, the celebrated grandson of Baber, was born in 1542, and succeeded his father, Humayun, in 1556. His reign (1556–1605) just overlapped that of our own Queen Elizabeth. He gradually extended his dominion over the whole of North India, then into Rajputana, Orissa, and Berar, thus ruling over a larger portion of India than had ever before been ruled absolutely by one man. But Akbar's fame rests largely on his successful civil administration, by which he combined his own soldier leaders and the native Hindu princes into one nobility, and extracted a larger revenue from the land than the British do now. This was due to his adopting a graduated tax, according to the value of the land; but it is surprising that he should have been able to exact one-third of the gross produce. Akbar's favourite wife was a Rajput; another wife is said to have been a Christian. This indicates that he had learned religious toleration; and, in fact, he went so far as to doubt the truth of his Mahometan faith, and to introduce a new eclectic religion of his own, formed of the best features of the religions known to him. "In this strange faith," says Sir W. W. Hunter, "Akbar himself was the prophet, or rather, the head of the church. Every morning he worshipped the sun in public, as being the representative of the Divine Soul that animates the universe, while he was himself

**Reign of Akbar.**

**Akbar's civil and religious policy.**

INDIAN GIRLS DANCING BEFORE A MAHARAJAH.

worshipped by the ignorant multitude." He died on the 13th October, 1605, and was buried in the magnificent mausoleum he had built at Sikandra, near Agra.

Shah Jahan, grandson of Akbar, was the next notable ruler of the Mogul empire; he reigned from 1628 till 1658, when he was deposed by his son, Aurungzebe. Shah Jahan was the founder of the modern city of Delhi, where he erected the celebrated throne in the form of a peacock with a spread tail, at a cost of six millions sterling. At Agra he built the marvellous Taj Mahal, a mausoleum of white marble for his favourite wife Mahal, at which twenty thousand workmen worked for twenty years; also the Palace and the Pearl Mosque of Agra, and many other magnificent public works.

**Shah Jahan.**

**The Taj Mahal.**

Aurungzebe, who reigned from 1658 to 1707, was the first of the Mogul emperors who conquered the extreme South of India, after numerous campaigns against the Mahometan Sultans of Bijapur, which fell in 1686, and Golconda, taken in 1687. Aurungzebe's capital was at Delhi, where it remained till the fall of the empire. During his time the Mahratta confederacy first began to attain importance. They were a numerous Hindu race, of comparatively low caste, centreing about Poonah, and extending considerably along the west coast of Bombay, from Surat to Canara. Though always more or less independent, they did not become united until the seventeenth century, under Sivaji, who was of Brahman descent, and who showed a remarkable power of uniting the Mahrattas and of making head against Aurungzebe; and in the next century his successors, the Peshwas, extended their rule over the greater part of India, with governments at Gwalior, Kolapore, Nagpore, Indore, Gujerat, and Tanjore. We must only mention the invasion of Nadir Shah, from Persia, the sixth great Mahometan conqueror of India, in 1739. The Mogul army was defeated at Karnal, Delhi was sacked, and Muhammad Shah, the Mogul emperor, submitted to Nadir. After this, the governors under the

**Conquests of Aurungzebe.**

**Rise of the Mahrattas.**

**Nadir Shah.**

Moguls became more independent, and we hear more and more of the nawabs or nabobs (Mahometans), and the maharajahs (Hindus); while the Mahrattas held the western and central parts of the Deccan.

# CHAPTER II.

## The Europeans in India.

**Vasco da Gama—Portuguese conquests—Albuquerque—Invasion of the Dutch—The first Englishmen in India—First charter of the East India Company—Settlements in Surat and Bengal—Bombay ceded by Portuguese—Presidencies formed—Dark prospects in 1686–89—Resolution to gain territorial sovereignty—The French in India—Dupleix and Clive—Siege of Arcot—Vicissitudes of Pondicherry—Calcutta formed—Tragedy of the Black Hole—Battle of Plassey—Clive's conquests and reforms—Rule of Warren Hastings—First Mysore war—Cornwallis—Second Mysore war—The Marquis Wellesley—The Mahratta wars—War with the Ghoorkhas—Lord William Bentinck's governorship—Sind and Sikh wars—Second Sikh war—Introduction of railways, etc.—Hindu suspicions aroused—The Mutiny of 1857—East India Company abolished—Victoria, Empress of India.**

THE sea was the avenue through which the Europeans approached India; and the tardiness of maritime conquest long delayed their advent. Until after the voyage of Vasco da Gama, the Indies remained for Europeans a vague and exciting region of fabulous riches and wonders, although Ibn Batuta, the celebrated Arab traveller of Tangier (1304–78), had lived in Delhi eight years, and had given an account of it in his travels, which however have not been published till the present

**Vasco da Gama.**

century. Vasco da Gama landed at Calicut, on the Malabar coast, on May 20, 1498, when Afghan Mahometans were ruling at Delhi and in Bengal, when there were five independent Mahometan kingdoms in the Deccan, and the Hindu kingdom of Vijayanagar was in the height of its power.

Portuguese conquests.

The Portuguese were not slow to form ideas of a great Indian empire; and in 1500 they sent out an expedition under Cabral, the sum of whose instructions was, "to begin with preaching, and, if that failed, to proceed to the sharp determination of the sword." Cabral established factories at Calicut and Cochin; and in 1502 the King of Portugal procured from Pope Alexander II. a bull appointing him "lord of the navigation, conquests, and trade of Ethiopia, Arabia, Persia, and India." In 1509, Albuquerque became Portuguese governor in India, and seized Goa, which has ever since remained in the possession of the Portugueso. Albuquerque also took Malacca, and opened up trade with Siam and the Spice Islands; and from this period down to 1600 the Portuguese held the Indian and Oriental trade of Europe in their possession. Albuquerque endeavoured to gain the friendship of the Indian princes; but in general the bigoted Catholicism of the Portuguese, and their hatred of Mahometans, led them to behave most tyrannically and cruelly to the natives.

Albuquerque.

Invasion of the Dutch.

The Dutch, before the close of the sixteenth century, successfully invaded the Oriental supremacy of the Portuguese, and gradually expelled them from all their possessions but Goa. But the Dutch no more than the Portuguese were destined to maintain their sway; indeed, they had no higher aim than securing monopolies, especially of spices; and the English in turn supplanted them. The first Englishman apparently who visited India was Thomas Stephens, in 1579. He was a Jesuit, and his letters to his father greatly stimulated people to trade with India direct. In 1583, three English merchants—Fitch, Newberry, and Leedes—went to India overland; but the Portuguese imprisoned them. Finally, Newberry became

The first Englishmen in India.

a shopkeeper at Goa, Leedes entered the service of the Mogul emperor, and Fitch returned to England.

CASHMERE WOMAN.

Stimulated by the Dutch doubling and trebling the

price of pepper to the English, and on the 31st December, 1600, Queen Elizabeth granted a charter to the East India Company under the title, "The Governor and Company of Merchants of London trading to the East Indies." Of course the Portuguese opposed them actively; but the British were not to be daunted, and gradually established themselves in trade and influence. In 1614 an important factory was established at Surat, which became the chief British seat in Western India till Bombay was fixed upon in 1685. In 1634 the East India Company obtained from the Great Mogul permission to trade in Bengal, the Portuguese being at the same time expelled from Bengal. In 1645–6 the medical skill of Dr. Broughton, the surgeon of one of the Company's vessels, who had benefited both the Emperor Shah Jahan and the governor of Bengal, secured new concessions for the British. In 1661 Bombay was ceded by the Portuguese to the British as part of the dowry of Catharine of Braganza, queen of Charles II.; and in 1685 it became the capital of the Western Presidency, instead of Surat. Just before this, in 1681, Bengal was separated from Madras; and in 1683 Madras (Fort St. George) was formally constituted a Presidency. In 1684 Sir John Child was made Captain-General and Admiral of India, and Sir John Wyborne, Vice-Admiral and Deputy-Governor of Bombay. Thus the British Company had rapidly become developed into an important organised power. In 1686 there were many difficulties, the Company suffering much from the strife between the Mahrattas and the Mogul Emperors. Sir John Child was therefore made "Governor-general," with full power to make war or peace on behalf of the Company. So dark grew the immediate prospect that, in 1687, the Company retired from all its factories and agencies in Bengal to Madras; and in 1689 the factories at Vizagapatam and Masulipatam were seized by Mahometans, and the factors massacred.

**First charter of the East India Company.**

**Settlements in Surat and Bengal.**

**Bombay ceded by Portuguese.**

**Presidencies formed.**

**Dark prospects in 1686-9.**

Roused by these misfortunes, the Company at last saw

that its only salvation lay in establishing a territorial sovereignty in India, to give them a higher status in relation to the Mahrattas, the Mahometans, and the Hindus generally. This led ultimately to a severe contest with the French for political supremacy in India. The French had had an East India Company since 1604, and had established themselves at Pondicherry in 1672. For many years the French and English traded peacefully side by side; but in 1745 war arose in India in consequence of the concurrent European war, and under the governorship of Dupleix, the French almost drove the English out of India; but the peace of Aix-la-Chapelle, in 1748, restored to them their former possessions. Dupleix began now to be antagonised by a young opponent, the famous Clive. They took up the notable policy of favouring rival claimants to various Indian thrones, and thus gaining influence over the natives. This led to the capture of Arcot by Clive in 1751, and his subsequent heroic defence in it. For a long time, however, the French maintained great influence in the Deccan, and it was not till 1760 that Eyre Coote decisively defeated the French general, Lally, at Wandewash; the capitulation of Pondicherry followed in January, 1761. It was restored in 1763; but went through the singular fate of being thrice afterwards taken by the British, and afterwards restored, the last restoration being in 1816.

**Resolution to gain territorial sovereignty.**

**The French in India.**

**Dupleix and Clive.**

**Siege of Arcot.**

**Vicissitudes of Pondicherry.**

Meanwhile the centre of affairs had been shifting to Bengal. It was not till 1686 that the name of Calcutta was heard of, when the deputy of Aurungzebe expelled the British from the factory at Hooghly, and they made a settlement lower down the river, on a site formed by three villages, of which Kalighat (Calicut or Calcutta) was one, and Fort William was founded there in 1696. The varying fortunes of the English after this are too intricate to detail; but, in 1756, Surajah Dowlah became Nabob of Bengal, and marched on and took Calcutta,

**Calcutta founded.**

**Tragedy of the Black Hole.**

where the infamous tragedy of the Black Hole was perpetrated on June 20, 1756; and only twenty-three out of one hundred and forty-six came out alive after a night in a room only eighteen feet square, with two small barred windows.

Clive, then at Madras, promptly made for Calcutta, which he soon retook, regaining from the nabob all the Company's privileges. But, after taking the French town of Chandernagore, he was again attacked by Surajah Dowlah, whom he defeated with crushing effect, at Plassey, on June 23, 1757. Mir Jaffier, who had played traitor to his kinsman, Surajah Dowlah, was set in his place, and enormous sums extracted from him as the price. Here begins a record of deeds which were repeated for many decades, and which reflect little credit upon Anglo-Indian rulers.

**Battle of Plassey.**

In 1758 Clive was appointed first Governor of all the Company's settlements in Bengal. He successively conquered the Mogul forces, expelled the French from Masulipatam, established British influence at the court of Hyderabad, defeated the Dutch, obtained for the Company full power over the revenues of Bengal, Behar, and Orissa, and carried through a great reform of the Company's service, prohibiting the civil servants and officers from receiving presents or engaging in private trade. From this time British influence in India was predominant.

**Clive's conquests and reforms.**

Warren Hastings, in 1772, effected further reforms; and, from 1774 to 1785, was first Governor-General of India, with a Council nominated by Act of Parliament. He first employed Europeans as revenue-collectors and judges of civil courts. He engaged in long strife with the Mahrattas, and his officers conquered Gujerat and Gwalior; but the Mahrattas showed such prowess, that these possessions were restored in 1782. About the same time a great war with Hyder Ali and his son Tippoo, in the Mysore, ended, in 1784, in a mutual restitution of conquests. Lord Cornwallis (Governor-General from 1786 to 1793) first placed criminal juris-

**Rule of Warren Hastings.**

**First Mysore war.**

**Cornwallis.**

THE NIZAM OF HYDERABAD.

*From a negative kindly lent by Mr. W. Griggs, Elm House, Hanover Street, Peckham.*

diction in the hands of Europeans, and separated the offices of collector and judge. He also brought about a permanent settlement of the land taxes.

In the second Mysore war (1790–2) the British, for the first time, secured the alliance and aid of the Nizam and of the Mahrattas, and in 1792 Tippoo Sultan made peace on the hard terms of yielding one-half of his dominions, and paying three millions towards the cost of the war.

**Second Mysore war.**

After this time, and especially during the Marquis Wellesley's governorship (1798), the French were still seeking to undermine British influence with the Nizam, with the Mahrattas, and with Tippoo Sultan. Wellesley succeeded in getting the Nizam to disband his French battalion, and to take no European into his service without the consent of the English Government. In 1799 Seringapatam was stormed; and the third Mysore war ended with the partition of Tippoo's old dominions between the Nizam of Hyderabad, the Mahrattas, and the English.

**The Marquis Wellesley.**

But the Mahrattas afterwards gave much trouble, in consequence of the British insisting on their having no communication with other European powers. This led to a war with the powerful chiefs Holkar, Scindiah, and the Rajah of Nagpore. Sir Arthur Wellesley (afterwards the famous Wellington) defeated them at Assaye, and took Ahmednuggur; while General Lake won great victories further north, took Delhi and Agra, and posed as the champion of the weak Mogul emperor against the Mahratta chiefs. Again large territories were ceded to the British.

**The Mahratta wars.**

Consolidation, rather than conquest, now became the order of the day; and before long a new era opened with the sending of embassies to the Punjab, to Afghanistan, and to Persia. In 1814–15 we were at war with the Ghoorkhas, who for the last century have ruled Nepaul, being Hindu immigrants from Rajputana and Oudh. Although the hardy Ghoorkhas showed remarkable courage, they were compelled to submit to terms, and to give up their predatory expeditions. In

**War with the Ghoorkhas.**

1817–18 a third great Mahratta war arose, and after a fierce struggle entirely new relations were established with them. Their rulers consented to be feudatories of the British, and the Central Provinces, directly administered by English governors, were created. The strong fortress of Bhurtpore, in Central India, was taken by Lord Combermere in 1827, thus destroying its great reputation for impregnability.

**Lord William Bentinck's governorship.**

During the governor-generalship of Lord William Bentinck (1828–1835), much progress was made in reconciling the Indian populations to our rule. As Macaulay wrote, for the inscription on his statue in Calcutta, "He abolished cruel rites; he effaced humiliating distinctions; he gave liberty to the expression of public opinion; his constant study it was to elevate the intellectual and moral character of the nations committed to his charge." Among his great achievements were the abolition of suttee, or the immolation of widows; the suppression of thuggism, or bands of sworn assassins; and opening the Company's service to educated natives. In 1833 the East India Company's charter was renewed by the English Government for twenty years, on condition that it gave up trade, and allowed Europeans to settle freely in India.

**Sind and Sikh wars.**

From the government of Lord Auckland arose a new period of war and conquest. The Afghan wars, with their great calamities, we shall not here refer to. In 1843 came the war with the Ameers of Sind, who were defeated at Meeanee, Sind being annexed. Next came a trial of strength between the English and the Sikhs, a religious and military confederacy which, rising in the sixteenth century, had, in the eighteenth, become the rulers of the Punjab. Runjeet Sing, born in 1780, formed a powerful army, and established a kingdom at Lahore, extending to Mooltan, Peshawur, and Kashmir. On his death, in 1839, a period of turbulence followed; and the Sikh animosity against the British sepoys grew, and could only be satisfied by an invasion of British territory in 1845. No fewer than four fierce battles were fought in three weeks at Moodkee, Ferozeshah,

Aliwal, and Sobraon, the British army winning with heavy loss. Lahore surrendered, part of the Punjab was annexed, and a British garrison was left in the West. But a second Sikh war followed in 1848-9; the Sikh army was destroyed at Gujerat in 1849, and the Punjab was entirely annexed, since which it has been so completely pacified and so well governed, that it stood loyal during the Mutiny of 1857, and furnishes the most valued soldiers to the British army.

**Second Sikh war.**

Under Lord Dalhousie (1848-1856) very great progress was made in benefitting India. Railways were introduced, and the great Ganges Canal was made. Cheap postage and the electric telegraph were introduced. But numerous annexations (including Oudh and Nagpore) aroused a spirit of suspicion. The Hindu natives could not appreciate the setting aside of adoption, which was universally accepted by them on the failure of heirs to thrones.

**Hindu suspicions aroused.**

Although Oudh had long been shamefully misgoverned by the native rulers, and was annexed, in 1856, without any resistance, it is probable that this step hastened the mutiny of sepoys, which burst out in 1857 all through the Ganges valley, under a feeling of panic at the apparently approaching overthrow of all old Indian customs and powers. The wild excesses then committed rivalled the worst stories of Oriental cruelty. The British were taken by surprise, and were in many cases readily overpowered. Not to dilate on a long and sad history, the Sikhs were a tower of British strength, the Madras and Bombay native armies were staunch; Hyderabad supported the British power; but most of the rest of India, except Nepaul, supported the rebels, and a frightful war resulted. The massacre of Cawnpore, the relief of Lucknow, the capture of Delhi, will long remain graven on the memories of the British people. The Mutiny was practically suppressed in the year of its origin; but all rebels were not subdued till 1859.

**The Mutiny of 1857.**

The Mutiny was the death-blow to the East India Company, which, from 1853, only existed till Parliament should make a new settlement. In 1858 the whole administration of India was taken over by the Crown, the Governor-general's title being changed to Viceroy, and the title of Empress of India being adopted by the queen in 1877. The new government found it advisable to guarantee to the native princes their right of adoption of heirs. Since then the chief events in India have been peaceful. British rule has not been able to avert terrible famines, which, indeed, have been possibly made more severe owing to the great increase of population under our more peaceful rule; but much has been done by irrigation to avert them, and, by exceptional measures of relief, to mitigate them. The visit of the Prince of Wales, in 1875-6, stimulated loyalty to the British throne, his engaging manners rendering him very popular.

**East India Company abolished.**

**Victoria, Empress of India.**

The result of the history of India is, to establish it under British administration; twelve large provinces being directly governed, and one hundred and fifty feudatory states more or less directed by British residents. The vast population of two hundred and forty millions is composed of a great number of races, which we must now consider in detail, beginning with the less civilised.

# CHAPTER III.

## The Dravidian Peoples of India.

**Negroid tribes—The Nairs—Female succession—The Gonds—Their occupations—Their marriage customs—Language and clothing—The Todas—Toda village organisation—The Kurumbas—The Badagas—The Kotas—The Kandhs—Village organisations—The patriarch of the tribes--Kandh land system—Descent of property—Naming and marriage—Position of women—Kandh hospitality—Kandh agriculture—Drinking customs—British influence—The Oraon tribes—People of Rajmahal hills—Tamil-speaking people—Coolies—The Telugu—Telugu soldiers—The Canarese—The Malayalim—The Coorgs or Kodagas.**

DRAVIDIAN WOMAN.

WE cannot have a better guide in treating of the varied populations of India than Sir W. W. Hunter, the prince of Indian historians and statisticians, whose monumental works should be consulted by every one interested in our great Eastern empire. In his "Indian Empire," he treats in succession of the non-Aryan races, numbering about 18 millions in 1881; the pure Aryans (Brahmans and Rajputs), 21¼ millions; the mixed Hindus, 165 millions; and the Mahometans, 50 millions. These numbers include Assam and British Burmah as then constituted.

It is impossible to enumerate all the tribes to be found in various hill districts of India; a selection only can be made. In including these under the heading "Dravidian peoples," it must be understood that a very wide range is allowed to that term, and that subdivisions, or even quite distinct terms, may hereafter be shown to be necessary. We simply desire to emphasise, in this and the following chapters, the fact that non-Aryan races exist south of the Ganges in at least two main divisions, which we term for convenience Dravidian and Kolarian. The Anamali Hills of Southern Madras afford refuge to a number of these tribes, approximating to a negro or Australian type, thick lipped, small in stature, with curling hair tied in a knot behind, and having a curious marriage sign, the filing of the four front teeth of the upper jaw to a point. They call themselves "the lords of the hills," and live among great stone monuments, which may have been erected by their more numerous forefathers. They gather forest fruits and other products, and exchange them for rice and tobacco. Subordinate to them are the Mundavers and Puliars; the latter long-haired, wild-looking, living on mice and other small animals, and worshipping demons.

**Negroid tribes.**

The Nairs of the Malabar coast, to whom the royal family of Travancore belong, are at least partially non-Aryans, but follow the Hindu religion and claim to be of the Sudra caste. As in other tribes on that coast, female descent is the rule, perhaps originally owing to difficulty in tracing male descent. A man's heirs are not his own, but his sister's children, whom he regards with the affection which others give to their own. Coupled with this, is a freedom of the women totally inconsistent with European ideas. It is said that no Nair knows his father, and no father knows his son. A man's mother manages his household, and, after her death, his eldest sister takes the reins. Brothers almost always live in the same house; and family jealousies rarely occur. The Nairs are dark-complexioned, but otherwise well-favoured; often they are educated, are good accountants, and hold public offices.

**The Nairs.**

**Female succession.**

In the Central Provinces a series of tribes exists, of

whom the Gonds, a very numerous people, have made most progress. They have high cheek-bones, broad and flat noses, thick expanded lips, long shaggy hair, and little or no beard, nearly black skin, short squat figure, and much of the negro type. They are much given to drunkenness, and labour only fitfully, either hunting or growing grain. Around Nagpore and other British stations, they have entered the service of Europeans as grass-cutters. The Ojhyal division of them are bards and fowlers, and lead a wandering life; their wives tattoo the arms of Hindu women. They have seven different kinds of marriage, more or less binding. It is a regular thing for cousins to marry; but marriage does not usually take place till the pair are of full age. A betrothed youth in many districts serves an apprenticeship for his wife. Not unfrequently the girl runs off with whom she likes; but her first cousin has a right to take her from the man she has chosen. Often there is a pretended forcible abduction of a bride; and the bridegroom's foot is placed on the bride's back as a sign of her subjection. The Gonds do not appear to have any native chiefs.

**The Gonds.**

**Their occupations.**

**Their marriage customs.**

The language of the Gonds is very rudimentary, many of their words being borrowed from the Hindus; and the original language is fast disappearing. The men seldom wear more than a loin cloth, and women very little more. In some parts the women merely wear bunches of leafy twigs. Some of the wilder tribes used, till recent times, flint-pointed arrows.

**Language and clothing.**

The Todas, a Dravidian Tamil-speaking race, living in the Neilgherry hills, are not so deep-coloured as the preceding, but approach a copper colour. They are rather tall, somewhat long-headed, have hazel to brown eyes, long, well-formed nose,—generally aquiline,—rather thick lips, thick bushy beard, white, clean, regular teeth, hairy skin, and, on the whole, an attractive appearance. The women are fairly good-looking, with smooth clear skins, and of good height. They tattoo their arms, chests, and legs with dots. The Todas generally have frank and cheerful manners, are communicative,

**The Todas.**

yet watchful and shy, and somewhat indolent. They are of pastoral and not nomadic habits, and usually eat no flesh. They are distinguished for marrying strictly within the tribe, but their customs somewhat resemble those of the Nairs. The first-born child is reckoned as belonging to the eldest brother, the second to the next brother, and so on. The females, however, do not possess any property, as the Nair women do.

TODA WOMAN.

**Toda village organisation.** Each Toda village belongs to an intimately related clan; and the land is the property of the whole in common, although the cattle are private property. Disputes are decided by the priest, who affects to become possessed by the bell-god, and gives an oracular judgment in the matter. Cremation is their mode of disposing of the dead, a lock of their hair being first cut off, and one or two buffaloes being sacrificed at the same time.

The Todas have no sports or games, except something like tip-cat, and wear no weapons. It is a great reproach among them for a woman to be a widow, or childless; and chastity is very uncommon. Both men and women

TODAS.

IRULAS.

*From photographs kindly lent by* DR. BEDDOE, F.R.S.

wear nothing but a kind of cotton toga, or mantle, which is thrown across the right shoulder, passing over the left arm and trunk, and descending to the knee.

Subordinate to the Todas are the Kurumbas, Kotas, Badagas, and Irulas. The Kurumbas are a short, wild-looking tribe, with matted hair, slight whiskers, prominent teeth, thick lips, and general uncouth aspect. They are a sort of mountaineers, most agile in climbing. Their agriculture is very rudimentary, and their possessions are very limited. Yet, strange to say, the Badagas, who are a more numerous and settled tribe of agriculturists, are in a peculiar state of dependence on them, for every important thing they do requires the presence of a Kurumba, who performs the office of a priest, and many other functions. He must sow the first handful of seed, and gather the first sheaves, which he does with an abundance of ceremonial. He is the important functionary at marriages and funerals, and plays the part of a witch-doctor to drive off the fiends of the night. He is the musician at Badaga feasts, playing on the flute or the tom-tom. Of course adequate payments are made for these important services. Yet so great is the superstition with which the Kurumbas are regarded, that no Badaga would think of encountering one alone.

**The Kurumbas.**

**The Badagas.**

The Kotas, or Kotar, again, are a menial tribe, who perform all the lowest offices for the Todas and Badagas. They are very industrious, and have considerable skill in handicrafts. Yet they are extremely filthy in person, and devour putrefying carcases with glee. Drinking and opium-eating are prevalent among them.

**The Kotas.**

The Kandhs, or Khonds, of Orissa, are now a class of landless day-labourers in the plains; but in the hill country, between the Mahanudy and Godavery, they retain a tribal organisation, and a system of land law and religion of their own. Physically, they are of a very good type, fitted to undergo the severest exertion and privation. In colour they are light to dark copper-coloured; the cheek-bones high, the nose

**The Kandhs.**

broad at the point, the lips full and not thick, the whole physiognomy indicating intelligence, determination, and good humour. In many respects they have a high character, connected with the fierceness of the struggles they long maintained against the Aryan invaders. On first contact with the British, they showed a remarkable spirit of independence and love of savage freedom. A Kandh captured by our troops immediately tore his tongue out by the roots, thus killing himself; another, who had been made prisoner after a brave struggle, refused all food, and died on the fourth day.

**Village organisations.**

**The patriarch of the tribes.**

The Kandhs are remarkably devoted both to chiefs and to family. They look upon the tribe as proceeding from a common father, and governed by his representative, a sort of patriarch. Every branch of the tribe has its head; and each family is governed absolutely by the father, the sons possessing no property during the father's lifetime. Each village has an assembly of village elders chosen from the heads of houses, each tribe an assembly of patriarchs, and the whole of the federal tribes have a council of tribal patriarchs. The patriarch, or head of the tribes, is elected from one hereditary family, the fittest member being chosen. Though venerated and obeyed, he receives no pay, keeps no state, has no special residence, no assigned or extra property. He always consults the patriarchs of tribes on business; but he leads in war. "At home," says Macpherson, "he is the protector of public order, and the arbiter of private wrongs; conciliating feuds and dispensing justice, but depending for obedience to his decisions entirely upon his personal influence and the authority of his assessors." As regarded the outer world, they had till lately no intercourse but hostility. Murder was the duty of male relatives in certain cases of private injury, although money compensation was also accepted; but no payment could atone in cases of adultery. Stealing was leniently dealt with, if it was a first offence; a second was punished by expulsion from the tribe. The first occupier had the right to the soil, and no system of landlordism existed. When a piece of land appears to be getting exhausted, they choose a new settlement. In 1841 not an eighth part of the Kandh territory was appropriated by individuals. Sale could be effected by public offer, and handing over possession before witnesses; but in case of disputes about land, a council of elders sits and gives its decisions, after hearing both parties and their witnesses. Judicial ordeal, however, is also practised, it being believed, for instance, that rice steeped in the blood of a sheep killed in the name of the earth-god, will, if

**Kandh land system.**

KOTAS.

swallowed by the litigants, kill the perjured one on the spot. Oaths to purge an accused person are taken upon the skin of a tiger, which would certainly cause the destruction of the false swearer. If a tiger kills, or even wounds, a Kandh, his whole family becomes outcast; but the priest can restore them by taking away all the property in the man's house. When an oath is taken upon a leopard's skin, the perjured party is believed to suffer the penalty of scaliness. Other favourite ordeals are boiling water, hot oil, and heated iron. No court fees are paid, but the loser has to entertain the members of the council with rice, flesh, and liquor.

Property descends only in the male line; on failure of sons, agricultural property goes to a father's brother, while daughters only have a right to home personal effects and money, with a maintenance from their brothers while they remain unmarried, and the expenses of their marriage. When male heirs to a family fail, the land goes to the village, and is shared among the families.

**Descent of property.**

KANDH WOMAN.

"These people," says Macpherson, "have the easy bearing of men unconscious of inferiority, and rarely employ expressions of courtesy. In salutation they raise the hand perpendicularly above the head; in meeting on the road, the younger person says, 'I am on my way'; the elder replies, 'Go on.' Their most common boasts are: that they reverence their fathers and mothers; that they are men of one word; and that the Kandhs are one as a race, while the Hindus are endlessly subdivided."

Priests select names for Kandh infants by dropping rice-grains into water, mentioning, as each grain falls, the name of one of the family ancestors. According to the motions of each grain he is able to declare which of the various ancestors has reappeared in the infant, and name it accordingly. Marriage is forbidden between kinsmen or persons of the same tribe; and even when there is war between rival tribes, they suspend conflict to celebrate wedding feasts. The Kandh girl is married at about fifteen, while the boy husband may be only ten or twelve. A price is paid by the bridegroom's father for the girl, and she remains in his house till the young bridegroom sets up housekeeping for himself. The form of the wedding is an abduction in the middle of the feast, and evidently is a survival from a time when capture was the accepted mode of obtaining a wife.

**Naming and marriage.**

The wife occupies a considerable position in a Kandh's household; she does not become his property, and, if childless, can at any time quit her husband and return to her own family. There is very little unfaithfulness among these primitive people; and the wives are useful both at home and in the field. Cremation is the mode of disposing of the dead.

**Position of women.**

Kandh hospitality is extreme. "For the safety of a guest," says a Kandh proverb, "life and honour are pledged; he is to be considered before a child." "Every stranger is an invited guest"; and a guest can never be turned away. Hospitality is extended to fugitives from the battle-field, and even to escaped criminals. If a man makes his way into his enemy's house, he is allowed the benefit of refuge, even though his life is forfeited by the law of blood-revenge.

**Kandh hospitality.**

Agriculture and war are the only two professions the Kandhs respect; and only a few groups of hereditary craftsmen are hangers-on to their villages, doing the miscellaneous work which the Kandhs cannot do without degradation. None of them can hold land or rise to an equality with the Kandhs; and they are probably descendants of races long ago conquered by them. "Thirty years ago," wrote Sir W. W. Hunter, in 1872, "a true Kandh husbandman knew

**Kandh agriculture.**

nothing about money, and detested trade of every sort. Even the primitive shell currency had not reached his village; and, instead of a metal coinage, he reckoned the value of articles in 'lives.' As these lives might be either sheep or oxen, or even inanimate articles—such

KANDH HUMAN SACRIFICE.

as rice or peas—any traffic, except by actual barter, involved very complicated calculations."

Drunkenness is the one serious vice of the male Kandhs. "No event in his life, no public ceremony in his village, is complete without intoxication." **Drinking customs.** We cannot here detail their religious practices; but their human sacrifices, now happily abolished, must be briefly referred to. It was their belief that the earth-god, which they worshipped, demanded at seed-time and harvest, and on occasions of special calamity, a human sacrifice, which must be bought with a price. The sacrifice must be neither of Brahman nor Kandh race, but was kidnapped from the lower races in the plains, and often kept in reserve and well fed till the day of sacrifice. These rites have been abolished under British rule.

Moreover, by taking the place of their ancient feudal suzerain, the Hindu rajah of Gumsar, the British have taken the Kandhs into their own hands in a peculiar way, and have succeeded in converting isolated and mutually hostile tribes into a prosperous and peaceful people. Neither rents nor revenues are exacted from them; and we keep order by means of a special agent, who stops blood-feuds and adjusts dangerous disputes with the aid of a special force of police.

**British influence.**

TAMIL WOMAN; MADRAS.

The Oraon are a group of tribes in Chota Nagpore, closely in contact with the Kolarians elsewhere mentioned, but not intermarrying, and showing marked distinctions of language, features, and habits from them. The Oraon language is harsh and guttural, having much connection with Tamil. Those living in isolated positions are generally very dark and ill-favoured, approaching black. Their mouths are wide, with thick lips, high cheek-bones, nostrils wide apart, and low foreheads. They often approach a negro type, and show a negro-like gaiety. Like the Mundah Kol, they are very fond of dancing, and have special festivals in which dancing and music play a prominent part. They marry out of their own tribe, though within their own people.

**The Oraon tribes.**

Besides their small family huts, in each village there is a home for boys and young men, and sometimes another for the young girls, with an elder woman to look after them. Marriage is an imitation of capture. In many respects their habits are very interesting, but we have not space to detail them.

The people of the Rajmahal Hills, or Malé, closely resemble the Oraon, and contrast markedly with their neighbours the Santals, being better looking, though with the thick lips, flat faces, and small eyes of the Oraon. They are less cheerful and industrious than the Santals, and not devoted to dancing like the Mundah Kol. They are quiet cultivators of the hills, living in houses of wattled bamboo, a long bamboo being fixed in the ground in front of the house to guard against evil spirits. Some of them eat the carcases of diseased animals, while other tribes abstain from those which die a natural death, and from cow's flesh, and will only eat food cooked by themselves. They believe firmly in the transmigration of souls, and have their own set of deities, with priests and priestesses. They bury their dead, excepting the priests, who are carried when dead into the forest, covered with leaves and branches, and left there. Their language abounds in Telugu and Tamil words, though it has adopted many words of Kolarian origin from neighbouring tribes.

**People of Rajmahal Hills.**

The Tamil-speaking people themselves might furnish material for a volume; but they have so largely adopted Brahmanism and Hinduism, and intermixed with other races, that they may be best regarded as part of the common Indian people, local differences being here and there alluded to. The Tamil people are for the most part dark-coloured and short of stature, energetic, fiery, and quarrelsome. Some have described them as at once the least scrupulous and the least superstitious of the Indian races. They are ever ready to migrate wherever money is to be made, or "wherever a more apathetic or a more aristocratic people is waiting to be pushed aside." In the entire Deccan and Mysore, in Ceylon, in Singapore, Further India, and

**Tamil-speaking people.**

other places, the coolies, or hired labourers, are Tamil-speakers; and they now swarm to the Mauritius and the West Indies. They are variously estimated at from thirteen to twenty millions.

**Coolies.**

The Telugu-speaking people of South India are partly subjects of the Nizam of Hyderabad, and partly under direct British rule, beginning north of Madras, and extending north-west to Bellary, where Telugu meets Canarese, and north-east to Vizagapatam. In early times Telugu appears to have been spoken as far northward as the mouths of the Ganges. It was formerly termed Gentoo by Europeans, from a Portuguese word meaning heathen, or Gentile. The Telugu people are taller and fairer than the Tamil, and as bold and energetic as, though less restless than, the latter. Tamil and Telugu roots are mostly the same at bottom; but the lapse of time and dialectic changes have so modified both, that they differ from each other, much as Spanish from Portuguese or Irish from Welsh.

**The Telugu.**

CANARESE WOMAN: MANGALORE.

The Telugu people are mostly good farmers. They have supplied the British with many good infantry soldiers. Many are seafaring, and formerly possessed large islands in the Eastern archipelago. Their country is less thickly populated than the Tamil or Bengali countries; and this is partly due to the extent to which they have been oppressed by enemies and overrun by robbers. Their land has few large towns or temples, but rather abounds in forts and tracts of waste land. Caste is not observed among them to anything like the extent observable in other parts of India. Religiously, they take to Brahmanism, rather than Hinduism. Slavery is unknown among them, and they are very submissive to lawful authority. "They will evade, cheat, run away, appeal—anything but resist." Their numbers are stated at seventeen millions.

**Telugu soldiers.**

NATIVE OF COORG.

The Canarese-speakers are the next great division of the Dravidians, numbering between nine and ten millions. They are included in the Nizam's dominions, in Mysore, and under direct British rule. They are perhaps as purely a Dravidian race as can be found. They profess, for the most part, the Lingaet or Jangama form of Hinduism, and do not recognise castes, reverence Brahmans, nor acknowledge the Vedas. They are strictly vegetarian by creed, and will not even bring a living creature for sale to a member of a flesh-eating people. In other ways the Lingaet are most exclusive, and very few of them have entered the British armies. Consequent on their habits and quiescent nature, they have been continually overrun and subjugated by other powers.

**The Canarese.**

The Malayalim or Malealam language is spoken by about five millions of people of mixed race in South-west India, from the river Chandragiri to Cape Comorin; but Tamil is also spoken by 17 per cent. of these. The Nairs are the most prominent tribe among them, but a multitude of others are found in this region, including Semites and Aryans. Malayalim was separated from Tamil before the latter became refined and elevated. The Moplah are descendants of Arabs and Indian women, and are active and enterprising, and possess much landed property.

**The Malayalim.**

The Coorgs, or Kodagas, are among the most interesting of these Dravidian peoples. They occupy a small mountainous principality on the south-west of Mysore, and number less than 200,000, including subject and associated tribes. In 1837 a rebellion took place in the adjoining British Canarese territory; and the Coorgs took up arms and put down the rebellion, and recovered for us the treasure carried off. The Governor-general ordered the treasure to be divided among the Coorgs; but they refused to take it, declaring that they had not fought for loot. This led to a very liberal treatment of them by the British; and they are now among our best subjects.

**The Coorgs, or Kodagas.**

# CHAPTER IV.

## The Kolarian Peoples of India.

**Origin of the Kolarians—The Santals of Bengal—Character of the Santals—Habits of the Santals—Village system—Position of women—Expeditions for hunting and plunder—British influence—Santal rebellion—Second rebellion—Santal religion—The Bhils—Hostility to the Mahrattas—Physical characters—Clothing and caste—Ceremonies and oaths—Settlement of disputes—Character of Bhils—Bhil weapons—Occupations—The Juangs of Orissa—Their low condition—The Kol tribes—The Larka Kol.**

INDIAN EAR-ORNAMENTS.

**Origin of the Kolarians.**

THE group of peoples termed Kolarian must be clearly distinguished from the Dravidian group. Although both have an agglutinative type of language, they are radically distinct from each other, and are spoken by races of distinct origin, though both non-Aryans. We can say no more to determine the origin and relationship of the Kolarians. They may represent some of the earliest of all human peoples, or a later stage of their advance, of which we appear to have specimens in Europe in the Basques and the Lapps. But it certainly is true that the Kolarians neither resemble the Chinese nor the Malays.

Among the Kolarians the Santals of Bengal merit a prominent place. The Santal skull and face are rather round; but his lower jaw is not heavy, nor his lip much thicker than that of the Aryan; the body is more squarely built, hardy, and robust than that of the Hindu. They are certainly not good-looking. They inhabit the whole western frontier of Lower Bengal, from within a few miles of the coast to the hills of Bhagalpore, and number from a million and a half to two millions. They have no definite tradition of their origin; but they have a tradition of the creation and of a deluge, or a subsidence of waters, somewhat mixed up. But several features of this tradition point to the Himalayas as the district from which they migrated to Bengal.

**The Santals of Bengal.**

SANTAL (BENGAL).

"They have neither the sullen disposition nor the unconquerable laziness of the very old hill-tribes of Central India" (Hunter, *Annals of Rural Bengal*, 1868); "they have carried with them from the plains a love of order, a genial humanity, with a certain degree of civilisation and agricultural habits. Their very vices are the vices of an oppressed and a driven-out people, who have lapsed from a higher state, rather than those of savages who have never known better things."

**Character of the Santals.**

Near the sea, the Santals appear as an agricultural

people; in the mountain jungles they are fishers and hunters; in the highlands they breed buffaloes, cultivate a little Indian corn, and lead a semi-agricultural life. Santal hunting is conducted largely with bow and arrows, the bow made of very strong bamboo. They attain a surprising skill in its use against birds, as well as tigers and leopards; but against these latter they value guns if they can get them.

The Santal owes nothing of his husbandry to the Aryan. He has several kinds of grain not cultivated by the Hindus, although rice is his staple crop; but his system of cultivation, his implements, and his vocabulary of husbandry are peculiar to himself. His disposition is a truly happy one; he is as hospitable as the Kandh, and seizes every occasion for a feast. His form of salutation is to raise his hands gravely to his forehead, and then stretch them out towards the stranger, till the palms touch each other. Unlike the Hindu, he makes no attempt to profit pecuniarily by strangers; and in sales, names the true price at once.

**Habits of the Santals.**

Every Santal village is conducted on a purely patriarchal system. The head man for the time being is supposed to be a descendant of the original founder of the village; and every order he gives is undisputedly obeyed. A deputy looks after details, special officers look after the children, and there is a watchman for each village.

**Village system.**

Santal women are well treated, being allowed to join in festivals; but the man finishes his meal before his wife may begin. She does not shrink from speaking to strangers, like Hindu women, but joins in showing them hospitality. The Santals live as much apart as possible from the Hindus, and only tolerate necessary workmen among them, such as blacksmiths or basket-weavers.

**Position of women.**

Until the close of the last century the Santals were accustomed, after harvest was over, to descend to the plains *en masse*, combining hunting in the forests with plunder in the open country. The devastations of tigers and elephants combined with those of the Santals to render more and more of the country waste.

**Expeditions for hunting and plunder.**

As soon as the British, in 1790, undertook the task of restoring order, the re-settlement of the district began; and since then the population of all the districts has more than doubled, and in those more directly under British administration has increased manyfold. The Santals were hired to rid the lowland forests of wild beasts; and finding that their profits were much greater than in the old freebooting days, they gradually accepted regular agricultural employment during the cold season, and became the day-labourers of Lower Bengal. As Sir W. W. Hunter remarks, "The same tribes that had turned cultivated fields into a waste during Mussulman times, were destined to bring back the waste into cultivated fields under English rule."

LOW-CASTE WOMAN WITH WATER BOTTLE.

**British influence.**

An enlargement of territory granted to them in the hill country to the north of them, enabled them in less than twenty-five years to found 1,500 new townships. Unfortunately the grasping Hindu money-lenders and tradesmen appeared among them, cheated them in every direction, and got them so completely into their power, that an insurrection broke out in 1855 against the British Government, which afforded sanction to such oppression. Unfortunately the British power was not then represented by skilled students of the people, and a much too small staff were in command; thus very serious measures had ultimately to be taken before the insurrection could be quelled. Then all was changed, a more effective administration established, and the people were soon as contented as ever. In fact, some said the Government had granted all that the rebels had asked for; a concession which many other governments might with justice and wisdom have made.

**Santal rebellion.**

INDIAN STREET DANCER.

In 1881, however, the Santals again became disturbed, one Bhagrit Mangi having, in 1875, given out that he was commissioned by Heaven to deliver the Santals from British rule. He acquired great influence, and was accorded both royal and divine honours. Although ultimately captured and imprisoned, his religion spread, and his disciples came near to raising an insurrection in 1881.

**Second rebellion.**

We cannot refer in detail to the Santal religion, which is one of fear and deprecation. They have no idea of a beneficent God, but propitiate multitudes of demons and evil spirits by many complex rites. They have both family, tribal, and national spirits, the latter being "the great mountain," who is invoked with bloody offerings, formerly human. In many respects

**Santal religion.**

this god resembles the Siva of the Hindus, who resort in large numbers to his temple in the hills of Beerbhoom.

The Bhils, or Bheels, are an equally important tribe on the western side of the peninsula, in the Vindhya, Satpura, and Satmala Hills. They formerly held much wider territories, but were driven to the hills by the Aryan invaders. A strange relic of their former predominance appears in the fact that the chief in many Rajput States, on succeeding to power, must have his brow marked by blood from the thumb or the toe of a Bhil. They were in great hostility to the Mahrattas, who flogged, tortured, and hanged any Bhil they caught, multilated their women, and cruelly killed their children. Being more restless and violent in disposition than the Santals, they were skilful hunters, and could readily support themselves in a marauding life. Both the Rajputs and the British at first failed to subdue them, until the British won over some of the Bhils to aid them, and many Bhils settled down peacefully. But many still remain troublesome, and likely to resume plunder when any excitement arises.

**The Bhils.**

**Hostility to the Mahrattas.**

When living a wild life, the Bhils are slight, spare, short, and wretched-looking; but under civilisation they soon come to resemble the Hindus in size and plumpness. The wild woodsmen of the Satpuras are dark, short, and well-made, active and hardy, with high cheek-bones, wide nostrils, and in some cases, coarse Negroid features; but their hair is not at all woolly, though thick and dishevelled.

**Physical characters.**

The hill Bhils have seldom any clothing but a strip of cotton cloth round their loins; the women, however, wear a coarse tattered robe. The lowland Bhils wear a turban, coat, and waist-cloth; and the women a robe: both men and women wear brass or silver earrings and anklets. In many respects they have become assimilated to the Hindus, and adopt caste fashions, and are particular as to what they eat; whereas the Bhils of the hills, when they cannot get grain, feed on wild

**Clothing and caste.**

roots and fruits, vermin, and animals that have died a natural death.

According to Lieut. Mildmay, there are some oaths and ceremonies which no Bhil will venture to break. One is, swearing by the dog; another is, by the *joar* grain; a third is, by placing his hand on the head of his son. In many instances, when these oaths are sworn, a written document is given, by which the person swearing agrees that, in case of any extraordinary injury happening to himself or his family within a certain time, he will consent to be considered guilty. They believe strongly in witchcraft and in the power of witch-finders, who exhibit the usual cunning of their kind. Witches are tried by ordeals from which few can escape.

**Ceremonies and oaths.**

Disputes are often settled among the Bhils by joint assemblies of the villages concerned. When the question is settled, or sentence is passed, one party pours a quantity of spirits into the hand of his opponent, who, after praying that if he ever again quarrels on the point now settled, the curse of the deity Mata, or small-pox, may fall upon him, drinks it off; the other party then goes through the same ceremony.

**Settlement of disputes.**

Bhils are generally very abstemious as to food, but immoderately fond of drink and tobacco. They are kind and affectionate parents, and very faithful to their chiefs. Their word can usually be thoroughly depended upon. Marriage is usually by purchase, and polygamy is allowed. Brahmans usually officiate at their weddings. Heavy compensation is exacted from seducers; and they are very suspicious of their wives. The Bhils bury boys and virgins, and those who have died of small-pox; but all others are burnt. The bones or ashes from the pile are scattered in one or other of the sacred rivers. Their worship is modified Hinduism.

**Character of Bhils.**

All the Bhil chiefs of the Vindhya mountains belong to the Bhilala, a cross between Bhil and Rajput; they keep strictly to their own caste, not intermarrying with the Bhils.

Besides guns and swords, which the well-to-do possess, the Bhils use principally bows and arrows; the bow being of bamboo, the arrow a reed tipped with an iron spike. The fine for murder is 240 rupees; and until this is paid, a blood feud is carried on between the relatives of the murderer and his victim. Plundering expeditions are now comparatively rare, and the Bhils live by cultivating Indian corn, keeping cattle, and manufacturing baskets, screens, and winnowing fans out of bamboos. Their agriculture is very

Bhil weapons.

Occupations.

TELUGU WOMEN POUNDING GRAIN.

primitive, the ground around the hut being simply scratched, and the seed thrown broadcast. Irrigation is not attempted by them.

The Juangs of Orissa.

The Juangs are a tribe speaking a Kolarian language, living in Orissa to the number of ten thousand; and the women till lately wore nothing but leaves as clothing. They neither possess nor till land, but live by hunting deer, hogs, etc., even eating snakes, though not eating cattle. They are small in stature, and physically weak. They have flat noses and wide nostrils. Instead of wearing blankets at night, the women sleep between two fires. They have a very mixed primitive religion, with nameless spirits of the wood and mountains, to which they make offerings. They bury their dead.

Till foreigners came among them, these people had no knowledge of metals, nor any words signifying metals. Flint weapons are still used by them abundantly. Their huts are among the smallest constructed by any tribe, measuring only six feet by eight, into which the head of the family and all the women crowd. The boys and young men of the village live in a building apart.

**Their low condition.**

These may serve as types of the Kolarians, who number in all perhaps three millions, being scattered in the hills of the northern Deccan and Central Provinces, especially Chota Nagpore. Amongst the tribes properly named Kol, man and wife eat together, contrasting with numerous other Indian tribes. The Kol and the Mundah tribes are passionately fond of dancing, and sing well, and have a great variety of simple melodies. These especially come into play in the great national festivals and fairs.

**The Kol tribes.**

The Larka Kol preserve a sort of savage independence. The Mundah call themselves Ho, though generally known as Kol. They, like the Santals, are the reverse of good-looking, approaching to a Hottentot type. Some have very high cheek-bones, small orbits, flat faces without much beard or whisker, and they vary in colour from brown to tawny-yellow. Much yet remains to be discovered respecting the past history and true relationship of these interesting peoples.

**The Larka Kol.**

# CHAPTER V.

## The Inhabitants of Ceylon, etc.

**Early history of Ceylon—Hinduism and Buddhism—Portuguese and Dutch conquests—The British take Colombo—The king of Kandy dispossessed—The Singhalese—Tamil-speaking people—Arabs—Buddhist worship—Agriculture—The Kandians—Roman Catholics—Various occupations—The Weddas of Ceylon — Physical characters — Intellectual state of Weddas—Primitive high morality—Language—The Andaman and Nicobar Islanders.**

STATUE OF BUDDHA.

THOUGH practically a portion of India, only separated by shallow channels and ridges, Ceylon has a separate government and history, which must gain for it a separate chapter. It is about one-sixth smaller than Ireland, but has not half its population. Little is known for certain of its early history; but it was known, at least by name, to the Greeks and Romans; and the Hindu epic, the Ramayana, relates its partial conquest by Rama. In B.C. 543, an Indian

**Early history of Ceylon.**

prince, Vijaya, is said to have established himself as sole ruler of Ceylon and introduced caste. Hinduism in a very pure form was set up; and by wise rule Ceylon became comparatively highly **Hinduism and Buddhism.**

SINGHALESE WOMEN.

civilised. Asoka, in B.C. 307, sent a mission thither to establish Buddhism. From this time for many centuries Ceylon was subject to incursions from the natives of the Malabar coast of India, who conquered various portions of it.

The modern history of Ceylon begins in 1505, when the Portuguese adventurer, Almeida, landed at Colombo. The Portuguese established a factory there in 1517, and during all that century strengthened their hold and displaced their wonted fanaticism and cruelty. The natives sought the aid of the Dutch in 1602; and after a succession of victories over the Portuguese, they at last drove them out of the island in 1658.

**Portuguese and Dutch conquests.**

The Dutch showed both enterprise and commercial wisdom, greatly increased the Singhalese trade, undertook public works, and developed education. But they in their turn were fated to give way before the greater British power. After various partial enterprises, Colombo and all the Dutch possessions in Ceylon were taken by the British in 1796, and placed under the East India Company. In 1802 all the seaboard of Ceylon was allotted to the British Crown by the treaty of Amiens; but the centre of the island remained under the king of Kandy, the last of the Malabar line. His cruelty and tyranny, however, invited conquest; and in 1815 the British, at the request of many natives, dispossessed him and took possession of his kingdom. Since then, with the exception of some minor attempts at revolt, Ceylon has remained a crown colony of Great Britain.

**The British take Colombo.**

**The King of Kandy dispossessed.**

The great majority of the Singhalese are of Aryan Hindu descent, and speak Singhalese, a language allied to Pali, the language of the Buddhist scriptures. These live largely in the South, while the North and East is inhabited to a considerable extent by Tamil-speaking people, mainly of Dravidian descent, including many immigrants from Southern India, and also some of Arab descent. The inhabitants generally are not tall, but of good proportions, light to dark-brown, dark-eyed, and black-haired. A large number of the people of Arab or Malay descent are Mahometans, although not very fanatical; but the Tamils are Hindus in religion. The Singhalese generally are Buddhists. re-

**The Singhalese.**

**Tamil-speaking people.**

**Arabs.**

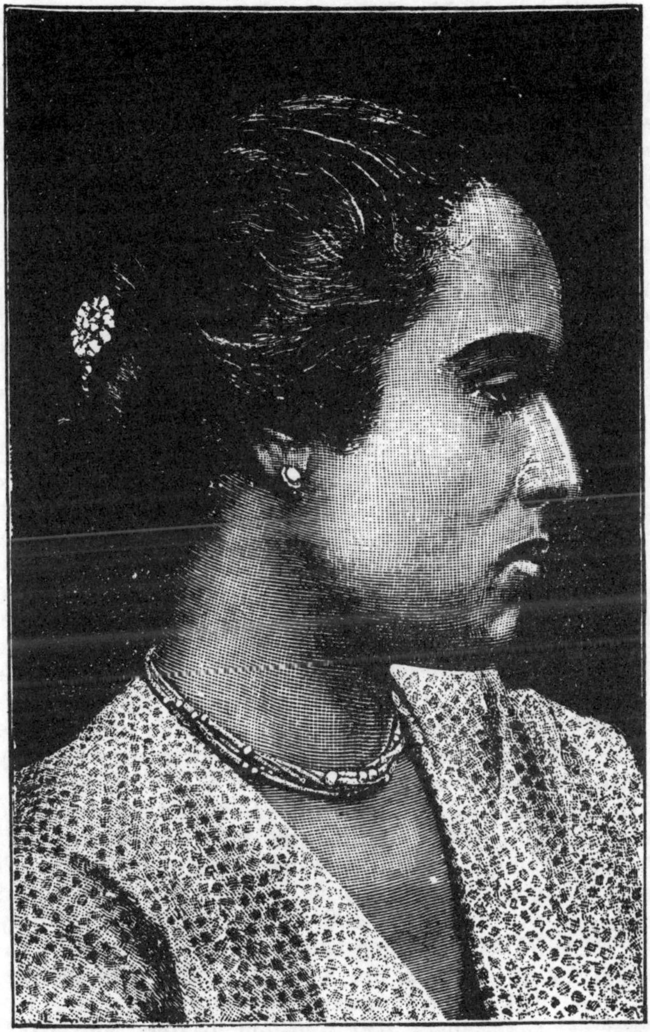

SINGHALESE LADY.

presenting a highly developed form of it. It must be acknowledged that nowhere is a pure Buddhism better practised than in Ceylon, and it leads to a very favourable moral state. Caste is not maintained with great rigour; but it retains its position as socially convenient, all classes being eligible to the priesthood, though not intermarrying. Agriculture, carried on in a very primitive manner, is the main pursuit; but lately European enterprise has been endeavouring to make improvements, and large crops of tea are now raised, while coffee has greatly degenerated, owing to disease. Of course rice, so necessary as a native food, forms a very large portion of the crops. On the coast, fishing is a considerable pursuit; and many natives engage in manufactures of decorated fabrics, and gold, silver, and lacquered ware.

**Buddhist worship.**

**Agriculture.**

The Kandians of the hill country form a vigorous branch of the Singhalese, somewhat peculiar in their customs, and till lately isolated from the rest. Among them polyandry is prevalent, a woman being the common wife of all the brothers of a family, the eldest brother being called the father of the children. And strangely enough, the first husband can introduce others, not brothers, to share in his home. In Kandy, in the Beena marriage, the husband went to reside in the wife's house, and could be dismissed summarily by the wife's family. In the Deega marriage, the wife goes to live in her husband's house, and cannot be divorced unless by her husband's consent.

**The Kandians.**

It is worthy of note that the Roman Catholics have acquired and kept a considerable hold on the people of Ceylon, having started their work early in the sixteenth century, under the Portuguese. Their adherents are said to number 220,000, while Protestants are only 50,000. Among the classes of occupations revealed by the census, are such as 1,532 devil-dancers, 121 snake-charmers, 240 astrologers and fortune-tellers, 640 tom-tom beaters, and 5,000 fakirs and devotee-beggars.

**Roman Catholics.**

**Various occupations.**

The Weddas of Ceylon, though few in number, are a

most interesting people. Being distinctly non-Aryans, they speak an Aryan language; and a portion of them,—

WEDDA.

the Jungle Weddas,—retain a most primitive mode of life in a vast extent of forest. The latter are now reduced in number below 400. The Village Weddas are more numerous, and have been led to cultivate land and build houses. The Jungle Weddas, on the contrary, live entirely in the open air, sheltering during storms under rocks or in trees. Their food is very limited, though they have hunting dogs. They drink nothing but water, and do not use tobacco. Their height is small, seldom reaching five feet four, and sometimes as low as four feet one inch; but their arms are very strong, due to their great use of the bow. They do not show any monkey-like tendency to climbing, though living in the forest; and they exhibit no special hairiness of body. Besides bows and arrows, their only implement is a small axe.

**The Weddas of Ceylon.**

Physically, they appear very distinct from the Singhalese, being marked by flat noses and rather thick lips, with somewhat short thumbs and sharp elbows and coarse long hair. They never wash, believing that would make them weak, and wear but little clothing, not caring for bright colours, and indeed having no words to express differences of colour. Their voice is excessively loud and fierce; and they look extremely unhappy, and never laugh. Indeed, the sight of a person laughing excites their disgust. Being asked whether they ever laughed, they said, "No; why should we? What is there to laugh at?" Yet they are quite capable of tender feelings, and even of tears.

**Physical characters.**

In intellectual capacity the Weddas are very low. They cannot count, or understand the meaning of counting; they do not even use their fingers to express number. Their memory is very bad; and it is literally correct to say, they cannot put two and two together. The Jungle Weddas have no deities nor form of worship. They have the notion that after death they become yakko, or devils. They bury their dead in a skin, males alone being present. Nothing is buried with the body, and the spot is never revisited. Offerings of roasted flesh and roots are made to the departed spirit, which has become a devil, that it may not visit the survivors with fever.

**Intellectual state of Weddas.**

Singularly enough, the Weddas exhibit perhaps the highest form of primitive morality to be found anywhere. They cannot imagine that any one should say what is not true, or take what is not his, or strike another. They do not practise polygamy, although marriage with sisters and daughters is allowed (though not with the eldest sister). They are very constant to their wives and affectionate to their children. The marriage ceremony consists in nothing but the present of food to the bride's parents, who give her to whom they will. There are no castes among them.

**Primitive high morality.**

The Weddas have no written characters, and a most limited vocabulary, expressing only the most elementary ideas. The words have no Dravidian affinities, and appear to be predominantly Hindu.

## *THE ANDAMAN AND NICOBAR ISLANDERS.*

The Andaman and Nicobar Islands, situated in the Bay of Bengal, and included in our Indian Empire, may be fitly described here, although the population is not directly related to any of the Indian peoples, as far as can be ascertained. The Bengal government established a convict settlement on the Andamans in 1789; but it had to be abandoned after seven years. Until 1858, the islands remained in the hands of the aboriginal inhabitants, who promptly killed any strangers who landed or were shipwrecked on their coasts. In 1858 a new convict settlement was established, and the islands were annexed; but many difficulties were encountered in bringing the natives to tolerate the invaders. There are now more than 10,000 convicts on the islands.

The Andamanese are among the most interesting subjects of investigation to anthropologists. They belong to a very peculiar type, and have apparently been long isolated, owing to their inveterate hostility to all intruders. It is possible that they may come of a cognate stock to the various Negrito tribes of Malacca, the Philippines, etc. They are among the darkest-skinned races, and of small stature—few exceeding

**Physical characters.**

five feet, and many not more than four feet six. Their woolly or frizzly hair distinguishes them markedly from the native Australians. They are round-headed (brachycephalic), with broad, flat foreheads, narrow noses, and jaws not prominent,—thus contrasting with the long heads, prominent brow-ridges, wide noses, and projecting jaws of the Australians. The proportionate length of their limb bones differs from that of Europeans, and agrees more with that of negroes; but most negroes have projecting jaws, wide nostrils, and long heads, and the Papuan negroes have also very long and high skulls. They may, as Prof. Flower suggests, be the unchanged or little-modified representatives of a primitive type, from which the African negroes on the one hand, and the Oceanic negroes on the other, have sprung.

ANDAMAN ISLANDER.

The Andamanese live in small groups, scarcely to be called tribes; and they appear to be fast decreasing. They are unclothed, except in the neighbourhood of the

Indian settlements; but they are much tattooed and painted, and they also rub themselves with red ochre and with various unguents, as a protective against mosquitoes, etc. Their huts are mere palm-leaf sheds, and frequently they dwell under trees or in caves. They generally establish themselves not far from the sea, which they fish with great skill, being clever boatmen, divers, and swimmers. They feed largely on fish, turtle, and wild roots and fruits, and also on hogs and birds, which they shoot with bows and arrows. Their settlements are not permanent, for they are compelled to move occasionally by the odours of their fish and other remains which accumulate about them. At present, at any rate, they are not cannibals; but it is difficult to be sure that they were not formerly, and their passionate mobile nature gives countenance to the idea. They are equally accessible to pleasing and to mournful ideas; and they weep readily in either case.

**Habits and dwellings.**

These strange islanders have but one wife, who rarely has more than two children. Wives and children are kindly treated. When the period of marriage approaches, the young people undergo various tests to form their character, such as deprivation of favourite food. Although robust, the people are not long lived, probably owing to their damp climate and exposed life; and few of them live beyond forty years. The dead are allowed to decay, and afterwards the bones are kept in memory of them. Usually a widow carries by her side the skull of her late husband, and uses it as a treasure box. The Andamanese have no idea of a god, except that of an evil spirit that spreads disease. The natives of Little Andaman are still quite inaccessible to intercourse with strangers, showing unconquerable hostility. The Andaman language appears to approach some Dravidian and Burman dialects, but it is very poor in expressions, having no numerals. The inhabitants of Little Andaman do not understand those of South Andaman. Their total number is perhaps now scarcely more than five thousand; but they are of much importance as relics of an old and peculiar type of humanity.

**Marriage and mortality.**

The Nicobar Islands, lying between the Andamans and the North of Sumatra, have had a very chequered history.

NICOBAR ISLANDERS.

Again and again, from the time of the French Jesuit missionaries, Faure and Bounet (1711), European powers have attempted to hold or to colonise them; but their efforts were frustrated by the unhealthy climate or by the hostility of the natives. French, Danes, English, and Germans in succession failed, until, in 1869, the islands were added by the British to their Andaman Islands settlement.

**The Nicobar Islanders.**

The Nicobar Islanders are not at all of the same race as the Andamanese. They are of middle height, and bronze or copper coloured. They neither tattoo nor paint their bodies, and do not smear themselves with ochre or clay. Their bodies are well proportioned, with slightly oblique eyes, small flat noses, large mouths, thick lips, and straight black hair. Thus it is evident that they are of Mongoloid affinities, and are related to the Malays or to the Chinese. Their teeth and lips are blackened by excessive betel-chewing. The women flatten the heads of their infants. The men wear their hair long, the women shave their heads. The people are intensely vain, and greedy of European clothing. The English black silk hat is an almost priceless possession. They are lazy, cowardly, treacherous, and drunken. Their chief occupation is fishing; but they have plenty of other food, such as poultry, turtle, and many fruits. Their houses are built close to the shore and raised upon pillars, being entered by a trapdoor and ladder, the latter being drawn up at night. Each house is inhabited by a score or more of people; it is beehive-shaped, thatched, and without windows. The Nicobarese greatly dread evil spirits, and are very

NICOBAR GIRLS.

superstitious. They have some idea of life after death, and imagine that the soul of the dead remains for a time near where it had lived. They bury their dead, erecting over each grave a post on which the deceased's utensils are placed. They only have one wife, though she may be dismissed very readily.

# CHAPTER VI.

## The Hindus.

**Hindu religiousness—Mixed character—Great religious originators—The Brahmans and Rajputs—Lowered character of Brahmans—Priestcraft—Changes, with permanence—Physical characters of Brahmans—Distinct tribes—Varied employments—Religious rites—Brahman dress—Women's dress—The poor housewife—Low position of women—Early marriages—Widows—Female influence—Seclusion of women due to Mahometanism—Abolition of Suttee by the British—The Rajputs—A feudal aristocracy—The Hindu masses—Eclecticism of Hindu religion—Multitude of castes—Hindu village communities—Village organisation—Various village functionaries—Castes in towns—Hindu manipulation—Masterly workmanship—Introduction of factories—Criminal castes—Caste rules—Boycotting—Polluting glances—Caste a general Aryan feature—Character of Hindu villagers—Discordant views about Hindus—Village temples—Goddess worship—Self-immolation—Idol festivals—Drowning and burying alive—Self-torture.**

RAJPUT'S GRAVE.

**Hindu religiousness.**

IN considering the Hindu people generally, our first and our most permanent impression should be, that the Hindus are extraordinarily religious in many ways, that their religions in their pure forms include many of the highest conceptions and principles, and that multitudes of their peculiarities and practices are inseparably bound up with religion. A mixed people, compounded of pre-Aryans of more than one type, of Mongoloids to a certain extent, and of Aryans and Semites of several different stocks, they have, in spite of numerous permutations, preserved among them by caste distinctions many comparatively pure specimens of ancient races, while yet being a people externally impressed with marked common characteristics of Orientalism. Their religious temperament, their readiness to devote themselves to worship, expensive, self-sacrificing, devout, and serious, is shown by their having originated such great religions as Brahmanism, Buddhism, and Hinduism, with their many modifications, and their having so widely accepted Mahometanism.

**Mixed character.**

**Great religious originators.**

Although we cannot here dwell fully on the various Hindu religions, our remarks must have some referenc to religions; and first we will describe briefly the pure Aryans—the Brahmans and Rajputs. We may name Agni, the heat-giving god, as originally the most invoked of their gods, giving place to Indra, the rain-giver, as the Aryans progressed southwards; while in the Ganges valley the great Brahmanical triad became prominent—Brahma the creator, Vishnu the preserver, and Siva the destroyer and reproducer. Originally, however, the Brahman creed was both a lofty and a bright one: even their sense of sin found a corresponding assurance of pardon on repentance. Many Hindus of the present day recognise Brahma as supreme creator, preserver, and destroyer of the universe, from whom all souls come, and to whom all return—infinite, eternal, incomprehensible. Yet among the mass of the people he is the least important of the deities.

**The Brahmans and Rajputs.**

The Brahmans of the present day are the descendants of those in whom priestly functions became concentrated in early times, or of others who, as a great privilege, obtained admission to their number. Notwithstanding the lofty theoretical religion which they have inherited, they have very largely lent

**Lowered character of Brahmans.**

themselves to the superstitions and the abuses of Hinduism, with absurd mythologies and revolting rites. They undertake the conduct of sacrifices, the reading and teaching of the Vedas, and the making and accepting of gifts—a most important function in Oriental courtesy; and where these occupations fail, they may occupy themselves in certain trades. As has so often happened,

THE HOLY CITY OF BENARES.

however, the "craft" has gained upon the sacred profession; and, while abating no jot of their sacred pretensions, the Brahmans engaged in money-making far outnumber those occupied in the temples, and the former look down upon the latter. So far is it from being true, that the Orientals never change; they do change most vitally, only they pretend not to

**Priestcraft.**

know it; and by keeping up some external forms and customs, they appear at first sight to be as unchanged as the lancelet or the lamp-shell from time immemorial. The brief history of India that we have given is a record of continual and mighty changes; and whoever takes up the idea that Orientals do not change, will make a disastrous mistake.

**Changes, with permanence.**

The Brahmans, as a rule, are tall, well-made men, of a light-yellow colour. Very many of them are incapable of conversing in Sanscrit, and use the vernacular of the people among whom they are. Sir W. W. Hunter ("Indian Empire," 2nd edition, p. 96) well describes them as "the result of nearly 3,000 years of hereditary education and self-restraint; and they have evolved a type of mankind quite distinct from the surrounding population. Even the passing traveller in India marks them out, alike from the bronze-cheeked, large-limbed, leisure-loving Rajput or warrior caste of Aryan descent, and from the dark-skinned, flat-nosed, thick-lipped low castes of non-Aryan origin, with their short bodies and bullet heads. The Brahman stands apart from both; tall and slim, with finely-modelled lips and nose, fair complexion, high forehead, and somewhat cocoa-nut shaped skull—the man of self-centred refinement. He is an example of a class becoming the ruling power in a country, not by force of arms, but by the vigour of hereditary culture and temperance. For their own Aryan countrymen they developed a noble language and literature. The Brahmans were not only the priests and philosophers, they were also the lawgivers, the statesmen, the administrators, the men of science, and the poets of their race. Their influence on the aboriginal peoples, the hill and forest races of India, was not less important. To these rude remnants of the flint and bronze ages, they brought in ancient times a knowledge of the metals and of the gods. Within the historical period, the Brahmans have incorporated the mass of the backward races into the social and religious organisation of Hinduism."

**Physical characters of Brahmans.**

Brahmanical tribes are as much separated from one another as any other castes. Although some of them may eat together, they may not intermarry. They are perhaps most numerous in Kashmir, where the population is most purely Aryan, and the Brahman pundits form an educated aristocracy, occupying all important offices in the State. They eat meat, and

**Distinct tribes.**

BRAHMANS.

are excluded from the regular ten tribes of Indian Brahmans. They are, it is confessed, much more secular and loose in their observances than the priestly Brahmans. They make their way, and show their cleverness, versatility, and energy all over North India. Indeed, in some parts the Brahmans condescend to menial and servile employments, saving their caste by refusing something or abstaining from certain kinds of contact. They may, for instance, refuse to put their

**Varied employments.**

HIMALAYA WOMEN.

hands to the plough, while performing every other kind of agricultural labour. In Bengal they are largely employed as clerks and accountants, in learned professions, as merchants and bankers, and show themselves acute, but not often energetic.

A modern orthodox Brahman will even now, according to Sir Monier Williams ("Religious Thought and Life in India"), devote several hours a day to religious forms, including bathing, worship, and meditation at two services, worship by the repetition of the first words of every sacred book, oblation of water to the secondary gods, sages, etc., sacrifice to fire by fuel, rice, clarified butter, etc., and worship of the gods in the domestic sanctuary. There is also a service before the midday meal, with offerings of food to all beings, including animals; daily homage to men, by the offering of food to guests and beggars; daily visiting of the neighbouring temple, to bow to the idol; solemn fasts are kept twice a month; a pilgrimage is made, whenever practicable, to some holy shrine; and the last sacrifice is the burning of the body by the sacred fire originally lighted by husband and wife on the domestic hearth.

**Religious rites.**

The good Brahman always rises before sunrise; but his wife rises long before him, looks after the children, prepares fuel, and pays attention to the family clothing. The orthodox garments are of white calico, an under or waistcloth tucked round the waist and reaching to the feet, the outer a shawl-like upper garment without seam from top to bottom. The turban is only worn by the better classes, the rest doing without any head-covering. In Western and Northern India the turban-cloth may be from twenty to fifty yards long, folded according to caste. The great majority never use shoes or stockings.

**Brahman dress.**

The women's dress is a sort of bodice, covered with a garment often ten or fifteen yards long, and first tucked round the waist with many folds in front, then brought gracefully over the shoulder and frequently over the head. It is in jewellery of all kinds that both men and women in India display most extravagance. Nose-rings, ear-rings, necklaces, bracelets, or bangles, armlets, finger-rings, anklets, and toe-rings are worn in great profusion and variety. The children of the rich go naked till about the third year, while the poorer classes are naked till six or seven years old.

**Women's dress.**

The poor housewife has to bruise rice her family, or to grind some kind of grain. She attends personally

**The poor housewife.**

to the kitchen, making it a model of cleanliness and purity—one of the features in which the Indians so markedly excel the Africans. A somewhat strange function of wives, is to keep all bad omens out

ZEBU CARRIAGE.

of the husband's way, or to contrive to make him look at something lucky in the early morning.

**Low position of women.**

Besides keeping the home, the chief function of an Indian high-caste woman, is to give birth to male children, who are desired more ardently perhaps than anywhere. To have no boys, is a shame and a disgrace; to have girls, is a misfortune. This feeling results in the existence of one hundred millions of Indian women unable to read, deeply ignorant. A feeling exists, says Sir Monier Williams, in most Hindu families, that a girl who has learnt to read and write, has committed a sin which is sure to bring down a judgment upon herself and her husband. She will probably have to atone for her crime by early widowhood—the greatest possible misfortune.

**Early marriages.**

As a rule, girls are betrothed at three or four years old, sometimes earlier; married at six or seven to boys of whom they know nothing; and they are taken to their future homes at the age of ten or eleven, often becoming mothers at twelve. They cease to have any but the smallest domestic interests or importance, being not even allowed to pronounce their husbands' names. All upper-caste women are practically prisoners in their zenanas, have no companionship with men, and lack every means or incentive to improvement or to a healthy moral tone. Can it be wondered at that a Hindu woman is often worn out and decrepit at thirty?

**Widows.**

We have abolished the long-standing custom of suttee—the widow being burnt on the funeral pile of her dead husband. The widow with a family now has a tolerable existence. But we have not abolished the blank existence of the childless widow, forbidden to re-marry, and treated as a household drudge, with much contumely, so that often she would cheerfully resign herself to be burnt, if the law permitted.

**Female influence.**

This same system gives rise to the opposite extreme of excessive female influence in numerous cases. The woman's craftiness and desire of power exist in India as elsewhere; and, where the husband is well-to-do, and a numerous family of grandchildren and great-grandchildren grows up around the heads of the family, there is scope for great exertion of influence by the female head, though she may have lost all personal charms. Scheming has its full play in her proceedings; superstition and caste observances find a stronghold in her; and this secret life of the zenanas, closed to all but the family, is an almost impregnable barrier m-provement. Many English women turn their ey s to obtaining access to the zenanas, as affording the most hopeful chance of conferring education on and emancipating Indian women from the chains in which they are bound, too much with their own consent. It must be acknowledged, too, that not a few Indian women have

THE RAO OF CUTCH (A RAJPUT).

shown remarkable skill in management, even of the higher political order, and have wielded, and still wield, great power in many States.

Strange as it may appear, the seclusion and isolation of women in India are no part of original Brahmanism. The laws of Manu, dating from about 500 B.C., show a diminution of liberty and social consequence, woman being declared unfit for independence. Even up to the Christian era women had many rights and privileges from

THE THAKORE SAHIB OF MORVI, GUJERAT (A RAJPUT).

which they were excluded at a later period; and they were certainly not secluded nor veiled. It was the introduction of Mahometanism which gave the strongest impulse in this downward direction. The practices in fashion among the conquering race had a stamp of authority which propagated them extensively among those who never became Mahometans; and finally it came to be laid down that "a man both day and night must keep his wife so much in subjection that she by no means be mistress of her own actions. If the wife have her own free will, she will behave amiss. A woman must never go out without the consent of her husband. She must never hold converse with a strange man; she must not stand at the door; she must never look out at the window; she must not eat till she has served her husband and his guests with food. She may, however, take physic before they eat. It is proper for a woman, after her husband's death, to burn herself in the fire with his corpse." So deep was the feeling that the latter practice rested on inspired authority, that the British for many years dared not forbid it. It was happily abolished in British India in 1829; but, even up to recent years, it has occasionally been repeated in native principalities. Its abolition was facilitated by the discovery that some Brahman pundits had falsified a verse of the Rig Veda, which was supposed to inculcate suttee, by inserting the word "fire" for a closely similar one meaning "first."

**Seclusion of women due to Mahometanism.**

**Abolition of suttee by the British.**

The Rajputs, literally sons of rajahs or princes, represent the warrior caste of the invading Aryans, and in numerous tribes extend very widely through India, being most numerous, however, in Rajputana. But their race origin is obscured at present by the fact that almost all Hindus who have taken to soldiering, whether Mahrattas, Jats, or aborigines, claim a Rajput origin. The advent of the Mussulmans was a great blow to the Rajputs, driving them from their ancient seats of power on the Ganges, to the much less attractive and valuable lands of Rajputana; and even here the Mahrattas gained predominance over them in the last century. Since the decline of the Mahratta power, the Rajputs have emerged into comparative brilliancy; and in Raj-

**The Rajputs.**

putana at any rate constitute a powerful feudal aristocracy, as also in the North-east Punjab. In the Ganges valley they still form a considerable proportion of the cultivators of the soil, but are very little distinguishable physically from the Brahmans. The modern Rajput is quite as strict a Hindu, and even more prejudiced, than many Brahmans; and many of them took a violent part in the rebellion of 1857-8. Even the humbler Rajputs have a fine, dignified look, and their women are very handsome. The Rajput is very proud of his warlike reputation and of his noble ancestry. Each clan marries into some other, marriage in the same clan being regarded as incestuous. There is much celibacy and infanticide among them. As a specimen of their subdivisions, we may note, that in Oudh alone, in 1871, there were found 439 Rajput clans or divisions of clans, some divisions having only one or two living members. Their great desire is to marry their daughters into a higher clan, and to avoid misalliances.

**A feudal aristocracy.**

NATIVE OF OUDH.

In connection with the Rajputs, we may here refer to the Aryan people of Cashmere (or Kashmir), which is in many respects most interesting, both for its exquisite scenery and for its manufactures and people. After having been ruled by a Naga dynasty for a long period, it was annexed to the Mogul empire by Akbar in 1586. Later it was ruled over by Afghan chiefs, and in 1819 was taken by Runjeet Singh. When we conquered the

RAJPUT WOMEN.

Sikhs, we appointed a Maharajah of Cashmere who was already ruler of the adjacent district of Jummoo, and who was of Rajput descent. The majority of the people of Cashmere have long been Mahometans. The Aryan inhabitants are among the finest and most European-looking of the Hindu races, their features lacking the prominent cheek-bones, thick lips, and other unpleasing elements of many Hindus. The women are also in many cases beautiful, with something of a Jewish appearance. In fact, those of the well-to-do classes are little darker than Italians. A large infusion of them are of Brahman descent, and retain their religion, while excluded from the Indian Brahman tribes, and distinguished from them by eating meat. Their pundits are extremely clever, and are known all over Northern India as an energetic race of office-seekers. In and around Jummoo the Rajputs are the predominant race, of a slender type, with high shoulders, curiously bow-legged, and with turned-in toes. They are light-brown in complexion, with small features and frequently hooked nose. They are very particular in caste observances, conceited, avaricious, and grasping. They do not work at any trade, touching a plough being considered a disgrace. Very many of the Brahmans, however, are cultivators.

**The Hindu masses.**

The mass of the Indian people,—something approaching two hundred millions,—are Hindus by religion, with local and racial variations which priest-craft has most skilfully adapted or has itself suggested. On the whole, the Hindu people may be said to be divided between the worship of the two gods—Vishnu, with other personal deities, faith in whom secures salvation, and Siva, a sterner deity, propitiated by works, penances, and austerities. But what is most remarkable in Hindu religion, is the extent to which it has absorbed and tolerated almost all forms of religious ideas. Yet, with all its inclusiveness, and notwithstanding the long predominance of Buddhism, with its anti-caste doctrines, nothing is more remarkable than the extent to which caste regained its ground and increased its domination on the decline of Buddhism, showing that it rested on some basis very deeply seated in the Indian nature.

**Eclecticism of Hindu religion.**

Instead of the four early castes already referred to, a multitude of castes has arisen, partly through the inter-marriage of men of the higher castes with women of the lower, to whom distinctive occupations have been assigned, and partly by a tendency to form trades' guilds, which was almost equally influential in Europe in the middle ages, and has by no means died out among ourselves. Why it should have gained such remarkable ascendency in India we cannot tell. It may be simply because the struggle for existence was so keen, that each group protected itself as far as possible, and jealously excluded others. No doubt the skill acquired by those who exclusively devoted themselves to particular crafts, and whose sons showed special and increasing aptitude for the same pursuit, aided this powerfully. The word caste was a Portuguese term, indicating the divisions or creeds they found among the Indians. The Hindu word for caste is 'jat,' or 'birth,' which, however, has become identified with occupation; and castes in this sense are now innumerable, and constantly being formed.

**Multitude of castes.**

Of course the vast majority of the Hindus are agriculturists, and, according to some, castes have arisen essentially out of the primitive constitution of village communities. The Indian village or township, extending over three or four square miles of territory, is in many respects a little republic; and its organisation has lasted practically for more than two thousand years, testifying to the excellent elements it contains. If the agriculturist's implements are rude, his social system is complex and very satisfactory.

**Hindu village communities.**

The community has little to do with Government, beyond paying a joint produce-tax and obeying general laws. It elects its own headman, or president, who is the paid chairman and magistrate, presiding at the sittings of the local council, which often assembles under a large tree. He settles labour questions, payments, disputes, etc. Of course a notary and a priest are high in office in the village; and the latter abates no jot of the pretensions of the priesthood. A schoolmaster is found in many villages, though the instruction he gives is very rudimentary; but he has a good stock of punishments at command for his scholars, such as stand-

**Village organisation.**

ing on one foot for a long period, sitting on the floor with one leg turned up behind the neck, hanging head downwards from a branch of a tree, knocking heads together, etc. The barber, who shaves every man most regularly, cuts nails, cleans ears, cracks joints, etc.; the carpenter, sawing with both feet and hands; the blacksmith, dairyman (who never makes cheese), weaver, shoemaker, potter—all are found in the villages, being regularly appointed or hereditary, and paid jointly by the council out of the village contributions.

**Various village functionaries.**

But it is in the towns that caste institutions present themselves in all their variety and rigour. There, all who practise a trade live in the same quarter of the town; and it is possible to find whole streets devoted to particular trades, and known as bazaars. The shops are open to the street, the owners being seated on the ground among their commodities, and by no means resembling English shopkeepers in their eagerness to sell their wares. At the same time the workers are to be seen plying their occupations in open workshops. The patience, perseverance, and endurance of these native workmen is simply marvellous. Here they reap the full advantage of their fine, lithe, supple fingers. If their manipulation is slow, it is also first-rate, though only in a few cases are modern scientific improvements introduced. Perhaps it is the European machine which is destined to break up caste more than any other cause. The steam-engine and the railway have already opened the eyes of the Hindu marvellously. He has taken to travelling as one of his greatest enjoyments, and thus has learnt to migrate easily and cheaply in search of work. In spite of caste, he crowds the third-class carriages.

**Castes in towns.**

**Hindu manipulation.**

The Indian workman's mastery over his materials is marvellous. English people are now familiar, through exhibitions, with the exquisite carvings, filigree work, gold and silver weaving, inlaid-work, gold and silver plate, embroidery, needlework, muslin, and other manufactures of India. In architecture, in

**Masterly workmanship.**

clay-modelling, in miniature paintings on wood, talc, and ivory, the Indians have shown mastery in forms quite original. But we cannot explain why they should not have shown similar tendencies to sculpture and painting in the forms generally known to us; nor is it easily comprehensible why there should be so little fine furniture

HINDU WORSHIPPING THE GANGES.

in India. It is not for want of perseverance or ingenuity. In Benares Sir Monier Williams found a man making a set of twenty toy boxes, some lacquered, some coloured, all neatly constructed and furnished with lids, and fitting one inside the other, so that the smallest box in the interior of all was not bigger than the head of a knitting needle. The price of the whole nest of twenty boxes was not more than sixpence, although twenty-three different manipulations were needed to complete each box. In Benares the most exquisite patterns are graven on brass with no other tools than a hammer and a nail; and purchasers always weigh the articles and only pay a trifle more than the cost of the brass; and indeed, most things are made to order; the keeping of large stocks is almost unknown. Nowadays, however, factories with English machinery have been established in India; and it is possible that Indian frugality and low wages may revolutionise the cotton industry, and lead to our being surpassed in cheapness of production by Eastern manufacturers, producing a similar effect on our cotton industries to that which cheap corn has produced upon farming in England. At any rate, the English must not send worthless and rotten goods to India, if it is desired to keep a hold on the Indian market; for the Hindus have found them out.

**Introduction of factories.**

So far does the idea of caste, depending on birth, prevail in India, that there are certain criminal castes organised to prey on others. The thugs and dacoits belong to these, with professed poisoners and thieves. Most of the crime in India is committed by these criminal castes. There are even religious mendicants who accept alms only from certain castes.

**Criminal castes.**

Contact with certain castes or people gives rise to ceremonial uncleanness, only to be purged by complex rites. A Hindu visitor to a European house changes all his clothes on his return home, and purifies himself in a prescribed manner very repulsive to us. Every workman is clean in his own trade, that is, the actions necessary in his trade do not render him unclean; but no Hindu will use an article of earthenware which an English barbarian has touched. Such vessels are at once broken, and brass or copper utensils scoured with sand. Small brass pots are kept at roadside watering-places for people of caste; but the out-caste people or pariahs, must catch in their mouths the water that has passed through a bamboo, not daring to put their lips

**Caste rules.**

close to it. Not one of the out-castes can enter the house of a Hindu; but he stands at a distance and shouts any message he may have. If a man of caste offends against the rules of his caste, a meeting of the members, or of the council, is called, and, on proof of the offence, the offender is punished by a severe form of boycotting, which proves that the Irish were very late in the field in putting into practice that form of persuasion.

BENGALI WOMAN.

Sir Monier Williams gives an instance that came under his own notice in 1875, of a man, a cloth merchant, who had committed the crime of marrying a widow of his own caste, who was sentenced to excommunication. No one of his own or any other caste was to associate with him, eat with him, deal with him, or marry any of his children. No temple was to receive him as a worshipper; if he died, no one was to carry his body to the burying-ground. The day after the sentence, he had the hardihood to go into the bazaar, but found it impossible to transact business; not even his debtors would pay him what they owed, nor would any one give evidence before the courts to support his claims. He was a ruined man, and had to leave the country.

**Boycotting.**

It is held, theoretically, that a Brahman is polluted if even the shadow of a low-caste man falls upon him, or if he even glances into his superior's pot. A Brahman will turn aside and spit, if a low-caste man passes him in the street; but the low-caste man has his advantage in the unimportance to him of any

**Polluting glances.**

such occurrences; and if he accumulates a little money, he can even hire a high-caste man to work for him. Many a Brahman is thus engaged as cook.

Instead of decrying caste as an odious Orientalism, we should recognise that it is a general Aryan feature, which has attained its greatest development in India. It is one of man's devices for preserving that which he has gained in the struggle for existence—a conservative expedient. But, like all other of man's devices, it may be abused and carried to extremes which are evil and retard progress. It readily becomes a tyranny; and those whose great care is to preserve caste, irrespective of merit, are really self-condemned to extinction. However, caste in India is really giving way before European institutions and the spread of free thought; but it may long continue to exercise a more or less real sway.

**Caste an Aryan feature.**

All impressions of Hindu character must be founded on local and limited knowledge; but the following is worth considering as the experience of an officer of long residence in India — Lieut.-Colonel Monier Williams, father of the distinguished Oxford professor who has given his life to making India known in this country. About sixty years ago, he recorded that he found the villagers in Western India, of every caste, simple and temperate in habits, quiet and peaceful in disposition, and obedient and faithful in the fulfilment of duty. They had no conspicuous vices; the parents were affectionate and tender, the children habitually dutiful. Hospitality towards strangers was carefully observed. There were no beggars, except those who were religious mendicants by profession. The indigent and diseased were always provided for by internal village arrangements. No written documents were required in transactions involving money payments. No receipts were given or needed for rents. Money and valuables were deposited without any security. On the occasion of a great religious assemblage on the banks of the Nerbuddah, where two hundred thousand people assembled, there was no rioting, no quarrelling, no

**Character of Hindu villagers.**

drunkenness, nor disorder of any kind. Under the protection of the village watchmen, the Indian survey officers were never robbed, nor was the smallest article even pilfered from their tents.

It would be taking too rosy a view to apply this picture universally; yet much of it is true. The Hindus among themselves are habitually just and honourable. In our courts they appear as constantly guilty of deception, concealment, and false swearing, much as too many Europeans conduct themselves towards tax-gatherers and magistrates. And he who thinks evil of the Hindus will probably find sufficient justification for his thoughts in his experience; while those who look at the best side, and seek the good features, always find much to commend and admire.

**Discordant views about Hindus.**

Every village in India has its temple or temples, rude though they may be, either to Siva in his character of Father of all beings, Dissolver and Regenerator, with his son Ganesa, lord of demons; to Vishnu, the god who shows his sympathy with human suffering and his interest in human affairs by numerous avatars, or descents upon earth, among whom Krishna and Rama are very important; or to some one of the numerous classes of goddesses, mostly impersonations of the female energy of Siva, such as Kali, the terrible destroyer, the Matris, or mothers of the universe, including Vaishnari and Lakshmi. While the worship of Siva and Vishnu includes many comparatively good features, it is in connection with the worship of goddesses that the most degrading and licentious rites are practised. If, on the one hand, the elevation of Hindu religion may be sought by laying emphasis on the pure doctrines embodied in it and found in the sacred books, there can be no elevation for those who practise most of the forms of goddess worship, except by total abandonment of such degrading superstitions. No doubt British influence is gradually breaking up a great deal of superstition; and infanticide, fanatical murder, and human sacrifice are far less common than they were. Even the practice of self-immolation under cars of the gods has

**Village temples.**

**Goddess worship.**

*Self-immolation.*

greatly decreased. Such cars are attached to every large temple, and are drawn forth on particular days by large numbers of devotees. Although now and again people are crushed under the wheels, this is often accidental, owing to the great crowd, and anxiety to get near the sacred god. Our rule may be said to have increased the attendances at religious festivals, by largely facilitating communication; and accidents not unfrequently happen in most large assemblies. It is well known that the most celebrated of these assemblies is that of Juggernaut (properly Jagan-nath, or Krishna), at Puri in Orissa. There is no doubt that self-immolation is discouraged in Vishnu worship. Accidental death within the temple renders the whole place unclean. "The ritual suddenly stops, and the polluted offerings are hurried away from the sight of the offended god."

*Idol festivals.*

*Drowning and burying alive.*

Self-immolation by drowning was formerly very common at Benares. The Ganges is the sacred river beyond all others; and to end one's days in it was the most certain of all modes of securing salvation. Often Hindus would paddle into the stream between two large empty pots, which they would then fill with water, and so sink themselves. Burying alive was another practice we have succeeded in putting down, though even up to recent years it has been occasionally practised.

*Self-torture.*

Voluntary self-torture is another considerable feature of Indian life. Many forms of it have been prohibited by law, such as swinging in the air, fixed by a rope and hook passed through the muscles of the back and attached to a lofty pole, boring the tongue with a red-hot iron, etc. Some infatuated men would formerly sit for years over a hot fire, or with eyes open looking at the sun, or stand with heavy weights suspended to their naked bodies, or hold their hands closed till the nails pierced through them, or keep their arms vertically raised till the joints became fixed, or lie on beds with iron spikes. Sir Monier Williams saw a man at Allahabad who had sat in one position for fifty years on a stone pedestal, exposed to sun, wind, and rain, never moving except once a day, when he was led to the Ganges. Of course he was an object of veneration. He also saw a man prostrating himself and measuring every inch of his body round a mountain, and apparently intending to go on till he had completed a circuit of twenty miles one hundred and eight times. Such are a few of the acts which show how intense is the religious and self-sacrificing spirit of the Hindu.

# CHAPTER VII.

## The Hindus (*continued*).

**Buddhist influence on Hinduism—The Jains—Jain temples and pilgrimages—The Parsees expelled from Persia—The towers of silence—Moslem attitude to the British—Various Moslem races—Mahometan soldiers—Rise of the Sikhs—The Gurus—Theistic religionists—Rammohun Roy—Keshub Chunder Sen—Christians—Eurasians—Variety of languages—Hindustani—Sanskrit—Pali—The prakrits and modern vernaculars—Native literature—Forms of marriage—Polygamy—Essentials of Hindu marriage—Torchlight processions—Desire of male offspring—Property laws—The ryot, or cultivator—Modes of agriculture—Indian sports—Jugglers and snake charmers—Results of British rule.**

DANCING GIRL: HYDERABAD.

**Buddhist influences on Hinduism.**

BUDDHISM has, as we have said, almost disappeared from India, surviving only in Ceylon, where it flourishes. But there is no doubt that it exerted great influence on Hinduism itself, "in bringing forward the principle of the brotherhood of man, with the reassertion of which, each new revival of Hinduism starts; in the asylum which the great Hindu sects afford to women who have fallen victims to caste rules, to the widow, and to the out-caste; in that gentleness and charity to all men, which take the place of a poor-law in India, and give a high significance to the half-satirical epithet of the "mild Hindu."

Buddhism is also represented in India by the Jains, a sect of over a million, differing from Buddhism in recognising in the Jina Pati, or Adi Buddha, a divine personal ruler of all, denying the divine origin of the Vedas, and distinguished by an extreme tenderness for animal life. Their holy men of the past are admitted as true deities. They believe in a sort of pantheism; and spirits are condemned to continual migration. There are many Jains in Rajputana, in Benares, in Gujerat, and the Mysore; and they possess a large share of wealth and influence, so extensive that it is said one half the mercantile wealth of India passes through their hands. Their tenderness to animal life, however, is against many of their enterprises, for they will undertake nothing by which animal life may be destroyed. Some of the noblest architectural remains in India were erected by the Jains in the past; and they still make pilgrimages to five holy hills where they have shrines—pilgrimages being, according to them, the only means by which the devotee may attain to their heaven of complete annihilation.

**The Jains.**

**Jain temples and pilgrimages.**

The Parsees of India, though few in number, not more than seventy thousand,—of whom fifty thousand are in the city of Bombay alone,—are a most important and influential group of people, possessing much wealth, and following European practices to a large extent. They are Aryans of Persian descent, whose ancestors were expelled from Persia by the Mahometan conquerors in the seventh and eighth centuries. They speak the Gujerati vernacular, but all also speak English. Yet they maintain the observances of the Zoroastrian religion. Their mode of "burial" in the "Towers of Silence" on Malabar Hill at Bombay, is most peculiar. They proceed on the principle that every effort must be made to protect mother earth from the pollution which would result if putrefying corpses

**The Parsees expelled from Persia.**

**The towers of silence.**

SCENE IN THE (MAHOMETAN) MOHURRUM FESTIVAL: BOMBAY.

were allowed to accumulate in the ground. Hence they build solid and massive circular stone platforms, or low towers, on which the dead are exposed, and speedily devoured by vultures, which always surround the parapet of the towers. The Parsees defend this practice on the highest sanitary grounds. On the whole, however, the Parsees are more important as a caste of civilised traders than as religionists, for they do not proselytise. They have but one wife, who enjoys a degree of freedom unknown to Hindus or Mahometans. They neither eat beef, pork, nor ham, nor do they eat food cooked by a person of another religion.

The Moslem, or Mahometan, population of India, though by no means homogeneous in race, constitute a vast population of over fifty millions, whose political attitude is a most important factor in our Eastern dominion; for by their religious faith they naturally feel hostility to Christianity and its professors, while the attitude of the latter has been for the most part equally hostile, not admitting the good features in the Moslem faith. It is not sufficiently remembered, moreover, that the advent of the British has practically expelled the Mahometans from the vast share they formerly possessed in the administration of Hindu as well as Mahometan States. It is asserted by Sir Richard Temple that the Mussulmans nowadays find themselves beaten by Hindus in the open competition of mind with mind. Consequently there is amongst them a considerable disgust at the results of British rule; and this requires continual watchfulness on our part not to offend their prejudices, nor to do anything which might give them a pretext for hoisting the standard of a religious war.

**Moslem attitude to the British.**

The Mahometans are most numerous in Bengal, the North-Western Provinces, and the Punjab, although they are largely distributed all over India, and include people of Arab, Persian, Scythian, Tartar, Mongol, Turk, and Afghan descent, with many converts from the Rajputs, Jats, and pre-Aryan tribes. Many of these races keep distinct, religiously as well as racially; but all are liable to be united under the standard of Allah.

**Various Moslem races.**

The Moguls, or descendants of the last conquering race, do not number a quarter of a million. The Afghans, known as Pathans, approach two millions. The Sayyids, who claim lineal descent from Mahomet, are over three-quarters of a million; while the Shaikhs, or those of Arab descent, number nearly five millions. The Bohra of Gujerat, Cutch, Sind, and the Rajput states, represent

HINDUS BATHING IN THE GANGES.

themselves as the followers of the Shaikh-ul-Jabl, or Old Man of the Mountain. They are chiefly mercantile in pursuits, and are active and intelligent people. In Bengal the vast proportion of the Mahometans plainly are of the same race as the low-caste Hindus. They have become subdivided into many classes with hereditary occupations, much resembling the Hindu castes, and having many polytheistic customs and festivals. In the Punjab too the Mussulman is not strongly marked out from the Hindu racially. In the Deccan, the ruling power at Hyderabad is Mahometan, depending on a mixed Arab, Negro, Abyssinian, and Northern Hindu soldiery. In Southern India they are divided into three distinct races. (1) Labbai, tall and well made, deep bronze in colour, merchants and pedlars, using the Tamil alphabet, having the Koran in Tamil, and only speaking and reading Tamil. They, like (2) the Moplah, are said to have originated from trading or sailor Arabs and Indian women. The Moplah of South-western India and Ceylon are of a more restless disposition, and have had various agrarian disputes with us. The Moplah of North Malabar follow the local practice of descent of property in the female line. (3) The Nao-aiti (or new comers), a small slender almost fair race with handsome women, are Arab immigrants, and are not military, but exclusively engaged in trade.

**Mahometan soldiers.**

The Mahometans furnish something like one-fourth of the British army in India; and they have shown both steadiness and dash in warfare. The bulk of them may be said to hope for a return of their former glories, and dwell with pride on their past successes. They usually speak Hindustani, although the educated speak Persian. They are far less characterised by learning than the Hindus. The great Mahometan capitals are Gaur, Rajmahal, Dacca, and Moorshedabad; but it is not around them that the Moslem faith is most professed, but in thickly peopled agricultural districts, where the equalising creed of Mahometanism has made many converts among those who otherwise had the lowest social position as out-castes.

**Rise of the Sikhs.**

The Sikhs form another religious group, often in England supposed to represent a nationality, but in reality a theistic sect founded by Nanak, a Hindu, born in 1469. The word Sikh means "disciple." Nanak's great idea was, to bring about a union of Hindus and Mahometans on the basis of a common belief in one God; but his teaching was also largely pantheistic. He denounced caste and prohibited image worship, but attached great sanctity to cows, like the Hindus. Under Nanak and his successors many converts were made; and the Sikhs began to be influential in a worldly sense and to develop military abilities. This led the Mahometans to fiercely oppose them; the Sikhs gradually grew stronger; and formed powerful bands under independent chiefs.

HINDU LADY OF HIGH RANK, WITH PET ANIMALS.

As they grew more powerful they purchased the tank called Umritsur, where they built the famous lake temple and established their chief centre. Gradually the sayings and teachings of their leading teachers (Gurus) were collected, and they formed a sort of Bible, or Granth. The ninth Guru was imprisoned and tortured by Aurungzebe, and induced a fellow-prisoner to put an

The Gurus.

end to his sufferings. From this time the Sikhs became actively warlike, and under the tenth Guru, Govind, were organised on principles of hostility to Mahometanism, and of active propagation of the Sikh faith by the sword. Aurungzebe was more than a match for the Sikhs; but after his death they became more powerful, and in 1767 they were masters of the country between the Jumna and Rawul Pindi. We have already referred to the achievements of Runjeet Singh, who still further moulded the Sikhs into a nation. Since their successive defeats by the British, they have settled down quietly, entered our military service, and stood loyally by us in the great crisis of 1857. They now number nearly two millions. Many of them, however, adopt caste, wear the Brahmanical thread, keep Hindu festivals, and even make offerings in Hindu temples. Thus they are being drawn back into Hinduism.

Theistic religionists.

A slight mention must here suffice for the Theistic religionists who have arisen within the last century in India, many of whom take the pure teachings of the Vedas for their guide, and believe in the abolition of caste rules, the cessation of child marriages, and the remarriage of widows, and have given up Hindu domestic ceremonies. Rammohun Roy, who died at Bristol in 1833, was one of the most notable reformers.

Rammohun Roy.

He was the real founder of the Brahmo Somaj, or Theistic Churches, of Bengal, Keshub Chunder Sen, who died in 1884, being equally eminent. Although the Native Marriage Act of 1872, obtained largely by his influence, introduced civil marriage at a proper age into India, legalised marriage between different castes, and permitted the remarriage of widows, it has not as yet been largely taken advantage of.

Keshub Chunder Sen.

Keshub Chunder Sen's doctrine cannot be better described than as "the Fatherhood of God and the brotherhood of man." It represents the daily growing ferment of disbelief in and rejection of Hindu idolatry which is permeating Indian society as it becomes more educated, and is a sign of hopefulness for India's future, if it do not degenerate into mere negation of all religion, a feeling which is also growing in India.

The Christians of India must not be left out of account. They are variously estimated at from one to two millions, being most numerous in Southern India. A considerable number of these are however Europeans or descendants of Europeans. The Roman Catholics report the largest number of converts; but their tolerant inclusiveness makes the reality of their claim doubtful. Tinnevelly is a centre round which the largest numbers of Protestants are found. Very many of the Christians are Eurasians, of mixed European and Asiatic blood, a large number being Indo-Portuguese. The Eurasians, however, do not yet manifest the solid qualities of either Europeans or Hindus; and the problem whether a permanent European cross can be established in India is yet unsolved. It appears certain that pure-blooded Europeans cannot become acclimatised in India.

**Christians.**

**Eurasians.**

The great number of spoken languages in India is a bar to unity of feeling in India. It may perhaps be created in the future by the diffusion either of English or of Hindustani, a mixed dialect first used by the Mahometans of India, and since widely employed as a sort of *lingua franca.* It is essentially Hindi, or the vernacular of the North-West Provinces, with many words of Sanscrit, Persian, and Arabic origin. It has been a great question whether pure Sanscrit was ever a spoken language; but authorities of eminence believe that it was, and that it was once a vernacular language, giving way later to various dialects, called Prakrits. Others, however, regard Sanscrit as the sum of the Vedic dialects, constructed by the labour and zeal of grammarians, and polished by the skill of learned men. Modern investigation seems to have shown that the vernaculars are not derived directly from Sanscrit, but from an Aryan speech older than Sanscrit. By degrees the main Prakrits became subdivided into local vernaculars, each spoken in a limited area. Pali, the literary language of Buddhism, is a development of the spoken

**Variety of Languages.**

**Hindustani.**

**Sanscrit.**

**Pali.**

Prakrit of the Gangetic kingdom of Magadha (Behar); while similarly the Jains used the Maharashtri Prakrit of Western India for their sacred books; and these are very

BENJARI (WANDERING TRADERS) ON A JOURNEY.

valuable for comparison with their present representatives in the vernaculars of Behar and the Mahratta country.

The change that has occurred in the interval is of the following nature. The Prakrits had synthetic inflections;

the modern vernaculars are analytical, have disjointed particles to indicate time, place, and relation, and post-positions where we have prepositions. They have incorporated a considerable number of non-Aryan or aboriginal words, and also many words from the Persian court language of their Mahometan conquerors.

**The Prakrits and modern vernaculars.**

The principal Aryan vernaculars are Sindi, towards the north-west frontier; Punjabi, in the valleys of the Indus and its tributaries; Gujerati, south of the Punjab; Hindi, east of Punjabi; Marathi, south-east of Gujerati; Bengali, east Bengal and delta of Ganges; Urija, Mahanudy delta to northern parts of Madras. Each of these vernaculars has a literature of its own, as yet very partially investigated. In Rajputana the poetry and hymnology of a single sect are said to amount to 540,000 lines. Most of these literatures find their main impulse in religious movements. Bengali appears in modern times to have most vitality, and has both drama and fiction, as well as periodical literature, now firmly established and growing.

**Native literature.**

We have already referred to the languages of the Dravidian peoples. Four of these have considerable literatures—the Tamil, Telugu, Kanarese, and Malayalim. The Tamil owed many excellent works to the activity of the Jain Buddhists from the ninth to the thirteenth centuries. The Sanscrit epic Ramayana was also paraphrased or imitated in Tamil. There are two encyclopædic collections of Tamil hymns, in praise of Siva and Vishnu respectively. The printing press has greatly stimulated Tamil literature. In 1882 no fewer than 558 vernacular works were printed in Madras, the great majority being in Tamil.

The forms of marriage and ideas respecting it naturally constitute one of the richest fields of study in India, with its variety of races and castes. We can only refer to the subject briefly. Marriage in India is essentially based on the idea of the father's right to dispose of his daughter in marriage, while the husband purchases her. Mahometanism modifies this to

**Forms of Marriage.**

the extent that the bridegroom purchases the bride from herself, by means of the dower he offers. Marriages usually take place between persons of different tribes or sections of tribes; although Brahman girls may only marry with those of their own caste. Although polygamy is lawful both to Mussulmans and Hindus, it is only practised by the richer classes, and especially by the princes. The results, in intrigue and murder, have too frequently been scandalous. Among Indian Mahometans a man can only marry one wife with full rejoicings and ceremonial, and she receives full deference, although the children of first and subsequent marriages are on an equality in their father's home; yet the offspring of the latter are not similarly dowered, nor equally regarded with those of the first marriage outside their home. Among Hindus in general, it is rare to find more than one wife in a house; but the very numerous female devotees of the temples are almost always immoral. These temple women are not held by the Hindus to pursue a disgraceful vocation; indeed, all classes of Hindus, in time of trouble or in the hope of offspring, have been known to vow their daughters to the temples. Until lately they included almost the only educated women in India, and were often very accomplished. This is but a melancholy instance of the low estate of women in India, far below their ancient position. The whole ritual of their marriages, indeed, is based on a high idea of woman.

**Polygamy.**

Five things are considered essential in the Hindu marriage ceremony—the betrothal, the gift of the girl, the acceptance, the seizure of the girl, and the seven steps, or Sapti-padi. The giving away of the girl by her father or guardian, in the presence of the Brahmans, to the bridegroom's father, is in these words: "I give you, for your son, my beautiful virgin daughter, accept her therefore." The bridegroom's father replies: "With my mind, with my voice, and with my body I joyfully accept thy daughter for my son, and religiously receive her among my own kindred." The girl's father then declares his tribe, and gives the bride-

**Essentials of Hindu marriage.**

SERPENT CHARMERS IN INDIA.

groom grains of rice tinged with red and betel leaves, declaring again that he gives him his daughter, and promising to pay the marriage expenses. The girl's father next declares: "O Brahmans, to this youth, very learned in the Vedas, the son of N., to him I give my daughter, dressed in gay apparel, and adorned with gems." The Brahmans answer, "So let it be." The girl's father now puts her hand into the bridegroom's, and pours over them water sacred to Vishnu, making the gift irrevocable. The wooden yoke of a ploughing bullock is then laid lightly upon the bride's head, signifying her subjection. A veil being now held up between the pair, the eight auspicious verses are recited, calling upon the gods, the saints, the trees, the hills, and the rivers to witness and bless the union. The veil being then let fall, the bridegroom binds the Tali, a golden ornament, round the bride's neck, never to be removed unless she becomes a widow. Then follows a sacrifice to Agni, in which the wedded pair take the Sapti-padi, or seven steps, together, amid loud chanting of the Vedas. Next, grains of parched rice are eaten. On the fourth night after the marriage, a torchlight procession sets out; and the newly-married pair are carried round the village in a palanquin with music and dancing. The details and cost of these processions vary much, according to the ideas and wealth of the relatives. They may even include camels and elephants. At sunrise the pair are conducted home, being received at the threshold by some married woman; when seated, a lamp is waved round their heads, to avert the evil eye. Wedding cards are represented by the distribution of betel leaves with areca nuts and grains of rice coloured red. This may serve to give an idea of marriage in India, but the details and local customs vary greatly.

**Torchlight processions.**

A whole series of religious forms was formerly gone through by Hindu women before the birth of their offspring, to secure the due purification of the child; and these were largely connected with the desire for male offspring, which we can understand when it is considered that the well-being of

**Desire of male offspring.**

the parent's soul after death is believed to depend on the proper performance of certain ceremonies by a son. The Rig Veda says, "When a father sees the face of a living son, he pays a debt in him, and gains immortality. The pleasure which a father has in his son exceeds all other enjoyments. His wife is a friend, his daughter an object of compassion, his son shines as his light in the highest world." The birth and name-giving ceremonies are still important and solemn functions, succeeded by food-giving, tonsure, and ear-boring. Children are suckled sometimes to the age of five or six years.

**Property laws.**

So far is entail from being a Teutonic invention, that the Hindu's boy from birth has a vested interest in his father's property; and the son, when he comes of age, can compel him to give him his share of the property.

Cremation is almost invariable, except among the Parsees, or when drowning is voluntarily preferred. Dying people are frequently taken to the banks of the Ganges or other sacred river, and the last settlement of affairs takes place upon its banks; and the dying person repeatedly calls upon his gods by name.

**The ryot, or cultivator.**

Agriculture is so important in India, that some further description of it may be permitted. Mr. Clements Markham describes the Bombay cultivator, or ryot, as "a lean man, with prominent muscles, and small hands and feet, with eyes full and black, cheek-bones high, and teeth stained with betel. He forms one in a population of 600 to 1,000, which cultivates some 4,000 acres, and lives in a village surrounded by a mud wall, with two gates. The 150 to 200 houses are of sun-dried bricks, with terraced roofs, and there are open porticoes along their fronts; but the few small dark interior rooms have no windows. The furniture of a cultivator's house consists of a copper boiler and a few other copper vessels, about twenty earthen pots, to hold stores of grain and other food, a large wooden dish for kneading dough, a flat stone and rolling-pin for powdering spices, two iron lamps, and two beds laced with rope. The whole will not cost much more than forty shillings. But his agricultural implements and bullocks are his most valuable possessions. The plough, consisting of beam-head and handle, but having no share, and leaving a mere scratch, is made of babool wood (*Acacia Arabica*), and costs only a few rupees. The cart is a rude frame on two solid

BENJARI WOMAN.

wooden wheels, and there are also a harrow with wooden teeth and a drill plough. A pair of good oxen is indispensable." The arable land includes that of which the crops depend on rains, irrigated lands, and garden ground with fruit-trees and vegetables. There are two crops in the year; for the one, spiked millet and two kinds of pulse are sown; for the other, wheat and grains. The land is ploughed only once in two years, having first been drag-hoed. At the beginning of harvest, a level place is chosen for the threshing-floor and made dry and hard. "A pole five feet high is stuck in the middle, the grains are stacked round the floor, and the women break off the ears and throw them in. Six or eight bullocks are then tied to each other, and to the post, and driven round to tread out the grain; and the winnowing is done by a man standing on a high stool, and submitting the grain and chaff to the wind from a basket. The cultivator requires but little food. It consists of cakes made of millet flour, with water and salt, baked on a plate of iron; green pods or fruits cut in pieces, boiled and mixed with salt, pepper, or turmeric, and then fried in oil; and porridge of coarsely ground millet and salt."

**Modes of agriculture.**

We can do no more than glance at the amusements by which the Indians vary their life. Naturally surrounded as they are by jungles containing great quadrupeds, by poisonous snakes, such as the cobra di capello, which do not keep to the jungles, but invade the privacy of homes, and by rivers in which crocodiles abound—hunting must be a somewhat serious amusement; and it is pursued, frequently under the auspices of Europeans, with an ardour and a pomp of circumstance which partake of the nature of real war. Elephant hunting and catching alive, tiger and panther-hunting, are among the most notable forms of sport; while the cheetah, or tame leopard, is made use of as a hunting animal in pursuit of antelopes. In those pursuits the Hindu often shows himself very daring and courageous.

**Indian sports.**

The other side of the Hindu character is exemplified in his devotion to chess; while gambling finds as many devotees as in our own favoured land, for instance among the Rajputs. The performances of jugglers, who are marvellously skilful, afford great amusement to the Hindus; while allied to these

**Jugglers and snake-charmers.**

are the snake-charmers, who by music and various arts sometimes attain a remarkable command over snakes, even without their fangs being extracted. It often happens, however, that the snake-charmer meets with his death from a snake which he has long charmed. Music, of a kind too noisy to be quite appreciated by a Western audience, cock-fighting, athletics, wrestling, dancing,—often of an indecent character, according to our ideas,—all find many votaries among the Hindus, who are neither deficient in intelligence nor in capacity of amusing themselves, though they do not show their amusement by the same facial expressions which we employ.

**Results of British rule.**

Altogether, India has prospered greatly under British rule, has increased largely in population and wealth, and has ceased to suffer from endless wars and fear of wars, with their attendant devastation and death. Tyranny, too, has been very largely done away with; and the lives and liberties of the people are now safe, instead of being, as at most former periods, precarious, and depending on the will of despots and the intrigues of self-interested persons. The manner in which local peculiarities are studied, local interests are guarded, and native ability is utilised under British rule, is on the whole admirable. Although much remains to be done before the natives of India can be extensively admitted to government offices, large advances in this direction have been made. Railways and irrigation works have greatly diminished the risks of famine, which, however, are still very considerable; but the population increases faster than the means of irrigation or of distribution of food supplies.

India, we have shown, is a most interesting field of study, a perfect storehouse of novelty, the result of a panoramic succession of influences, and a motley combination of races such as the world cannot parallel elsewhere. The Queen's reign, as an able writer has said, found the people of India a collection of heterogeneous races. It has moulded them into the beginnings of a nation. "We have taken the young princes of India out of the seraglio, and placed them under high-minded English officers or in schools of chiefs. For the perpetual flattery of women, we have substituted a training in manly sports and in manly arts." Hence it has come about that many of the native Indian princes of the present day are among our most devoted supporters.

# CHAPTER VIII.

## The Tibeto-Burmese and Tibetans.

**Races of Mongoloid stock—Inhabitants of Ladakh and Baltistan—The Nepalese—Growth of Ghoorkha power—Jung Bahadur—The Khas, Gurung, and Magar tribes—Tibetan tribes of Nepal—The Lepchas of Sikkim—Dress—Habits—Character of the Lepchas—The Bhutanese—The Lhopas—The Assam tribes—The Khasias—Dolmen and cromlech builders—The Garrow tribes—Female property and privileges—Human sacrifices—Festival dances—Witchcraft and demonology—The Kukis—Dress and habits—Marriage customs—Ideas of Heaven—The Naga tribes—Physical characters and habits—Skulls and scalps—Women and marriage—War-whoop and hoo-hoo—Naga Agriculture—The Ahom of Assam—Burmah—The Burmese—Influence of Hindu thought—Bravery—Dacoits—The Burmese women—Marriage—Burial—The late despotic government—The Burmese language—Injurious influence of Buddhism—Amusements—The Talaings, or Mons—The Karens of Burmah—White, Red, and Black Karens—Religion and funeral customs—Marriage ceremonies—Will-making—Karen dwellings—Mode of government—Karen war-song—Food—Introduction of Buddhism—The Grand Lama—Lamasseries—Dress of Lamas—The Prayer cylinders—Universality of the prayer machine—Wealth of the Lamas—Physical aspect—Clothing—Food—Cattle—Tibetan jewellery—Tibetan houses—Exposure of the dead—Chinese authority.**

**Races of Mongoloid stock.**

DWELLING in the Himalayan valleys and uplands, and the slopes on both sides, are races which in the main belong to the great Mongoloid stock, with which we shall presently deal. From Cashmere to Assam and Burmah, the majority of the people belong to the same type, which may be called Tibeto-Burman.

**Inhabitants of Ladakh and Baltistan.**

A great number of the inhabitants of Cashmere, especially in the extensive districts of Ladakh and Baltistan, are of Mongoloid origin, belonging to the Bhot division of the Tibetans. They are strong, hardy, short and square built, with the characteristic Mongol features, flat faces, broad cheeks, snub noses, large ears, oblique narrow eyes, and black hair. Most of them are Buddhists. Agriculture is their principal occupation. Polyandry, or one woman having several husbands,—usually brothers,—is quite common among them; and the children recognise all the husbands as father. The men do not average more than five feet two inches in height, the women four feet nine inches. The population is scanty, except in Baltistan, where the people have become Mahometans, have adopted polygamy, and are increasing in numbers.

A GURUNG (NEPAL).

**The Nepalese.**

In Nepal there is a great mixture of races; but the Tibetans have penetrated into most parts. The warlike Ghoorkhas, who are the ruling class in Nepal, are a mixed Tibetan people, but have conformed to Hindu speech and religion. During the last century they grew rapidly in numbers and power, and extended their dominion widely;

**Growth of Ghoorkha power.**

and in 1814, their repeated inroads on British territory made it necessary to attack them. They fought very bravely, and were reduced with difficulty, a British resident being received at Khatmandu, the capital; but there were frequent occasions on which the rulers of Nepal helped our enemies, until Jung Bahadur seized power in 1845, and ever after supported British influence, greatly assisting us during the Mutiny of 1857.

**Jung Bahadur.**

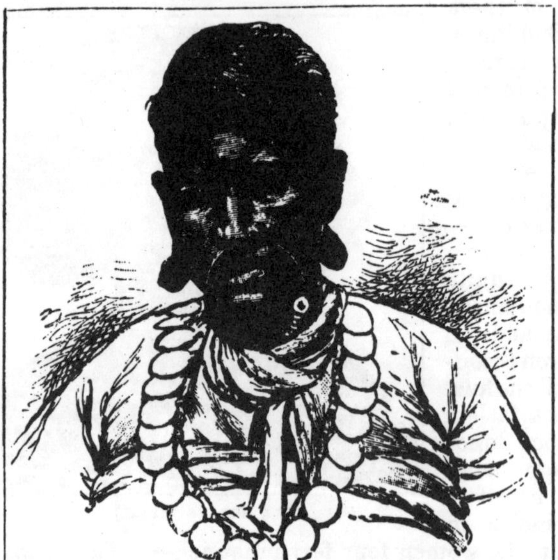

SAMWAR WOMAN, NEPAL.

Besides the Aryan immigrants from India, the bulk of the population of Nepal consists of Tibetan (Mongoloid) tribes. The Khas tribe, which includes many of the dominant people, are descended from Hindu rajputs and Nepal women, and are tall, robust, and energetic, with many Aryan characteristics. The Gurung and Magar tribes, sharing with the Khas the name of Ghoorkha, are much more Mongoloid

**The Khas, Gurung, and Magar Tribes.**

in type and feature, with broad Chinese face, small eyes, flat nose, and meagre whiskers. Their energy and martial character has made them very acceptable in the British Indian army. The inferior Tibetan tribes of Nepal are chiefly agricultural and pastoral, and are mostly Buddhists; but the Hindu caste system has taken root considerably, and Buddhism is strangely combined with bloody sacrifices and polytheism. There are many peculiar languages and dialects in Nepal, and some of the hill-tribes are still very imperfectly known.

**Tibetan tribes of Nepal.**

LEPCHA WATER CARRIER, SIKKIM.

Sikkim is a small native State east of Nepal, subject to British control, containing the interesting Tibetan (or Bhot) Lepchas, markedly Mongoloid in feature, and short of stature, rarely exceeding five feet, small-boned but muscular. They have a cheerful expression and laughing eye, unusual among Mongoloid races. The total absence of beard, parting the hair in the middle, and dressing in a loose bedgown sort of jacket, add to the womanly look of the men; the women dress in silk skirts with a sleevelcss woollen cloak. Brides are

**The Lepchas of Sikkim.**

**Dress.**

purchased by money or service before maturity. The men carry a long, heavy, straight knife, which they use for all purposes possible. Although the Lepcha men are not industrious, leaving that department to the women, they are of an inquiring mind, and have considerable intelligence. They are pretty good marksmen with bow and arrow, but use poisoned arrows; they are also expert in catching birds and fish. A displeasing quality is their dirtiness of person, for they seldom wash; but they take great pride in their hair, the women often dressing the men's hair, "Thus," says a distinguished traveller, "one may often see, the last thing at night, a damsel of discreet port demurely go behind a young man, unplait his pig-tail, tease the hair, thin it of some of its lively inmates, braid it up for him, and retire." The women always wear two braided pigtails.

**Habits.**

Dr. Campbell says of the Lepchas, "They are wonderfully honest, theft being scarcely known among them; they rarely quarrel among themselves. I have never known them to draw their knives on one another, although they always wear them. They fly bad government rather than resist it, and used to prefer digging for yams in the jungle, and eating wretchedly innutritious vegetables, to enduring any injustice or harsh treatment. They are singularly forgiving of injuries, when time is given them, after hasty loss of temper. Although they were ready enough to lodge complaints before the magistrate against one another in cases of assault and other offences, they rarely prosecuted to a decision, generally preferring to submit to arbitration, or making mutual amends and concessions. They are averse to soldiering, and cannot be induced to enlist in our army, even for local service in the Hills." So far as they have any religion, they are Buddhists, and bury their dead. They are gross feeders, eating all kinds of animal food, including monkey, elephant, rhinoceros, besides many uncommon vegetables and roots. Tea is a favourite beverage, and they had no native distilled liquor.

**Character of the Lepchas.**

Still less known than the people of Sikkim are the

natives of Bhutan, the large mountainous tract lying east of Sikkim, north of Assam, and south of Tibet. The population is somewhat scanty, under a temporal ruler, the Deb raja, and a spiritual ruler, the Dharma raja, who is supposed to be an incarnation of Buddha; under these are a spiritual council of Buddhist monks, and a secular council. There is an appearance of systematic government, which has been sufficiently active to occasion much trouble to us in dealing with them since we annexed Assam. After finding the Bhutanese to be quite untrustworthy, we were compelled to annex the borderland between Assam and Bhutan, called the Doars, in 1865. The upper classes and rulers are described as shameless beggars, bullies, and sycophants, while the lower classes bear a much better character. They weave a coarse cloth, make a kind of paper from bark, distil spirit from various grains, and drink it freely. Marriage is a very loose ordinance; brothers usually have one wife between them; and the women have no sense of delicacy.

**The Bhutanese.**

The Lhopas form a considerable portion of the Bhutanese. They are tall, and quarrelsome and cruel rather than brave. Their eyes and hair are black, and their broad flat face approximates very considerably to the Chinese.

**The Lhopas.**

Assam is remarkable for the number and variety of the races it contains; and little more than a summary account of them can be attempted. Assam was annexed by the British in 1829, after the first Burmese war; and many traces of Burmese domination remain. Indeed, many of the people are of the Shan (or Siamese) race. Half the population have adopted the Hindu religion, including the Shans, while one-fourth are Mahometans.

**The Assam tribes.**

The Khasias, inhabiting the Khasia and Jaintia Hills of Southern Assam, are a peaceable tribe, numbering 170,000 at the census of 1881. Although Mongols, they approach to a fair complexion, having, however, the straight black Mongolian hair. They are honest and truthful, though superstitious. They

**The Khasias.**

deem a twin birth unlucky and degrading, and used to kill one of the twins. They have a great belief in omens;

MISHMI WOMAN, ASSAM.

one of their methods is, to break eggs on a board, and divine coming events from the way in which the yolk and the pieces of shell arrange themselves. They raise remarkable cromlechs, dolmens, etc., as memorials of their dead, of great events, etc. In some cases these rise to thirty feet high in a single block. The mode in which they cut these blocks from the mass is very ingenious. They cut grooves, along which fires are lighted, and into which, when heated, cold water is run, causing the rock to fissure along the groove. Levers and ropes are their simple means of transplanting the blocks to the required situation. Their marriage ceremonies are of a very simple character, merely consisting in the couple sitting on one seat and receiving their friends at a marriage feast. It is not surprising that such a union is very readily dissolved. The house belongs to the woman, who retains it if separated from her husband, or if he dies. To these women proprietors naturally falls the greater part of the work, both domestic and agricultural; yet they are not devoid of feminine vanity, and wear gold ear-rings and necklaces, and heavy silver bracelets (not anklets). Both sexes chew a mixture of betel-nut and lime, which swells and colours the lips, making them hideous. The men are expert at fishing, often catching large numbers by poisoning the fish. They are courageous and fight well, some of them having great muscular development.

**Dolmen and cromlech builders.**

The Garo or Garrow tribes (about 100,000 in number) inhabit the hills in South-western Assam. Some of them have habits like the Khasias. They build large houses, with a bamboo floor from four to ten feet above the ground. The lower chamber serves for the cattle. It need hardly be said that such houses are filthy. Only the girls remain at home with the parents, one corner of the house being reserved as a bedroom; while the boys and bachelors sleep in a bachelors' hall. The men are lively, good-natured, hospitable, and truthful. Women are the holders of property, and make the first advances towards marriage, the bridegroom being taken to the bride's home. The divisions or clans of the people are so many motherhoods. The man who marries the favourite daughter of a house must also marry her mother on the death of her

**The Garrow tribes.**

**Female property and privileges.**

father. The Garrows till recent times had many slaves; and it is to be doubted whether the practice is yet extinct.

Cotton is the chief crop of the Garrows; but they also rear cattle, goats, pigs, dogs, cats, and fowls. Among their food are tortoises and dried fish, deer, wild hogs, frogs, and snakes; but they dislike milk, believing it to be a product of disease. In the past they have been very turbulent, being very difficult to persuade of the excellence of civilised ways. They were very unwilling to give up human sacrifices, and only in 1848 consented to discontinue hanging human skulls in their houses. Their mania for human skulls, to appease the spirits of their mountains, and even for use as a sort of currency, has with difficulty been repressed. In 1871 they were greatly disturbed by the census arrangements, and in 1872–3 had to be forcibly put down. Somewhat like the Khasias, the Garrows erect carved posts as monuments.

**Human sacrifices.**

The feasts of the Garrows are occasions of much drunkenness, combined with dancing. "Twenty or thirty men, standing behind one another in a row, hold each other by the sides of their belts, and then go round in a circle, hopping first on one foot and then on the other, singing and keeping time with the music, which is animating, though harsh and inharmonious. The women likewise dance in rows, but hold out their hands, at the same time lowering one and raising the other, as the music beats, and occasionally turning round with great rapidity."

**Festival dances.**

Religiously, the Garrows are chiefly believers in witches and demons, combined with the idea that the souls of certain persons can leave their bodies and take up their abode in the body of a tiger or other animal. But they have adopted a number of practices and gods from the Hindus, who have largely influenced them.

**Witchcraft and demonology.**

The Kukis, of the Chittagong Hills, south of the Gar rows and Khasias, and adjacent to the Nagas of Assam, also known as Tiperah on the eastern frontier. They resemble the Khasia tribes, being much more muscular than the Bengali, and nearly as fair as an average dark European. Many of them have only adopted clothing during this century. Their endurance of fatigue is something marvellous. "I have seen a [Kuki] boy of not more than ten years of age," says Stewart, "carrying a burden weighing about thirty pounds for a long march of some fifteen or sixteen miles, on a footpath rugged and difficult, over country where high mountains had to be ascended and descended, lifting his legs as lightly as a cat, never making a false step, and his skin being perfectly dry and free from perspiration. Nor was this done only for one day, but for ten, one after the other; and I believe any other Kuki boy could do the same." **The Kukis.**

KHANTI: ASSAM FRONTIER.

As in others of these tribes, the boys and young men sleep in a bachelors' chamber; but each family, independent of the unmarried males, has its own house. The men wear a large cloth wrapped loosely round the body, and hanging from the shoulder to the knee; the women wear a short striped petticoat, and unmarried girls, in addition, wear a cloth round their chests. These garments are made by the Kukis. Like the last tribe, they are very fond of skulls, which they use in the funeral ceremonies of their chiefs, whose bodies they smoke dry and keep for two months before burial.

**Dress and habits.**

The Kuki chiefs exact the entire labour of their people for four days a year on their private land, besides a percentage of their crops and of all game caught. They migrate to new pastures and fields whenever they consider the old ones exhausted.

**Marriage customs.**

Marriage does not take place in childhood; and near relatives, even cousins, cannot marry. The chief may have as many wives and concubines as he can keep. Wives are purchased either by cash or by service for a term of years in the house of the wife's parents. The wedding ceremony is performed by the chief of the village. The pair place their feet together on a large stone, the chief sprinkles both with water, exhorts them to fidelity, and blesses them, after which a grand feast follows. Property does not descend to or through women. Like most of the hill people, the Kukis are pre-eminently dirty, washing being an operation unknown to them.

**Ideas of Heaven.**

The Kukis have very vague ideas of religion, ascribing all evils to the anger of gods or demons, whom they endeavour to propitiate. Their Heaven is for themselves alone, for they believe other peoples have heavens for themselves. They think they shall assume their old forms after death, and inhabit a world of shades. They have numerous beliefs, not constituting a formal religious system, which we cannot recount here.

**The Naga tribes.**

The Naga tribes inhabit the hills of that name in the eastern border of Assam, and really include a large number of peoples with different dialects; but, being practically of one Mongoloid or Tibeto-Chinese race, we must speak of them together. They have become unfavourably known to the British in consequence of their frequent destructive incursions into the plains. They are described as brave and martial, but vindictive and treacherous. In 1875 they treacherously murdered Lieut. Holcombe and his followers, and in 1879 killed Mr. Damant, our deputy commissioner.

The Nagas are a short, active, large-legged race, with

GROUP OF BAUTPARA NAGAS, ASSAM.

Tartar faces, wonderfully long-winded, sure-footed, and strong-backed. They have brown complexions, large mouths, flat noses, high cheek-bones, and a cunning, severe expression. They eat every kind of flesh, but do not drink milk. Their houses, though of considerable size, have very small

**Physical characters and habits.**

rooms, allotted to women, little children, pigs, fowls, etc. In addition to a youths' house, each village has a girls' house, in which the girls live till married. The young people, however, take their meals with their parents, and work for them during the day, returning at night to their respective houses.

The Nagas have bloody quarrels between different villages, in which they display much treachery and cruelty. Contrary to the Kukis, they have a love for the particular villages they inhabit, and retain them permanently. They bury their dead at the very doors of their houses. Scalps or skulls are held in high esteem, and they are not particular as to how they are obtained. The number of people killed gives the men their chief claim to distinction. The warrior wears round his neck a collar reaching to the waist, made of goats' hair dyed red, mixed with long locks of the persons he has killed, and bedecked with cowrie shells.

**Skulls and scalps.**

Naturally, among such fire-eaters, the women do all the work, while the men lie idly in the sun, unless they do a little work in the fields. Marriage is a very simple arrangement, without any ceremony except a feast; the family of the bride, also, is presented with cows, pigs, fowls, or spirits.

**Women and marriage.**

Naga cries are very extraordinary. The war-whoop is something indescribable, fearfully shrill and prolonged, with variations. A more peaceful cry is the "hoo-hoo," a mode of honouring an individual or a village. From ten to fifty natives cry in chorus, making only the sounds "hoi" and "hou" alternately, with the full force of the lungs, about a hundred times, and finished off with a "howh": this is the Naga way of hurrahing. But it is done with a strict eye to business. Every person or village thus honoured is expected to give a liberal present in return; and woe to the deficient giver!

**War-whoop and "hoo-hoo."**

The Nagas cultivate rice, cotton, and tobacco, as well as the more common Indian vegetables. They cut down the jungle, leaving the roots and stumps, and setting the cut wood on fire. After the wood is burnt, the soil is scratched with a hoe, to mix the ashes with it. Seeds are then dropped in indiscriminately. The results of such agriculture, combined with their habit of only cultivating the same patch of ground for two years following, are of course very inferior.

**Naga agriculture.**

Both sexes among the Nagas wear ear-rings, but not nose-rings, of brass wire; but they often wear flowers as ear-rings, as well as coloured pieces of paper or cloth, a blue beetle wing, or even a blade of green grass or a leaf.

ANGAMI NAGA.

Assam owes its name to its former possessors, the Ahom (the *h* being readily interchangeable with *ss* in Burmese), a branch of the Tai, which include the Siamese people. Intermarrying with the natives,

**The Ahom of Assam.**

their features became much improved, and they adopted Hinduism. They were subsequently conquered in 1810 by the Burmese, from whom we took Assam in 1829. The people largely speak Assamese, a vernacular closely allied to Bengali. They have responded very satisfactorily to efforts for improving their education and social condition, and have become largely assimilated to the Bengali.

**Burmah.** Burmah, or Barmah, is now entirely under the government of British India, the kingdom of Ava having been conquered in 1885, and added to the large portion, including Pegu, Arakan, and Tenasserim, which had been annexed in 1826 and 1853. The large increase of population under British rule is almost a sufficient justification for the successive annexations. The total population of Burmah may be estimated at 7,000,000, the old-established British provinces counting for four millions. Rangoon and Moulmein, in the Gulf of Martaban, are rapidly growing seaports, with four active vernacular presses at Rangoon, which is a Buddhist as well as a commercial centre. A cyclopædia of Burmese knowledge is even published at one of these presses.

BURMESE YOUNG LADY.

**The Burmese.** The Burmese people show considerable distinctness from the Siamese, having come as a conquering people from north to south. They are stouter and darker than their Eastern neighbours, and their head is oval rather than ovoid, the forehead being broad. Altogether their head has many resemblances to the coarse Malayo-Polynesian type.

The Burmese have been very largely influenced by Indian thought and culture, as must be evident from their having become zealous Buddhists; but their buildings also bear evident marks of Indian origin. They have great figures of Buddha (Gautama) in every pagoda, and believe in the presence of a spirit (La) in every animal, plant, or thing. Although so advanced in some respects, the Burmese tattoo themselves extensively, being perhaps the most civilised people who do so. They have no surnames, their single name having the prefix "Moung" signifying brother, or Nga, Koh, or Poh. In salutation, they bend three times to the ground.

**Influence of Hindu thought.**

Our troops have recently been compelled to realise once more the amazing muscularity, courage, and stamina of the Burmese. For true bravery and endurance of privation they are quite remarkable; and they are equally famous for ambushes and stratagems. The daring and the skill of the dacoits or bandits and murderous classes have been made unfortunately too familiar to us by the many deaths they have occasioned among our officers and men. When the late subjects of the King of Burmah have become as familiar with the benefit of British rule as their fellows in lower Burmah, it is probable that they may rank among our most intelligent and progressive subjects.

BURMESE ACTORS.

**Bravery.**

**Dacoits.**

The Burmese women are not kept in seclusion, but

mingle freely with the other sex, though treated as inferiors. Marriages are not arranged till the parties are grown up; and the negotiation is undertaken by the young man's nearest female relative. The bridegroom's present to his wife is three skirts, three sashes, three pieces of white muslin, and such jewels as he can afford; then, at the marriage feast, which is the only ceremony, the pair eat out of the same dish. Widows receive one-fourth of their husband's property, the rest being divided between the children. The higher ranks burn their dead, the lower bury them or throw them into a river. Priests' corpses are treated with especial ceremony, being embalmed with costly spices, and reserved for a grand ceremonial, the body being placed on an immense car, which is pulled in diverse directions by the multitude, towards water or fire, victory being to the strongest, and determining the mode of disposing of the body.

**Burmese women.** **Marriage.** **Burial.**

The government of the Burmese king and court was very despotic and tyrannic, and the cause of much oppression. The life and property of all subjects were at the king's disposal. White umbrellas and white elephants were among the special attributes of royalty; but our soldiers found the white elephants a mere sham, very little lighter than ordinary ones, and in no way worthy of the fuss made about them.

**The late despotic government.**

The characters of the Burmese language are formed of circles and segments of circles; there are thirty-three simple sounds or characters. Native books have formerly been made of pieces of prepared palm-leaf fastened together. For their religious rites and books the Buddhist priests use Pali, like their brethren in Ceylon.

**The Burmese language.**

In general accomplishments and intelligence, the Burmese are far behind the Hindus. Their manufactures are limited in number and are not highly advanced, although the possibilities for their development are considerable. The preponderating influence of Buddhism, with the exorbitant demands of its priests for their maintenance, and for the building and support

**Injurious influence of Buddhism.**

A BURMESE BAND.

of the temples, is responsible for much of the backward state of our new kingdom. To raise it to the level of Pegu and Tenasserim, still more to that of Calcutta and Bombay, will task the best endeavours of even the British government. The Burmese are far more attached to religious processions, exhibitions, and feasting, than to good government and industry; the latter they leave to the women. Puppets and marionettes, loud and coarse music, boat-racing and horse-racing, athletics, gambling, and cockfighting, are among the popular amusements.

**Amusements.**

The Talaings, or Mons, of the Irrawaddy delta are essentially of the same race as the Burmese, but preceded them in time, and speak a distinct language, founded on the Pali, and with considerable affinity to the Kolarian languages of India. They are of somewhat lighter colour and more delicate features than the Burmese, but are becoming more and more amalgamated with and assimilated to them.

**The Talaings, or Mons.**

Among the Mongolian peoples, few are more interesting for study than the Karens, who are widely spread in Burmah, especially in Tenasserim and Siam, but describe themselves as having originally come from the North. However, they inhabited their present territories long before the advent of the Burmese. They are divided into a number of distinct tribes, and vary considerably in physique and character according to the district in which they live—mountainous or lowland. They are of smaller stature than Europeans, but well proportioned and muscular, capable of much endurance. As with so many Mongolians, dirt, drunkenness, and deceit abound among them; but they are industrious, attached to home and family, and their women have a better moral character than some of their neighbours. Revenge is a cardinal idea with them. A father on his death-bed will charge his sons to avenge him on his enemies. They are very imitative, and can readily learn the use of tools, though they originate nothing.

**The Karens of Burmah.**

Various subdivisions of these people are known, as the white, red, and black Karens, from the colour of their clothes. The red Karens, however, now wear some black clothing. They inhabit some of the best land in the interior of Burmah, and in times past issued from their table-lands to plunder and kidnap in all directions, selling most of their captives—the Burmese to the Siamese, and *vice versâ*. Every man had a short knife; those who had not guns had swords or spears; with these, riding on their active ponies, they were sufficiently formidable as cavalry. Their character

**White, red, and black Karens.**

A BURMESE GENTLEMAN, WITH ATTENDANTS.

is further shown by the considerable amount of comfort in which they live. Their food is good, they have many implements, better than those of the Burmese, and they formerly made them all themselves.

Some of the Karen tribes are Buddhists, but others are Pagan. They burn their dead, but reserve a portion of the skull to hang from a tree, together with the clothing, armour, and ornaments of the deceased. Round these they dance and sing, after which the remains are buried. The Pagans have

**Religion and funeral customs.**

a sort of spirit worship, reverencing the *nats*, or good and evil spirits of rivers, hills, plains, and trees, and sacrificing to them buffaloes, hogs, and fowls. Some of them also worship the spirits of their ancestors.

The Karens usually marry within their own limited tribes, and second cousins are preferred. Children, especially girls, are betrothed early. A go-between often arranges marriages; open courting is considered discreditable.

HILL KARENS.

**Marriage ceremonies.** When the marriage takes place, the bride is led by her relatives, with a procession blowing trumpets, to the bridegroom's parents' house, where, while ascending the ladder to its entrance, she receives an abundant *douche* of water, and then takes a meal with her new relatives. The bride and bridegroom then give drink to one another, each saying to the other, "Be faithful to thy covenant." This is the essential part of the marriage ceremony. Polygamy is unknown, though divorces not unfrequently occur, the wife retaining the domestic hearth and most of the property. Before Dr. Mason visited them, now many years ago, a Karen of note made his will in the following manner, written wills

**Will-making.** being unknown. He invited every inhabitant of the village to a feast, at which he solemnly declared his wishes as to the disposal of his property, and begged that his wishes might be carried out after his death.

A number of the Karen tribes have only one great building, built of bamboo, to accommodate an entire village. This has an enclosed square or hall in the centre, and a walk extending round the four sides, with rooms opening into it on either side. The central hall is common property, but each married couple have a room and hearth of their own. Round the hall is a raised platform, which forms the sleeping quarters of the young men. This entire building is raised some eight or ten feet above the ground, pig-sties being arranged beneath. From this it may be expected, as is the fact, that the Karens are very dirty. If they could be cleansed, they would show a lighter skin, and the women would exhibit a capacity of blushing which would give them some attractiveness.

**Karen dwellings.**

KAREN CHIEF.

Government, among the Karens, is very indefinite. The strongest or most self-assertive man is chief of a village or district; but he loses his following when a stronger arises. The elders have considerable influence; but, on the whole, every man is a law to himself, and retaliation is looked upon as perfectly just. Cursing is a serious mode of treating evildoers; and selling them into slavery is a rather frequent practice. Villages are very often at war with their neighbours, and in proceeding to hostilities they give no quarter.

**Mode of government.**

As an illustration of war feeling among the Karens, we will give a war song recorded by Mr. Mason.

> "I go to war, I am sent;
> I go to fight, I am sent.
> Clothe me with the iron breast-plate,

Give me the iron shield.
I am not strong, may I make myself strong.
I am weak, may I make myself powerful.
I go with a multitude, many persons;
We will go to the house, the foot of the steps;
We will fire muskets and holloa,
The people come with wives and children;
Unsheath the spear, draw the sword;
Smite the neck, spear the side,
The blood flows purple.

I go to war, I am employed;
I go to fight, I am employed.
Employer, give me whisky to drink:
I drink till I am dizzy,
We march in order, like white ants;
We cross a stream, and trample it dry:
We arrive at the foot of the house,
We reach the foot of the ladder:
We go up into the bedrooms;
Blood flows like a stream of water;
The blood flows down under the house.
The mother cries herself to death.
The great hawk flies over the house,
Pounces down on the chief's red cock;
The great hawk sweeps around the house,
Carries off its prey at the foot of the steps;
Seizes the chief's white cock,
The great hawk flies away,
Leaving the chief behind weeping."

From this it is very evident how deeply the Karens are interested in their feuds and warlike affairs. The same author who has preserved this song tells us that the Karens eat every quadruped, from a rat to an elephant, excepting felines; and that reptiles are equally acceptable. All kinds of birds and fish and grubs are welcome in their bill of fare; while every plant serves as a vegetable.

Food.

## THE TIBETANS.

This people, one of the most isolated and little known in the world, is also one of the most interesting. Like the Chinese, long their racial antagonists, they afforded a home to Buddhism when it was almost expelled from the land of its origin; and Tibet now stands as the central abode of that religion, much as the States of the Church did till recently for Romanism. Buddhism was not introduced into Tibet until the seventh century, A.D., by a king of Sakya descent, whose dynasty ruled over the country for many centuries. Gradually the Buddhist priests increased their claims to influence and authority, and in the eleventh century were almost paramount. Until the fifteenth century marriage prevailed among the priesthood; and this party is still predominant in Ladakh, Bhutan, and Sikkim; while a celibate reformation gained possession of Tibet, the priests adopting the yellow robes, whose wearers are still predominant and are acknowledged by the Chinese emperor as practical rulers of Tibet.

**Introduction of Buddhism.**

The Grand Lama of Tibet is reverenced as an incarnation of Buddha, and holds sway at Lassa. At his death search is made for a child bearing certain signs or marks known to the Lamas, which identify him as the succeeding incarnation of Buddha.

**The Grand Lama.**

TIBETAN.

The lamas,—corresponding to some extent with Western monks,—exist in vast numbers in Tibet, congregated in hundreds and even thousands in huge "lamasseries." According to Captain Gill, who visited Eastern Tibet in 1877,* the lamas shave their heads, are filthy in their person, and dress in a piece rather than a garment of coarse red serge thrown over one shoulder, and another length wound round the waist and forming a sort of skirt. Many are bare-footed, while others wear high boots of leather and red cloth. A string of beads and a prayer-cylinder complete the costume. "The prayer-cylinder, or prayer-wheel, as it is often most inappropriately called, is usually," says Captain Gill, "about three or four inches

**Lamasseries.**

**Dress of lamas.**

**The prayer-cylinders.**

* "The River of Golden Sand," by Capt. W. Gill. 1880.

in diameter and in length; the mystical invocation, 'Om Ma-ni Pe-mi Hom' (O the Jewel in the Lotus! Amen.), is written on the outside, whilst a small weight at the end of a short string keeps the affair in rotation; and all day long, not only the Lamas, but the people may be seen muttering the universal prayer, and twisting their cylinders, invariably in the same direction with the hands of a clock. One or more great cylinders, inscribed with this sentence, stand at the entrance to every house in Tibet; and a member of the household or a guest who passes is always expected to give the cylinder a twist for the welfare of the establishment. At almost every rivulet the eye is arrested by a little building that is at first mistaken for a water mill, but which on close inspection is found to contain a cylinder, turning by the force of the stream, and ceaselessly sending up pious ejaculations tc heaven; for every turn of a cylinder on which the prayer is written is supposed to convey an invocation to the deity. Sometimes enormous barns are filled with these cylinders, gorgeously painted, and with the prayer repeated on them many times; and at every turn and every step in Tibet this sentence is forced upon the traveller's notice in some form or another."

**Universality of the prayer-machine.**

It is in accordance with the reverence paid to them that the lamas are rich, some lamasseries being enormously so. They own half the country, and constantly receive legacies, and grow rich by usury. They are untaxed; they scarcely ever do any work, the agriculture of the lamasseries being performed by large numbers of slaves; and they are generally profligates, though professedly celibates. They leave their retreats when they choose, and pray just as much or as little as they choose. Consequently recruits to their organisation are always forthcoming. Idlers and criminals are constantly entering them. It is said that the common people detest the lamas for their oppression, and that the country is getting depopulated by emigration to Yunnan.

**Wealth of the lamas.**

The Tibetans may perhaps be regarded as typical Mongols. In their own and surrounding districts they are known as Bot or Bhot, the same name which appears in Bhutan. Their ordinary complexion is tawny yellow; but the upper class are said to be almost as fair as Europeans, with the usual Mongol small black eyes, high cheek-bones, and snub nose. Their clothing is much more important to them than to Indians and Burmese, because of the great altitude of their table-land and mountains, the majority of the people living at a height of nine to eleven thousand feet above the sea level. Those who can afford them, wear Chinese satins in the warm season, and the same lined with fur in colder weather. The poorer people wear woollen, sheepskins, and any furs they can get. Ablution is as rare among them as with many Mongols; and their clothing is worn in an indescribably dirty and greasy condition, rendering proximity to them very disagreeable.

**Physical aspect.**

**Clothing.**

The principal food of a Tibetan is a kind of oatmeal porridge mixed with much butter. Their tea is taken with large lumps of butter in it. Sour cream, curds, and cheese are also eaten; but the milk, being kept in dirty vessels, turns bad very quickly. Mutton is their principal meat; and the long wool of the Tibetan sheep is well known to be excellent in quality. The Yak, or Tibetan hump-backed ox, is of course the most treasured animal, being the source of their abundant supplies of butter and milk. A man with three or four hundred head of cattle is rich, while one who has only twenty or thirty is poor. The richest people possess two or three thousand head, and let them out to cattle-keepers.

**Food.**

**Cattle.**

The Tibetan women, however poor, have large quantities of jewellery, often of solid gold. Not unfrequently they wear on each side of the head disks of chased silver about the size of a saucer, meeting above, and a third smaller one behind, all loaded with coral and turquoise. Necklaces and chains of beads, and elaborate charm boxes containing the mystical prayer, are frequent and abundant adornments. Another article almost universally carried is the polished wooden cup from which porridge or tea is drunk.

**Tibetan jewellery.**

Tibetan houses are rarely congregated, but are scattered over the country, often at intervals of two or three hundred yards. They are frequently very inferior and gloomy, with flat roofs and little windows. The lower area is a stable; a ladder leads to the upper storey, all being of wood. The idea of good fires does not seem to have occurred to them, for they are content in their cold weather with miserable wood or charcoal fires in pans giving far more smoke than warmth.

**Tibetan houses.**

The bodies of the dead are disposed of mostly by exposure; and not only are birds of prey admitted to the death enclosures, but also dogs and other beasts of prey. The bodies of Lamas and other leading people are however burnt, with a vast amount of ceremonial.

**Exposure of the dead.**

We must not omit mention of the suzerainty claimed, and indeed exercised, by the Emperor of China over Tibet. There are two Chinese residents at Lassa; and whether they interfere with local government or not, they keep alive the idea of Pekin authority, which is exercised to keep out foreigners who may not be palatable to them, and to claim a certain amount of tribute.

**Chinese authority.**

A conversation between a Tibetan Lama and a European traveller in 1886, gives the reason of their reluctance to welcome Europeans. The Lamas say that "Europeans have a good religion which they do not generally practise, and yet wish to force on others whose religion is as good and is practised. They are believed to be full of greed, for, living in a rich country, they always acquire other countries; and while they talk of their benevolent purposes, they destroy animal life every day for their own food, thus becoming clouded in intellect and in the perception of true morality. If they merely wanted to cultivate friendly relations, why not do so by letters? or would not one envoy be sufficient to propose trade arrangements?" In fact, the past ways of Europeans seem very evidently to forebode new conquests.

# CHAPTER IX.

## The Siamese, Cochin Chinese, Cambodians, etc.

**The Kingdom of Siam—The Tai, or Thai—Chinese immigrants—Four dynasties of kings—Constantine Phaulcon—Burmese attacks—The late king Monk-gut—King Chulalonkorn—Abolition of prostration and slavery—Slave-debtors—Physical characters of Siamese—Lao physical characters—Dress of both sexes almost alike—Jewellery—Tattooing—Ear ornaments of Laos—Work and habits—Siamese and Lao character—Houses and furniture—Reception of visitors—Marriage ceremonies—Education—New-born children—Treatment of mothers—Siamese temples—Cremation—Albino or "white" elephants—Siamese processions—Manufactures and productions—Language—The Cochin-Chinese—Physical characters and dress—Food and drink—Marriage—Religion—Sorcerers—Christian missionaries—The Tonkinese—Language—The Cambodian kingdom—Former civilisation—The Khmer—A Caucasian people—The Malays—Negritos.**

LAO.

**The kingdom of Siam.**

THE kingdom of Siam includes several racial elements, mostly Mongol, but also, according to recent researches, a distinct infusion of a Caucasian stock, more abundant in Cambodia. Our knowledge of Siam is still rather imperfect owing to the unwillingness of the people to admit foreigners, even as travellers. Bangkok, the capital, near the mouth of the river Menam, is the only place where Europeans are permitted to reside.

The Siamese people form a distinct Mongolian group, the Tai, or Thai, the dominant people who throng the Menam valley. The Laos are a variety less numerous, occupying chiefly the valley of the Meikong, or Cambodia river. The Shans are another variety in Northern Siam and Eastern Burmah. Siam also includes many Mons, or Peguans, and Malays; also a large number of Karens and other mountain tribes. But next to the Siamese or Tai proper, the most numerous of all the inhabitants are Chinese, who have so insinuated themselves as to gain a large proportion of the trade of the country. They are constantly immigrating, and never bring Chinese wives, but marry Siamese women. If they return to China, their Siamese wives and children remain behind. They have their own temples, and worship Buddha according to the Chinese fashion.

**The Tai, or Thai.**

**Chinese immigrants.**

In ancient times Siam appears to have been an appendage of Cambodia; but there are records of four dynasties of Siamese kings, extending from A.D. 1350. The seat of government was formerly Ayuthia, a few miles further up the Menam than Bangkok, which is quite modern; a large portion of its population indeed living on the river in boats, Chinese-fashion. In the sixteenth century the Burmese king of Pegu conquered Ayuthia, but did not retain his capture many years. In the reign of the enlightened king Narai (1657–1683), many European merchants established themselves in trade in the country, one of whom was the remarkable adventurer Constantine Phaulcon, Venetian in origin, his father being the son of a governor of Cephalonia, his mother a native of that island. Phaulcon, having visited Siam to trade, became a great favourite with the king, through his mechanical and business skill, and his introduction of many European novelties, such as telescopes. He erected forts for the king, selecting the site which Bangkok now occupies. He induced the king to repair the old city of Louvo, and construct a palace there in European style; near which Phaulcon built a palace for himself, as well as a Romish church. His innovations were so far-reaching that accusations were made against him, and he was assassinated by order of a rebel prince. Many of Phaulcon's works are still to be seen in ruins.

**Four dynasties of kings.**

**Constantine Phaulcon.**

THE LATE KING OF SIAM, MONGKUT.

The Burmese again attacked the Siamese in the middle of the last century, and took and burnt Ayuthia in 1767.

**Burmese attacks.** Finding it difficult to retain full authority in Siam, the Burmese contented themselves with plundering and murdering for some years, till an extraordinary man of Chinese origin, named Pin Tat, established himself as king at Bangkok under the name of Phya Tak. The present dynasty is descended from a notable Siamese general under Phya Tak, who became king in 1782. **The late King Mongkut.** The late King Mongkut (1851–1868) was a most enlightened monarch in many ways. Like not a few of his predecessors, he had decided literary tastes; he could speak and write English, and had many English surroundings and tastes. He was especially fond of scientific instruments and mechanical devices.

The present King Chulalonkorn continues the intelligent traditions of his father and predecessor. His palace **King Chulalonkorn.** is a mixture of different forms of European architecture with the characteristic Siamese roof. In his library are to be found the leading English and American periodicals and newspapers; and he works as hard as any European monarch, supervising the affairs of the entire kingdom. One of his first acts was to abolish the old etiquette which required every one to **Abolition of prostration and slavery.** approach the king in extreme prostration, and forbade any subject to see his face. All classes may now have audience of the king, and approach him standing. He has also abolished slavery (the order taking effect gradually) in the tracts under his immediate control; but this does not apply to northern Siam, with which his relations are indirect. But slave-**Slave-debtors.** debtors are very numerous, namely, debtors who are in service till a debt is worked off. As Carl Bock says, in his "Temples and Elephants," 1884, giving an account of a journey through Upper Siam and Lao, the king is a century in advance of his people, encouraging education and research in every way. At his own expense he has sent a considerable number of young Siamese noblemen to England, France, and Germany, to be educated and improved by contact with Western civilisation. A European doctor is one of his intimate friends; and in every matter in which he can employ Europeans without arousing too much jealousy among his subjects, he does so.

**Physical characters of Siamese.**

The Siamese, or Tai proper, are intermediate in colour between the Chinese and the Malays, the upper classes being decidedly light yellow, the hair and eyes being black, and the latter small and somewhat dull-looking. The nose is small, and the teeth are often dyed black, the lips being deep red from the universal habit of chewing betel. It cannot be said that the face has any beauty in our eyes, though the children are better looking. A considerable number of the people of Bangkok, influenced by the example of the king, now wear their hair all over the head, and cut short in both sexes; but the majority of Siamese men, especially away from the coast, retain the fashion of shaving it all off except a small tuft on the crown, while the women do not shave, but cut the hair short, and are also addicted to painting their eyebrows and eyelids. The Laos are of a lighter complexion than the Siamese, and much more exclusive. They are decidedly better looking, with high foreheads and well-shaped noses. Often the young women have fat round faces, and the lips are somewhat protruding. Many of the Lao women are able to bend their forearm and wrist outwards, so that the back of the hand touches the upper arm; this is acquired by early practice and the use of some force.

**Lao physical characters.**

**Dress of both sexes almost alike.**

Perhaps it is among the Siamese that the least difference of dress between the sexes is discernible; but no, we were forgetting the Esquimaux. Their principal garment is similar, namely, a long piece of cotton cloth or silk worn round the waist and passed between the thighs, one end being fastened in front and the other behind, thus producing the effect of a pair of short trousers. The upper part of the body is girt with a long scarf passed round the chest and over one shoulder in a variety of fashions. Under this the more advanced now wear a close-fitting white jacket, and even white stockings and dress shoes. The Siamese

**Jewellery.**

women are very fond of jewellery, though little partial to ear-rings. Rings and gold chains are abundant; and even children, though otherwise quite undressed, wear heavy bracelets and anklets.

SIAMESE WOMEN AT DINNER.

The western Laos for the most part content themselves with a much more limited garb, often only a small metal

**Tattooing.**

plate, while the appearance of clothing is given to the male by very elaborate tattooing. This extends from the waist down to the knees, and represents a variety of birds and other animals, including peacocks, pigeons, vultures, lions, tigers, elephants, as well as some fabulous creatures or monsters, the interspaces being filled in by wavy lines. The pigment used is the soot from burning lard, mixed with bile, and pricked into the skin. The operation is very painful.

Both sexes in Lao have their ears pierced and the aperture stretched to a remarkable extent, by pieces of wood, ivory, or metal successively inserted. The men either wear a fresh flower in the ear, or use it as a convenient place for carrying a cigarette or cigar, tobacco being universally smoked by both sexes and young children. The women's ear-ornament is a rolled plate of gold, or, among the poor, a thin cylinder of gold filled up with lead.

**Ear ornaments of Laos.**

Throughout a great part of Siam and its dependencies the women do the principal part of the work, even in the fields. The men are on the whole idle, disposed to sports and amusements, without ideas of improvement or even enriching themselves except by hoarding secretly what they can keep from the chief's eyes. The Siamese character has been described as "gentle, cheerful, timid, careless, and almost passionless"; but this does not apply to the northern people, who are mostly mean, selfish, and untruthful, and hate and distrust foreigners to an absurd degree. Credit must, however, be given to them for more than average morality between the sexes. They are certainly very expressionless in countenance, seldom laughing or crying; when roused, however, they can show anger or irritation as plainly as most people, but largely by movements other than those of the face.

**Work and habits.**

**Siamese and Lao character.**

Both Siamese houses and furniture are very slight, being built of bamboo, usually raised some feet above the ground, unless built out of the reach of inundations. "An ordinary Lao householder," says Bock, "thinks his dwelling well appointed if he has a few plaited rattan or bamboo mats and cushions ready to spread upon the floor; for, when not actually in use, they are kept piled up in a heap in some convenient corner. The best mats are edged with a red border;

**Houses and furniture.**

and the cushions, which are either oblong or three-sided, have their ends embroidered in silk or gold. When a visitor enters, a mat is spread on the floor, with a cushion either behind to lean against or at the side as a support to the arm—the quality of the cushions and mats selected depending entirely upon the rank of the visitor. The **Reception of visitors.** Chows (chiefs) have, as a rule, a table and a few chairs, but seldom use the latter except when visited by 'distinguished strangers,' when they look very uncomfortable as they sit cross-legged on the seat. Of bedsteads there are none, the people sleeping on home-made mattresses stuffed with cotton-wool, and surrounded by a mosquito-curtain." The utensils are limited to a few earthenware pots and pans, with wooden spoons. The better houses have lamps, and even clocks and looking-glasses; the poorer have cotton wicks to burn in vessels of oil. The infant's cradle is a sort of basket swung from the roof by long cords.

Both Siamese and Laos employ go-betweens in arranging marriages, about which there is much palaver. The astrologers are usually consulted as to favourable ages **Marriage ceremonies.** and other compatibilities. Dowries are given from both sides in equal proportion, and large presents, which are taken in stately processions to the bride. The priests read an extract from the Buddhist Scriptures, and pray for a blessing on the couple. After this, the curtain which has concealed the bride is lifted, and the pair, seated near each other, are sprinkled with holy water. After further prayers, followed by two days of feasting, the marriage is complete. Until the birth of the first child, the newly-married pair live with the parents of the bride.

It is the Siamese rule to have but one wife; but the upper classes keep as many subordinate wives or concubines as they can afford. The duly married wife has a **Education.** good deal of influence, though little or no education; but the male sex are little better educated, except in Bangkok, their education being confined to imperfect reading and writing and the precepts and legends of Buddha.

The Laos believe that children are the offspring of the spirits; and when newly born they are placed on the top of the ladder leading to the house, and the spirits are called to take away the child at once or not to molest it afterwards. Various offerings to the spirits are made; and on the second day the child is considered out of their power, and is nominally sold to some relative for a trifle, it being supposed that the spirits would not take what has been thus sold. The mother unfortunately is submitted meanwhile to horrible torture, being surrounded by bamboos and twigs, which are set on fire, literally roasting her. This is supposed to be a means of recovery, but often ensures death; the king even lost his wife in this way, being unable to overcome the prejudices of his officials. As this performance is repeated for some days,—among the Siamese for a month, in the case of a first-born child,—the woman is fortunate who escapes. Children are suckled for three years, and after receiving their natural food, they frequently have a cigarette to smoke.

**Newborn children.**

**Treatment of mothers.**

SIAMESE DANCING GIRL.

We have left till now two of the most notable features

of Siam, namely, temples and elephants. Both are certainly numerous, the temples of course belonging to the dominant Buddhist religion. The great temple, "Wat Poh," in Bangkok, contains an enormous gilt figure of the dying Buddha, about 160 feet long, constructed of bricks, lacquered and heavily gilt. The huge foot-soles are inlaid with mother of pearl figures illustrating stories of Buddha's life. The floor is of tesselated marble. Another great temple,—the "Wat Chang," or Elephant Temple,—has a lofty spire with external decoration in remarkable patterns which at a distance look like mosaics of precious stones, but are in truth nothing but a mixture of broken glass, crockery, and shells. A representation of the three-headed elephant is prominently placed on each of the four façades of this temple.

**Siamese temples.**

Cremation is the usual mode of disposing of the dead. Priests pray day and night in the house until the body is removed to the temple-grounds. The interval between death and burial varies according to the rank and wealth of the family; it may even be protracted for months, during which the prayers go on continuously, the coffin being covered with flowers. But the devouring of bodies by vultures and dogs is not at all uncommon. From the prolonged keeping of dead bodies, it is not surprising that cholera is rife. The people are not by any means educated up to the king's standard, and persist in ascribing diseases to spirits, and in hindering sanitary reform.

**Cremation.**

Elephants are very numerous—so much so that to ride on a female elephant is esteemed a disgrace. Albino elephants are thought much of; and the more they approach perfection in that respect, the more they are valued and claimed for the king. Many of those called white are simply a little lighter than the average, or have uncoloured areas on the body or on the ears. Whenever a lighter one than usual is found, an extraordinary festival is held in his honour, at which the king is present. The most perfect discovered in late years is pale reddish-brown all over the body, with a few white hairs on the back, and eyes a pale yellow.

**Albino, or "white" elephants.**

The reception of a white elephant furnishes a grand opportunity for a pageant. Brass bands, Siamese bands playing on tom-toms, conch shells, etc., and artillery grace the occasion, with many processions of princes and nobles. "No Siamese," says Mr. Bock, "moves from his house, whether for a walk, or to make an offering at the temple, or to pay a visit, without two or more—it may be a dozen or more—'slave-debtors,' according to his rank, carrying, as the indispensable insignia of office, or of social rank, not only his umbrellas, but his betel and tobacco-boxes, tea-pot, etc., and I believe, always in one of the betel or tobacco-boxes, his seal, for the Siamese attach great importance to seals, which take the place of signatures in Western civilisation. These seals are mostly made of ivory, the devices representing an angel or a lotus-flower, etc. No sealing-wax is used with these seals, but always a vermilion-red dye. If the master stops on the road, his cavalcade, with their betel-boxes, umbrellas, etc., all sit down on the ground on their haunches at a respectful distance; and when he enters a house, these servants sit outside on the ground, or on the steps, or even on the verandah, some of them always quite near enough to overhear the conversation."

**Siamese processions.**

SHAN CUTTING TOBACCO.

The Siamese are chiefly occupied in agriculture—jewellery, though largely manufactured, being principally in the hands of Chinese settlers. Sculpture is very fairly represented, chiefly by the figures of Buddha, and of elephants and other animals. Many Siamese are employed in inlaid mother-of-pearl and lacquer work, in which they are well skilled. Bamboo work employs very many. The most abundant agricultural products, in addition to rice and tobacco, are teak, rose, and other kinds of wood, sugar, pepper, and other spices and aromatics, cotton, resins and gums, and beeswax. Of the latter many beautiful models of flowers, figures, and buildings are made, and offered at the temples. The minerals of Siam are abundant—gold, copper, tin, iron, and lead being among them. Precious stones, too, are by no means lacking. The manufacture of figures of Buddha is very extensive, there being a constant demand; they are made to suit all purchasers.

**Manufactures and productions.**

The Siamese language belongs to the same group as the Chinese, or the monosyllabic non-inflecting group; and tones and vowels have a preponderating influence in determining the special meaning of the root words. Many modified Sanscrit words have been introduced, and Pali, in the Buddhist scriptures, has considerably influenced the language. There is no article, and no distinction of number, gender, or case. The order of words is most important in determining the meaning. There is little literature in the language. Some metrical legends and romances, and a number of books of laws, are the chief books known.

**Language.**

The eastern and south-eastern portion of Further India, known as Tonkin, Cochin-China, Annam, and Cambodia, is inhabited by people of a more and more Chinese type, intermixed with Siamese and Shan or Tai elements. A large portion of these territories has in recent years been brought more or less under French domination. We may, perhaps, best speak of the inhabitants as Cochin-Chinese, giving separate mention to any sections needing it.

**The Cochin-Chinese.**

The Cochin-Chinese are comparatively fair Mongoloids

NATIVES OF ANNAM.

—the men short, but active; the women fairer than the men, and well formed. Their faces are not so large and straight, their mouths are not so small, nor their eyes so hard and staring as is seen in the Siamese. They are much more merry, lively, and talkative. The loose Chinese trousers and frock with large sleeves, made of cotton or silk, are worn by both sexes. The hair is not cut short, but worn of its natural length, and coiled at the back of the head. The highlanders, known as Moi, are taller, lighter, and less peaceable, but have a good name for truthfulness and honesty, which the inhabitants of the plain have not.

**Physical characters and dress.**

Tea is the national drink here, as in China; and spirits are little in vogue. Rice and fish are the chief articles of diet; but nothing comes amiss—dogs, cats, rats, tigers, snakes, earth-worms, etc., being devoured with gusto. Betel-chewing and tobacco-smoking are practised by all.

**Food and drink.**

Polygamy is largely in vogue; but the first wife has a special position. Purchase is the form preceding marriage; and adultery may be punished by death. From this it will be inferred that women are not well treated by their husbands, who not unfrequently beat them. Slavery for debt here includes possession of the wives and family of the debtor, who may also be sold.

**Marriage.**

Buddhism in a rather loose form is the predominant religion; but with it flourishes much paganism, including ancestor-worship. Indeed, much of their religion differs little from the Shamanism of Siberian natives. Exorcists and astrologers abound. Burial rites are very complex, great respect being paid to the dead. The greatest care is taken to prevent desecration of the body, which is placed in a coffin as rich as can be afforded, and often kept for months before burial. The charms of sorcerers are considered all-powerful, and are largely bought; the details of their practices are most elaborate. Tigers or serpents are, among others, beasts of ill-omen; and ghosts and spirits are believed to be universally present. It is in accordance with this state of superstition that Christian

**Religion.**

**Sorcerers.**

missionaries have been greatly persecuted. In recent years, however, the Romanist priests have gained better treatment, even beyond the French border, in consequence of the threats of the French authorities, as to punishment in case of any harm befalling the priests.

**Christian missionaries.**

In the districts approaching China, Chinese influence is naturally greater, and a large proportion of the Tonkinese people are a cross between Cochin-Chinese, or Annamese,

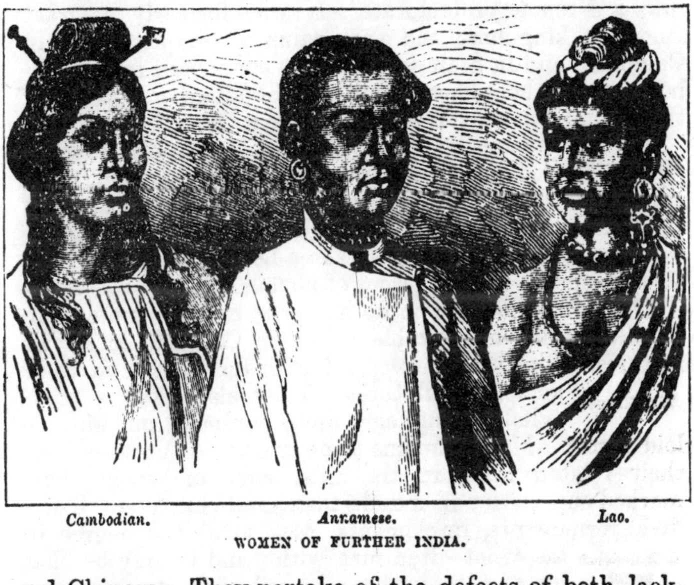

*Cambodian.* *Annamese.* *Lao.*

WOMEN OF FURTHER INDIA.

and Chinese. They partake of the defects of both, lacking the Chinese stability and industry. They do not cut or shave their hair, which they fix behind the head with a pin. Their cheek-bones project more than the Cochin-Chinese proper, and the nose is more prominent than that of the Chinese; they are also far more slender, and not prone to fatness.

**The Tonkinese.**

The Cochin-Chinese language may almost be called an early dialect of Chinese, being monosyllabic, and much of the meaning depending on the tone in which the words are pronounced. There is but little literary character in the language.

**Language.**

Cambodia, formerly a kingdom extending over a very wide extent of Further India, is now a small kingdom occupying only a small tract between Siam and Cochin-China, bounded on the north-east by the Me-Kong, or Cambodia river, which also flows through it, but not extending into the delta. After suffering much at the hands of the Siamese, it has subsided into a French protectorate. It was formerly a great Buddhist kingdom; and vast ruins of temples, both in Cambodia and in Siamese provinces conquered from Cambodia, show the ancient wealth of the kingdom. Some of the remains, however, of great extent, have been shown to describe the exploits of Rama and Vishnu, and must have been due to Brahmanism. The ancient palace of the Khmer kings (the national name of the Cambodians) has been explored, and is full of magnificent sculptures, the enormous three-headed elephant being there enthroned in all places of honour.*

**The Cambodian kingdom.**

**Former civilisation.**

The Cambodians, who do not now number more than a million, are remarkable for their Caucasic or Aryan features, which also correspond with the figures on their ancient sculptures. They also have a polysyllabic language, quite distinct from Mongoloid forms. Much remains to be known about them and their related tribes in the hills, some of whom show marked superiority in morals, taste, and character. Their dress, ornaments, implements, etc., exhibit a degree of taste not often met with; and it may be that long ago they were a branch of the same Aryans who conquered India, but have been themselves conquered and subdued, like the Hindus, by the invading Mongols, and have been unable, like the Hindus, to assimilate their conquerors. They seem now to be gradually getting absorbed by the combined Siamese, Cochin-Chinese, and Malay elements.

**The Khmer.**

**A Caucasian people.**

* Full details are given by Lieutenant Delaporte in his "Voyage au Cambodge," a magnificent volume published in Paris in 1880.

The Malay peninsula must be briefly dismissed here. A great part of the inhabitants are Malays, whom we can discuss better in their main home, the Malay Archipelago. The Chinese are largely immigrating, and may become the majority. A number of Siamese are also in the peninsula, becoming mixed with the Malays, and serving to uphold the Siamese power in the northern part of the peninsula.

**The Malays.**

But besides these, there are some aboriginal tribes, numbering about ten thousand, who belong to the Negrito type, found also in the Andamans and the Philippines. They are in a very low state of life, and live entirely on the chase, using poisoned arrows. Their hair is short and curly (not frizzed), and their skins are nearly black. Very little is known of them, as they shun intercourse with others.

**Negritos.**

# CHAPTER X.

## The Chinese.

**Chinese antagonism to Western ideas—Effects of trade—Modern breaking down of barriers—The Seres—Cathay—The Mongol empire—Cessation of European intercourse—Early Chinese history—Era of Confucius—Rise of Tartar power—The great wall of China—Introduction of Buddhism—Three Chinese kingdoms—An anti-religious emperor—Growing Tartar power—Jenghiz Khan—Kubla Khan—The Ming dynasty—Great disasters and insurrections—The Manchu Tartars subdue China—Literary and warlike emperors—British embassies—War with British—The great Tai-ping rebellion—Another war with Britain—Chinese Gordon—Prince Chun—The Chinese examination system—Rank conferred by examination—Severity of the tests—Graduated examinations—The highest tests—The Chinese classics—Strict fairness observed—The empire a patriarchal despotism—The kotow—Chinese princes do not travel—Prince Chun's journey—Poetical records—Visit to the British fleet—System of government—Mandarins—Peace and prosperity—Chinese punishments—Rarity of personal violence—Offences of women and children—Physical characters—Children and education—Chinese peculiarities—Food and drink—Chopsticks—Dress—Unchanging fashions—The pig-tail—Women's hair-dressing—Opium-smoking—A great opium den—Houses and travelling—Lantern festival—Imperial ceremonies—Marriage—Divorce—Death—Ancestor-worship—Funeral ceremonies—A Chinese funeral in England—Mourning—Division of property—Buddhism—Confucianism—Taoism—Fatalism—Remarkable inventions—Neglect of theory—Dislike of machinery—Manufactures—The Chinese language—Tones—Pigeon English—Chinese poetry—The Book of Rites—The classics—Encyclopædias—The streets of Canton—Shop-signs—Private houses—The Manchus—Diversity among Chinese—The hill tribes—The Formosans—The Coreans—Character of the people—The government—Long sleeves and long pipes.**

CHINA and Japan are, next to India and Syria (including the Holy Land), the Asiatic countries most interesting and important, commercially and philosophically, to Europeans. Although the Caucasian stock includes the vast majority of the inhabitants of

India, Europeans nevertheless find among the Hindu people a great contrast to Western ideas and practices in very many particulars; while in China and Japan a widely different stock, the Mongolian, is encountered, which has developed civilisations of extraordinary power, on principles an-

**Chinese antagonism to Western ideas.**

CHINESE MERCHANTS ON THE RIVER TIEN-TSIN.

tagonistic to our own. Long entrenched behind almost impenetrable barriers, they have resisted with fanatical repugnance the slightest contact with Western barbarians, manifesting the very spirit of the old Jews, Greeks, and Romans as to barbarians and heathens, and of some Englishmen as to "niggers." We may trace to merchandise, especially tea, the one indispensable article which China had to supply to the British, and to cotton cloth, the one great fabric which we could supply to China, the impulse which has led to the breaking down of many of the barriers between East and West; and now that India has begun to overtop China in exports of tea to this country, we may expect the persevering Chinaman, who has appreciated the money brought to his land by the Briton, to develop some other article into greater prominence, that he may retain his chief customer.

**Effects of trade.**

Even the victories of the British in India are not so great in their significance as those which are signalised by the gradual breaking down of prejudice and the adoption of Western practices in Japan and China. When China has a whole fleet of warships built in Europe and commanded by an English officer, when Japan establishes a university on the British model, we feel as if any wonder might take place, even the development of the Central African into something better than he is.

**Modern breaking down of barriers.**

Chinese history extends back to a period far beyond European records; and yet China was only vaguely known to the ancient Egyptians, Greeks, and Romans. They heard of the Chinese as the Seres, approached from Central Asia, a vast people, civilised and peaceful, already famous for silks. The Arabs seem to have known the country as Sin, a corruption of Chin, or China.

**The Seres.**

The Europeans of the middle ages knew China under the name of Cathay, derived from Kitai, still the Russian and Central Asian name for China. This knowledge was connected with the remarkable growth of the Mongol empire of Jenghiz Khan, leading to numerous enterprises of travellers into the far East, including many Dominican and Franciscan missionaries.

**Cathay.**

**The Mongol empire.**

Marco Polo was, however, the first European who visited China itself (in the 13th century); and his narrative did much to familiarise Europe with Cathay. At the end of the thirteenth century other Romish missionaries penetrated Southern China, and many converts were made. Trade, too, developed with the great Italian marts, Florence and Genoa.

**Cessation of European intercourse.**

It is not a little remarkable, that after this period European intercourse with China should have so far ceased, that no intelligence for centuries reached Europe directly from thence. In fact, when the Spanish and Portuguese, in the sixteenth century, lighted upon China, they regarded it as an unknown country, and gave new renderings of old names, so that for a long time it was not believed that China and Cathay were the same. The fact is, that Mahometanism had regained control over Central Asia, and China passed under rulers whose instinct was to keep foreigners out. Thus old maps of Asia, in the 16th and 17th centuries, placed Cathay as a large country to the north of China.

**Early Chinese history.**

Chinese history speaks of the early inhabitants of Chinese race as immigrants from the North and North-west; but they soon developed into a settled and agricultural people, cultivating rice and other grain, flax, and silk. It is undoubted that they long ago had the art of writing and some knowledge of astronomy, and it is probable that Chinese civilisation is older than any in Europe. There are some records by Confucius which may be considerably trusted for at least 2000 years B.C. They detail the gradual progress of the Chinese empire and vicissitudes of dynasties, until, in 936 B.C., we find the Tartars becoming invaders only shaken off with difficulty. The era of Confucius (551–475 B.C), of Lao-tze, and Mencius, was one of wisdom crying aloud, but unheeded; and a gradual decadence of the Chinese power took place.

**Era of Confucius.**

**Rise of Tartar power.**

The Tsin State on the North-west, in which we must recognise a Tartar people, gained the chief power in China about 255 B.C. Che-Hwang-te (246-210 B.C.) was the first great ruler of his line, extending his power widely, making roads and canals, building cities, driving back invading Tartars. He started the building of the great

**The great wall of China.**

wall of China in 214 B.C. to keep back the Tartars. As a reformer, he was unpopular; and in consequence of the authority of the ancients being always quoted against him, he ordered all books relating to ancient Chinese history to be burnt, and put to death all scholars who attempted to conceal them. Such actions were not likely to make his line permanent, and it came to an end with his son, a short time after his death. The succeeding dynasty of Han recovered as many of the old books as possible, and very many were found. The next dynasty,

CHINESE. SOUTH CHINESE.

that of the Eastern Han, added greatly to the Chinese domains in Tartary and Turkestan. Buddhism was introduced in A.D. 65.

**Introduction of Buddhism.**

For a good while China was divided into three kingdoms—northern, middle, and southern; which state of things led to constant wars. A succession of dynasties followed, some of which united the whole empire into one, and enlarged its borders; while others were marked by crime, profligacy, and decay. In the seventh century A.D. the frontier was said to extend to the Caspian and Eastern Persia; and ambassadors from

**Three Chinese kingdoms.**

Nepaul, Magadha (India), Persia, and Rome came to China. In 650 the emperor's wife, Woo How, gained practical supreme power, which became absolute on the death of her husband in 683. Her government was certainly vigorous and successful. The emperor Woo-Tsung, in the ninth century, found temples, monasteries, nunneries, etc., too numerous, and by decree abolished them all, and subjected priests of all kinds to oppressive treatment. But on his death Buddhism revived in great force. A period of great weakness of the imperial power followed, and China appeared likely to break up into independent States. The Tartars were extending more and more towards China proper, and were again and again bought off by tribute, which acted as an encouragement to come again. The result was, that they established themselves more and more in North China, especially as the Neu-che, or Kins.

**An anti-religious emperor.**

**Growing Tartar power.**

In the twelfth century the Mongol power was growing, and from 1212 onwards Jenghiz Khan overran a great part of China. His descendants continued the conquest of China until, about 1232, Ogdai, son of Jenghiz, destroyed the Kin dynasty of North China. His nephew, Kubla Khan, became in 1259 practically the first Mongol emperor of China, though his power was not fully established till 1279. This was the great Khan whom Marco Polo visited. The dynasty lasted only till 1368, when, after much bad government, it was displaced by Choo-Yuen-Chang, a Buddhist priest, son of a Chinese working-man, who showed great discernment in the measures he took to gain and keep the supreme power. His name was changed to Hung-woo, and his dynasty was known as the Ming, or "Bright."

**Jenghiz Khan.**

**Kubla Khan.**

**The Ming dynasty.**

In the fifteenth century the Ming emperors began by losing the province of Cochin-China. Later, one of the emperors was defeated and imprisoned by a Tartar chief. A serious insurrection occurred early in the sixteenth century, which was with difficulty suppressed. The Tartars devastated a large

**Great disasters and insurrections.**

province in 1542, and soon afterwards a Japanese fleet ravaged the sea-coast. The Tartars were bribed to depart in several reigns. In 1592 the Japanese defeated the Chinese army in Corea, and destroyed the Chinese fleet; but for some reason they failed to follow up their conquest.

**The Manchu Tartars subdue China.**

The Manchu Tartars now grew stronger, and in 1616 and 1619 were so successful against the Chinese that they kept possession of the north-eastern province of Leaou-tung. Meanwhile civil war arose in China, and became so fierce that one party called in the Manchus, who, when they had defeated the rebels, were unwilling to retire again. They took possession of Pekin, and proclaimed an emperor of their own in 1644. Nankin was soon after taken without a blow; and the Tartars confirmed the mandarins in their offices, and gave an amnesty to all who would lay down their arms. Thus was established the modern Chinese dynasty. It is generally asserted that it is descended from that known as the Kins in earlier history.

**Literary and warlike emperors.**

Kang-he (1661–1721) was one of the most notable emperors. He was a great student; and a great Chinese dictionary was published under his superintendence. Tibet was subdued during his reign; one of his successors, Keen-lung, added Eastern Turkestan to the empire, and rivalled Kang-he as a student and author. He even marched to Nepaul and defeated the Ghoorkhas in 1792; but he failed in Further India and Formosa.

**British embassies.**

Meanwhile, the East India Company had been coming in contact with the Chinese, who treated English subjects with gross injustice. Lord Macartney was sent as British ambassador to China, but gained little. Lord Amherst's embassy followed in 1816; but he refused to kotow before the emperor, and was quickly dismissed. The conduct of the Chinese to foreigners became more and more unbearable, and they

**War with British.**

endeavoured to stop all foreign trade, particularly the opium traffic. In 1840 the British declared war against China; with the result that Can-

CHINESE STUDENTS.

ton, Amoy, Shanghai, and other ports were taken by Sir Hugh Gough, and Nankin was threatened. In 1842 the Chinese found themselves compelled to cede Hong Kong, to open five principal ports, including Canton and Shanghai, to foreign trade, and pay a large indemnity.

Such a defeat was particularly disastrous to Chinese prestige, and rebellions were rife. The emperors were incompetent, and officials mostly corrupt. After the middle of the century, popular discontent found an energetic leader in Hung-Seu-tseuen, who aimed at founding a new Chinese dynasty, the Tai-ping, and expelling the Tartar rulers. He professed Christianity, and denounced the sins of the age with great vigour. So successful was he, that, in 1852, he took Nankin itself. His power extended yearly, and the weakened empire was still further threatened by the English declaration of war in 1857, in consequence of the "Arrow" outrage on British subjects. Canton was taken, and Lord Elgin determined to make his way to Pekin, and treat with the emperor in person. Having penetrated to Tien-tsin, where the Chinese made a treaty with him, a further attack followed, which led to a campaign in which the French joined us. Pekin was reached by the allied forces in 1860, and a fresh peace made, which was of great benefit to the Chinese rulers in opening the way for Major (the late lamented General) Gordon to take the command of their forces against the Taipings. His victorious career is well known, ending by the capture of Nankin in 1864: with it the Taiping cause fell.

**The great Tai-ping rebellion.**

**Another war with Britain.**

**Chinese Gordon.**

In 1873, when the emperor Tung-che assumed power, after his long minority, the right of personal audience with him, and "gazing on the sacred countenance," was claimed by and granted to the foreign ministers. Since this period, China has made much progress, and increased its foreign trade very largely. The present emperor, Kwang-sen, has been guided in his long minority by his father, Prince Chun, who is prime minister, and has shown much enlightenment. The existence of an emperor's father, nominally subordinate

**Prince Chun.**

to his son, comes about from the fact that by Chinese law the heir must be younger than the person from whom he inherits; and since the emperor Tung-che died young, without issue, the succession passed by his will to a son of one of his father's younger brothers.

**The Chinese examination system.**

To a large extent, China may be studied as representing the extreme development of an examination system—in fact, almost its worship. The respect we too often pay to mere wealth; or to powers of speech, impudent self-assertion, rank, or ownership of land, the Chinese pay to success in examinations.

CHINESE CHILDREN.

So much is thought of them, that an unsuccessful candidate has been known to go on competing till grey hairs have crowned him, and the emperor has given him an honorary degree.

**Rank conferred by examination.**

Europeans may almost be accused of having adopted a Chinese idea, in attaching so much importance to competitive examinations; and it is at least our duty to study carefully the system adopted by the nation which has carried these tests to the highest perfection, in some respects, in order that we may learn what errors to avoid and what plans to imitate. We can scarcely conceive what a sweeping change would be caused by our full adoption of the Chinese system. Imagine the rank of a duke to be conferred on the senior wrangler or senior classic; imagine the prime minister being selected as Indian civil service candidates are now; and, what is more important, imagine the respect given to titled and wealthy people transferred to the successful examinees, and we should have some idea of the possible effects of a further rise in the importance of the "great god, competitive examination."

CHINESE COIFFURE.

While we have learnt to groan over the misfortunes of the "plucked" man, he is met with far more abundantly in China. Successive tests exclude far more candidates than with us. Scarcely one per cent. are successful in the first, or local examination. The departmental examination, which is much as if a student went up to his county town, after having passed in his native place, cuts out many more; and then an Imperial examination takes place, beyond which the majority do not proceed; for the Imperial degree they gain gives them many privileges, including the much-valued exemption from corporal punishment if they chance to offend against the laws. Those who aspire to

**Severity of the tests.**

**Graduated examinations.**

CHINESE LADY: SHANGHAI.

higher successes pass on to the triennial examinations, held, as London University examinations are largely held, at important local capitals, like Birmingham and Manchester; again the total number of candidates, sifted though they have been, is very large, and only about one out of every hundred is successful. Most of those who succeed have reached the mature age of from thirty to fifty.

**The highest tests.**

Those who have succeeded so far, must, if they wish to proceed further, go to Pekin, where a few attain a Doctor's degree, and gain good posts in the administration. Finally, the Han-lin College is the limited body who have passed the last severe test, and are held competent to fill the highest ministerial posts. How competent these may be, all Europeans who have been brought into contact with them can testify, if only through the skill they can exhibit in foiling their wishes or finding reasons for non-compliance. The Marquis Tseng, who became so well known in Europe as the special Chinese envoy, is an instance of high appreciation of Western advantages, combined with the most admirable skill in Chinese matters.

**The Chinese classics.**

The great evil of these examinations, judged from our point of view, is, that they are founded so largely upon a knowledge of the ancient Chinese classics, such as those of Confucius, Mencius, and other sacred writings. Yet we British do not stand in a position to blame them, for our Universities long gave credit to scarcely anything but a minute study of the "classical" dead languages. Taken as examinations in Chinese knowledge, the native examination papers are in many respects admirable, and succeed in drawing out ability in addition to "cram," or book-work. Of course, no examination can discover tact, business ability, skill in ruling, or honesty; and as we fail in this quite as much as the Chinese, we are not entitled to cast a stone at them on that account

The utmost care is taken by the Chinese authorities to prevent tampering with the questions or the papers of the candidates, or the employment of illicit means of answering. Double-walled examination halls, guarded by strict sentries; searching of candidates to discover books or any illicit helps; no permission to go out till the examination is concluded, food being taken in by the candidates; the examiners knowing nothing of the candidates, whose names are kept from them till the adjudication has been made; these are some of the precautions adopted. Of course, examinees are sometimes found who are daring enough to attempt anything; and a story is even told of a secret tunnel being made into an examination-cell (for each candidate is secluded in a separate cell), by means of which books and other assistance were conveyed to a candidate.

**Strict fairness observed.**

Though the administration, and consequently the whole system of government, is carried on by successful examinees, the theory of the empire is an absolute despotism, which aims however at being as beneficial though as arbitrary as that of a parent over a child. The members of the Imperial family itself, who are now very numerous, do not gain or exercise authority by virtue of their descent. They do not even secure wealth, for many of them are very poor. There is no hereditary nobility; titles of rank are official only. It must be recorded, however, that notwithstanding the prevalence of examinations, corruption exists throughout Chinese official ranks almost to the same extent as in Turkey.

**The empire a patriarchal despotism.**

The divinity that "doth hedge a king" has nowhere been more evident than in China, where the emperor has ranked as a divinity, and has been accustomed to receive honours elsewhere paid to the gods. Even now, the amount of reverential "kotowing," or prostration, kneeling, etc., which subjects have to undergo in gaining an audience of his Majesty, is extreme; but the English and the Russian envoys have never bent their bodies to such signs of homage, and gradually they have ceased to be exacted of foreign ambassadors generally.

**The kotow.**

Up to recent times it has been recognised as inconceivable, and of course improper, that any prince of China, much less the sovereign, should travel extensively through the vast country, or quit the sacred dominions to enlarge his experience in foreign travel. External things were insignificant or barbarian, and could afford no true benefit to a Celestial. But in 1886 the almost incredible event happened; and the father of the Chinese Emperor, Prince Chun, who is also Prime Minister and Lord High Admiral, made a sea voyage along part of the coast of the empire. Notwithstanding the unfavourable prophecies indulged in by many Chinese as to the result of his journey, it certainly had a good effect in opening his eyes; and the sight of a fine British squadron taught him a good deal.

**Chinese princes do not travel.**

**Prince Chun's journey.**

So excited and interested was the prince in what he saw and heard, that he was constrained to write a series of poems which have been published, and of which some account was given in *The Times* of August 22, 1887. "What a change has taken place with the course of fate," he says; "during five reigns the sadness of our dynasty has been undispelled." He laments the decay of the old forms of submission to the emperor, and was very unfavourably impressed on hearing the mixed languages of the foreign consuls at Tien-tsin. But his reflections at this point are worth quoting.

**Poetical records.**

"Jabber, jabber, what a clatter of uncouth sounds to the ear!
One cannot accept all that General Tih said of the ends of the earth.
But, except a doffing of the hat, they have no other courtesies!
And what on earth is the history of this clipping of the hair?
Our gallant Tartar General stands here in his plumes.
There stands our Grand Secretary (Littung Chang) of eight-bearer quality.
It is really too ridiculous, this interpretation scene!
And then each man is followed by a walking-stick!"

The "walking-stick," apparently, is the small-sword worn by the consuls when in uniform.

Admiral Hamilton, with his ten British men-of-war, received from the prince the sentiment that China and England must both perfect their drill and cultivate the blessings of peace, so as to preserve a good state of things in Asia. His poetic address to the Admiral is another interesting effusion:

**Visit to the British fleet.**

**"From ancient times diplomatic intercourse has been our pride;**
**Let us not make our pride in exhibition of warlike power!**
**Thanks for coming so far, the bearer of your country's behests,**
**And for your conversation relating to untutored lands.**
**Be genuine, and you will reach the genuine hearts of others!**
**If you have hidden motives, you cause men to stand aloof."**

The reference to hidden motives in the last line looks

CHINESE LADIES RIDING.

like a dignified rebuke which diplomatists generally might take to heart. Altogether, the prince's journey and his comments are very significant.

Unlike the English practice, all Chinese laws are properly digested and framed into a code, which is capable of alteration only by the Imperial Edict. The criminal law, which is said to have lasted substan- **System of government.**

tially the same for two thousand years, is published at a very low price. Each of the eighteen provinces of the empire constitutes a complete government in itself. It is not generally known that the term Europeans use to designate Chinese officials, "mandarins," is a word brought to us by the Portuguese from the Malay "mantrin," a counsellor, this being also found in the Sanskrit. *kwan-fu* is the Chinese term. The button on the top of their hats is the mandarins' sign of rank, various colours denoting the several grades, the red coral one being the highest. Of course there is an appropriately rich dress for each grade; and a peacock's feather at the side of the hat is also a sign of high rank; while only those near the emperor can wear a feather with three eyes.

**Mandarins.**

Such as it is, the Chinese system has produced a state of comparative peace and prosperity among the people, which has been rivalled by no empire with so large a population. The Chinese certainly aim at governing by moral rather than physical force to a larger extent than some European governments; and they recognise the importance of securing and rewarding ability wherever it may be found. This last feature in itself removes many causes of discontent. An able man is practically certain to make his way to the front. Of course abuses occur in the system, but they are inherent to humanity in its present state of advancement.

**Peace and prosperity.**

The Chinese criminal law cannot be considered mild. Flogging with bamboos is a very ordinary punishment. The cangue is much more severe, involving confinement of the body in a sort of cage, through which the head, neck, and hands alone are allowed to protrude. The prisoner is thus unable to feed himself, and is entirely dependent on others. Ankle and finger squeezing, kneeling on chains, and banishment, are among their severe punishments; and the prisons are so objectionable as places of residence that prisoners not infrequently prefer death to a long term of imprisonment. Capital punishment is practised in several fashions rather too horrible to particularise.

**Chinese punishments.**

I undoubtedly to the credit of the Chinese and of th primitive system, that personal violence is very rare ai ong them, whether in private or in public. The fact is, the people in general take an interest in preventing it, and do not remain callous lookers-on or pass by on the other side when a quarrel is proceeding. Thus they become very skilful in quarrelling by means of words and gesticulations, and can continue a wordy war for a long time without coming to blows.

**Rarity of personal violence.**

Women are not usually imprisoned, except for the gravest offences; but when they commit minor offences are placed in the custody of their relatives, who are responsible for their good behaviour. Parents have great authority over their children, and may use considerable violence towards them; even killing them is not treated as murder, especially if the child has struck the parent.

**Offences of women and children.**

Physically, the Chinese scarcely need describing; we are all familiar with the shaven face and head, with only a portion of the black hair allowed to grow and form a pig-tail, the thick lips, and projecting ears, and the imperturbable gravity of their demeanour; the small feet and thin calves of the Chinese ladies, marking them off from the poorer classes as not needing to use them in labour or for walking; the extremely long finger-nails worn by both sexes, another sign of elevated position; the slenderness judged beautiful in women, while corpulence is equally the proper thing for a man who is valued.

**Physical characters.**

Children, notwithstanding the severity with which their offences may be punished, are well cared for and show much filial affection. The infanticide which occurs among the poorer classes is not more common than in countries that are supposed to be among the most advanced. That children do not grow up with any dislike of their homes is shown by the constancy with which they return to their native place late in life, or when they have a competency. They are taught to aid their parents in every possible way, to keep them in old

**Children and education.**

age, and perform due rites after their death. Schools are abundant, and under State direction; their chief fault is, the unvarying character of their teaching. After some very juvenile studies, the pupils learn by heart the writings of Confucius, and spend years in studying and writing exercises on them. The series known as the "Five Classics" follows. Of course reading and writing are carefully taught.

Chinese peculiarities.

Sir John Davis, in his work on "The Chinese," quotes the following from a work printed at Macao, in which a foreigner's perplexities on arriving in China are detailed. "On inquiring of the boatman in which direction Macao lay, I was answered, 'in the west-north;' the wind, as I was informed, being east-south. 'We do not say so in Europe,' thought I; but imagine my surprise when, in explaining the utility of the compass, the boatman added that the needle pointed to the south! Desirous to change the subject, I remarked that I concluded he was about to proceed to some high festival, or merrymaking, as his dress was completely white. He told me, with a look of much dejection, that his only brother had died the week before, and that he was in the deepest mourning for him. On my landing, the first object that attracted my attention was a military mandarin, who wore an embroidered petticoat, with a string of beads round his neck, and who besides carried a fan; and it was with some dismay that I observed him mount on the right side of his horse. . . . My attention was drawn to several old Chinese, some of whom had grey beards, and nearly all of them huge goggling spectacles. A few of them were chirruping and chuckling to singing birds, which they carried in bamboo cages, or perched on a stick; others were catching flies to feed the birds; the remainder of the party seemed to be delightedly employed in flying paper kites, while a group of boys were gravely looking on, and regarding these innocent occupations of their seniors with the most serious and gratified attention."

Rice is by far the most important food and crop in China. With the poorer classes it constitutes almost the

A CHINESE STREET-STALL.

sole food. Those who can get them, however, eat pork, game, birds, and fish freely. Beef is little eaten, owing to religious scruples. Both wine and spirits are made from rice; but tea is the national drink. Some extraordinary dishes are in vogue among the richer folk, but they are by no means to be despised, especially birds'-nest soup, well-fed cats and dogs, deer's sinews, and sharks' fins. Salted provisions are largely eaten.

**Food and drink.**

Chopsticks are the proverbial Chinese implements for eating; they are a pair of slender wooden, ivory, bone, or silver rods, about ten inches long, held in the right hand—one between the ends of the second and third fingers, the other between the thumb and fore-finger, and capable of being rapidly worked against the other. The use of these chopsticks, in which they are wonderfully quick, is connected with the custom of bringing all food to table ready carved.

**Chopsticks.**

Dress in China is largely made of cotton cloth; but silk is much used by those who can afford it. In winter, furs and cotton wadding are worn for warmth. Indeed, it is singular how little the people employ fires simply to warm themselves; their notion is, to put on more clothes till they are warm enough. Loose trousers, with a loose overgarment reaching below the knees, constitute the most usual dress of the men, finished off with felt-soled cotton shoes, leather being little in vogue. The women's dress, as far as it is seen, often looks like a long cassock surmounted by a mantle extending to the knees.

**Dress.**

The Chinese have the advantage in dress of unchanging fashions, ceremonial dresses being all ordained by an official board; thus the prevalence of handsome dress for great occasions is accounted for by the care taken of it, and the fact that the same may be used again as long as it will hold together. Gay fans and umbrellas, as in Japan, are important articles of costume: the art displayed in their manufacture and decoration is very considerable. A few adventurous Chinese have sometimes adopted European costume; but such a

**Unchanging fashions.**

change is very hard to make, and it cannot be said that it is altogether to be desired.

We might say that the Chinese women have all the advantage of their handsome hair, while the men get rid of the greater part of it, and indeed are slaves to fashion. It is believed that the Manchu Tartars first compelled Chinamen to wear the pigtail, as

**The pigtail.**

CHINESE GIRLS.

a mark of inferiority; but what was once a badge of servitude is now a national pride—a Chinaman would feel disgraced without it. Of course a lot of shaving of the head has to be done to keep the rest of the scalp free from hair, and barbers consequently are in great request. Beards are but slight, and very generally shaved off Women wear their hair long,

**Hair-dressing.**

often with other hair added; it is elaborately dressed, in various fashions, often making a great circular and hollow projection behind the head.

The evils of opium-smoking, as practised by the Chinese, have often been enlarged upon; no doubt with many great harm results, and the character is enervated. It cannot be said that it is so with all; and some doctors maintain that it is a craving like that for alcoholic drink in Europe, which may be and is greatly abused, but is not necessarily so harmful as many think. Anyhow, a large portion of the people have a great passion for it, and we cannot do better than give an account of the Nan-gin-tsin, in Shanghai, the greatest opium den in China, as given by the *North China Herald*. It is known throughout the length and breadth of the empire to the Chinese; and it helps to make Shanghai regarded as a city affording the same opportunities for pleasure and dissipation that Paris does the typical Frenchman. It is situated in the French Concession in Shanghai, within a stone's throw of the wall of the native city, within which no opium shops are supposed to exist. The character of the place could not be guessed from its external appearance, although the air of the people passing in and out might suggest it. The throngs visiting it represent all stations of life, from the coolie to the wealthy merchant or the small mandarin. It is with difficulty that one gets inside through the crowds of people hanging round the door. Those who have not the requisite number of copper cash to procure the baneful pipe, watch with horrible wistfulness each of the more affluent pass in with a nervous, hurried step, or totter out wearing that peculiar dazed expression which comes after the smoker's craving has been satisfied and his transient pleasure has passed away. One requires a strong stomach to stand the sickening fumes with which the air inside is thickened. The clouds of smoke, the dim light from the numerous coloured lamps, the numbers of reclining forms with distorted faces bent over the small flames at which the pipes are lighted, cause the novice a sickening sensation. But as soon as the eye

**Opium-smoking.**

**A great opium den.**

A STREET BARBER IN CHINA.

becomes accustomed to the scene, it is noticed that the place is got up on an expensive scale. In the centre of the lower room hangs one of the finest of Chinese lamps; the ceiling is of richly-carved wood, while the painted walls are thickly inlaid with a peculiarly-marked marble, which gives the idea of unfinished landscape sketches. Numerous doors on all sides lead to the smokers' apartments. In the outer portion of the building stands a counter covered with little boxes of the drug ready for smoking, which a dozen assistants are kept busy handing out to the servants who wait upon the *habitués* of the place. The average daily receipts are said to be about £200. The smoking apartments are divided into four classes. In the cheapest are coolies, who pay about fourpence for their smoke. In the dearest the smoke costs about sevenpence. The drug supplied in each class is much the same both in quality and quantity; it is the difference in the pipes that regulates the price. The best kinds are made of ivory, the stem being often inlaid with stones and rendered more costly by reason of elaborate carving; the cheapest kinds are made simply of hard wood. The rooms also are furnished according to class. In the most expensive the lounge upon which the smoker reclines is of fine velvet, with pillows of the same material; the frames of each couch are inlaid with mother-of-pearl and jade; and the whole air of these rooms is one of sensuous luxury. There are also a number of private rooms. In the poorer section will be seen many wearers of the tattered yellow and grey robes of Buddhist and Taoist priests. Women form a fair proportion of the smokers. The common belief is, that the opium sleep is attended by a mild, pleasurable delirium, with brief glances of Elysium; but this is the exception, not the rule. People smoke to satisfy the craving begotten of previous indulgence. There is accommodation for 150 smokers at a time, and there is seldom a vacancy very long. The stream of smokers goes on from early morning till midnight, when the place closes; the clouds of smoke go up incessantly all day long. Europeans do not often visit the place; but the seamen of American men-of-war visiting Shanghai sometimes seek solace in the drug.

The houses of the Chinese are not much to boast of, being chiefly of one or two storeys, and of wood. Their furniture is very simple, matting and sofas or low beds being the principal varieties. Travelling is largely done by means of rivers and canals, which abound. The introduction of railways meets with much official opposition, but they are gradually being introduced. Horses are comparatively little used. Sedan-chairs carried by bearers, as well as covered carriages, are however not infrequent. Any one going out after dark is compelled by law to carry a lantern.

**Houses and travelling.**

Lanterns form a considerable element in one of the great Chinese festivals, that of the Lantern, held at the first full moon of the year, when a vast variety of lanterns of various colours and materials are lighted. The New Year is another great festival, whereat debt-paying is not forgotten, and many entertainments and presents are given. One of the grand ceremonies, in which the emperor takes a part, is connected with agriculture; he actually ploughs a furrow or two in a field near the Temple of the Earth, and sows several sorts of grain. Similarly, the empress gives her patronage to silk-weaving, going through several of the processes of manufacture, and sacrificing to the inventor of silk-weaving.

**Lantern festival.**

**Imperial ceremonies**

Early marriages are much in vogue; and complex arrangements generally precede the ceremony, that the fitting wife may be selected. People of the same surname may not marry, being assumed to be related; near relationship between those of different name is also a barrier to marriage. Polgamy is not legal, but many of the richer have secondary wives, or concubines, who do not rank much above servants; but their male children are recognised, supposing the legitimate wife has no son—a disgrace of deep dye. The emperor has but one wife, who is empress; but he may have any number of Tartar concubines.

**Marriage.**

It cannot be said that Chinese women are very accomplished. The poorer women have the great virtues of being hardworking and domesticated; the richer learn embroidery, painting on silk, and perhaps a little music; but possibly there is "a good time coming" for them, as for their neighbours in Japan. A wife may be divorced for adultery, thieving, ill-temper, inveterate infirmities, disobedience to the husband's parents, talkativeness, and even barrenness; though this is rare, owing to the secondary marriages being always available. A widow does not usually marry a second time.

**Divorce.**

The phlegmatic Chinaman is not appalled by death, and is only too ready to commit suicide; he knows that his descendants will perform the proper rites for him, and keep his memory green. The regard which the people pay to their deceased parents and relatives is really like ancestor-worship. White is the mourning colour; and dressed in white the family sit weeping around the corpse of a father, which is washed by the eldest son, then dressed as in life, and placed in a massive coffin with plenty of quicklime, and carefully made air-tight and varnished. Usually after three weeks the funeral procession is carried to the cemetery, which is mostly in an out-of-the-way place in the hills. Offerings are carried for the deceased, and bands of music attend. In many cases paper is made to do duty for valuables in the burning which follows. The rites of the dead are repeated twice a year, especially in spring.

**Death.**

**Ancestor-worship.**

**Funeral ceremonies.**

As a specimen of Chinese funerals, one performed in 1887, in England, may be described. A sailor belonging to the *Lai Yuen*, one of the ships of the Chinese squadron anchored at Spithead, having died, the body was buried at the Portsmouth Cemetery. The deceased was named Chin Pit Luo, and described by his shipmates as the finest sailor in the Chinese navy. The corpse, which was contained in a leaden coffin encased in two wooden ones, and covered with the yellow ensign, was followed to the grave by a party of stolid-looking Chinese seamen under the command of a

**A Chinese funeral in England.**

petty officer. Arrived at the cemetery gates, the body was carried to the grave in the usual way, but without any ceremony. After the coffin had been lowered into the grave, four sailors, stationed at the foot of the grave, produced in succession a tin pail, a parcel of matches, a number of fagots, and various pieces of brown paper. A fire having been kindled, out of the pail were brought forth several plates, which were disposed round the fire, a lump of pork, various pieces of meat, a few eggs, and a quantity of salt and sand. These having been divided into fives, were cooked and placed on the plates, and on the consummation of the sacrifice they were all gathered together and returned to the pail. A sailor now partly filled in the grave, after which the captain of the ship and a couple of subordinate officers came forward and prostrated themselves three times, uttering a prayer at each genuflexion. This completed the ceremony.

Great attention is paid to the selection of the right place of burial, although those who can afford it are carried to their native place; yet the exact spot for burial is a subject for learned study by the astrologers. A parent is mourned for three years, during which period none of his children may marry. The eldest son gets two shares of the property, the rest being divided in equal shares; but so strong is family feeling that the children often remain together after the father's death. The bones of Chinamen who die in America and other places abroad, are often carried home for final burial, a service for which payment is made beforehand to the emigrant companies.

**Mourning.**

**Division of Property.**

The rites of burial are, as we have said, more connected with ancestor-worship than with national religion. Buddhism is known to have gained great hold in China; but its adherents cannot be accurately reckoned, because a Chinaman, as a rule, is so tolerant that he may be called a Confucian, a Taoist, and a Buddhist, all at the same time, without shocking him. Confucius, whose system we cannot here say much about, was born in the sixth century before Christ, and after long study drew up a code of morals

**Buddhism.**

**Confucianism.**

and politics which has become the chief standard of Chinese civilisation. Many of his doctrines appear to have anticipated those of Christ, especially in the incul-

CHINESE DEATH PUNISHMENT IN A CAGE.

cation of control over the thoughts, and of doing to others as we would be done by. His descendants have carefully preserved the purity of their line, if their genealogies are to be believed, and high hereditary honours are theirs.

The emperor does them special honour, and every city has a temple to Confucius.

The doctrines of Confucius gained such influence partly because he professed simply to revive the pure doctrines of past ages, and did not come forward as a novelty-monger. He taught that in former generations the obligations between ruler and people, father and son, husband and wife, friend and friend, were scrupulously fulfilled. He set out what he considered right methods of restoring these days, by individual training, self-restraint, and regard for duty. His teaching was seen by the ruling classes to be a most efficient support of their authority. Enlarging on these precepts, Mencius taught that it was the duty of the people to dethrone an evil ruler; and this maxim has almost rivalled those of Confucius in the extent of its adoption by the Chinese.

**Taoism.**

Taoism, which has a large and undefined influence, has been called the rationalism of China; but has degenerated into a system of superstition. It was founded by Lao-tsze, a contemporary of Confucius, whose philosophy was a sort of quietism, the control of desires and passions; but he added to this a conception of a spirit named Tao, in which, by which, for which all things exist, and to which all return; a sort of Pantheism, in fact. But his followers have sought for the philosopher's stone, have great beliefs in charms and amulets, and claim to be able to exorcise spirits of all kinds; so that their practice is little better than Shamanism.

**Fatalism.**

It may be questioned whether fatalism is not the actual religion of a majority of Chinese. What will be, will be; why take precautions? Anything that is to happen will happen just the same. This belief is evidenced in many ways.

**Remarkable inventions.**

When we consider that printing from fixed blocks was invented in China long before its invention in Europe, dating at least back to the tenth century A.D.; that gunpowder and cannon were used by the Chinese six centuries ago; that the mariner's compass was known to them at a very early date, as well as its deviation from the actual North Pole; that we have taken the name of their country as the title of our chief modern porcelain ware; that the steelyard and spectacles equally rank among their inventions, we shall be ready to concede that they deserve to rank high among inventive nations. But two things have kept them from completing their inventions, or gaining full advantage from them; the system of instruction, the sole regard for old knowledge; and their neglect of theoretical studies, the proper cultivation of which has enabled Western people to gain their modern ascendency. It is the practical in which they delight; but while practice can repeat, it can rarely invent new principles. Thus they have long rejected modern machinery, whether for weaving or porcelain; but we cannot doubt that the next hundred years will witness startling changes in China. With the development of the enormous deposits of coal, and the opening out of mineral treasures, China must change, though probably the Chinese individuality will impress itself deeply on the transformation. For silk-weaving, ivory-carving, the making of ornaments, and other manufactures, the Chinese, with their patient industry and excellent workmanship, are among the foremost peoples of the world, and no doubt will continue so as long as they are frugal and industrious.

**Neglect of theory.**

**Dislike of machinery.**

**Manufactures.**

We must not linger long over the Chinese language and literature. The language is monosyllabic to the last degree, and has no inflexion, no alphabet, no declensions or conjugations. Its written characters are thousands of distinct symbols, derived at first from natural objects; but one sound often represents a hundred different words, according to the characters in which it is written. The difficulty of learning the language is increased by the use of various tones in speaking, which have great influence on the meaning; and it is not surprising that where the British come in contact with the Chinese, a new sort of language has developed, called "pigeon English," perhaps the most infantile and ludicrous ever invented; but it gains ground, and will probably do so still

**The Chinese language.**

**Tones.**

**Pigeon English.**

more, for the English are proverbially intolerant of foreign languages, and make foreigners learn theirs, or at least some parody of it. To take an example from Miss Bird (now Mrs. Bishop) in "The Golden Chersonese," "if you order a fire, you say something like this: 'Fire makee, chop chop, here, makee fire number one'; chop being

RECEPTION ROOM IN A CHINESE HOUSE.

quick, and number one good, or 'first-class.' If a servant tells you that some one has called, he says, 'One piecey manee here speak missey,' and if one asks who he is, he very likely answers, 'No sabe,' or else, 'Number one, tink,' by which he implies that the visitor is, in his opinion, a gentleman."

True poetry is not likely to be greatly developed in so fixed a language as Chinese; and the most valuable parts of their literature are those which deal with facts. Still, their Book of Odes includes compositions dating back earlier than any other works, and breathing, as Professor Douglas says ("Encyclopædia Britannica," Vol. V.), "a quiet calm and patriarchal simplicity of thought and life. . . . We have brought before the mind's eye the lowly cottage where dwell a family united by the bonds of affection and of duty." Even where oppression is hinted at, the remedy sought is flight, not rebellion; and the essence of the people seems to have been, then as now, a strict subordination and patience. In later poetry, after the time of Confucius, superstition takes the place of monotheism, turbulence of subordination. Later, when the Chinese arms spread far in conquest, there was another flourishing period of poetry; but, after all, it does not reach any true greatness. Neither epic nor dramatic poetry has flourished among them; but plays are written in prose, and are very abundant. The stories are rarely such as we find interesting, and are not illustrated by scenery. Only two actors occupy the stage at one time.

**Chinese poetry.**

Chinese religious and philosophical books are on the whole disappointing, mostly composed of disjointed sentiments or statements; and some of them may be summed up in the sentence, "Walk in the old paths." The Book of Rites prescribes behaviour and ceremony for every minute circumstance of life; and one of the chief Boards at Pekin is occupied with seeing that its directions are faithfully carried out. Indeed, it has been said that the Book of Rites is the most exact and complete monograph the Chinese nation can give of itself. "Its affections are satisfied by ceremonial; its duties are fulfilled by ceremonial. Its virtues and vices are recognised by ceremonial; in a word, for it ceremonial is man." Confucius's Book of History is perhaps the next most influential work to the Book of Rites. It develops the patriarchal system of government in a series of conversations between kings and their minis-

**The Book of Rites.**

ters. Commentaries on the works of Confucius and his followers, particularly the Nine Classics, are numbered by thousands; but they are as devoid of original value and as servile to tradition as the teachings of the scribes and Pharisees. Finally, it is in the historical and topographical records of their own nation that Chinese literature is most prolific and most useful; and encyclopædias of all their knowledge have been compiled with astonishing completeness. One of them extends to 6,109 volumes. It might damp the ardour of those who believe in reading alone as a sufficient means of education, to see how much Chinese read, and to reflect how their intellect has been cramped and conventionalised by it.

**The Classics.**

**Encyclopædias.**

Giving ourselves space for just one glimpse at a Chinese city, Canton is replete with interest, whether in its water-habitations, in which a vast population is crowded, or in its closely-packed narrow streets. A strange contrast they present to Western streets, being often less than eight feet wide, and covered in at the level of the tops of the houses by boards or matting. A city without carriage ways, paved with granite; the streets all barricaded and blocked up at night; watchmen on the look-out for fires in elevated watch houses—a very necessary precaution when so many houses are built of wood. "In the streets," says Mrs. Bishop, in "The Golden Chersonese, and the Way Thither," "the roofs of the houses and shops are rarely, if ever, regular, nor are the houses themselves arranged in a direct line. This queer effect results from queer causes. Every Chinese house is built on the principles of geomancy, which do not admit of straight lines; and were these to be disregarded, the astrologers and soothsayers, under whose auspices all houses are erected, predict fearful evils to the impious builders.

**The streets of Canton.**

"There are few open spaces in Canton, and these are decorated, not with statues, but with monumental arches of brick, red sandstone, or grey granite, which are put up as memorials of virtuous men and women, learned or aged men, and specially dutiful sons or daughters. The public buildings and temples are extremely ugly, and are the subjects of slow but manifest decay, while the streets of shops exceed in picturesqueness everything I have ever seen. Much of this is given by the perpendicular

**Shop signs.** sign-boards, fixed or hanging, upon which are painted, on an appropriate background, immense Chinese characters in gold, vermilion, or black. Two or three of these belong to each shop, and set forth its name and the nature of the goods which are to be purchased at it. The effect of these boards, as the sun's rays fall upon them here and there, is fascinating. The interiors of the shops are lofty, glass lamps hang from the ceilings, and large lanterns above every door, and both are painted in bright colours, with the characters signifying happiness, or with birds, butterflies, flowers, or landscapes. The shop wall which faces the door invariably has upon it a gigantic fresco or portrait of the tutelary god of the building, or a sheet of red paper on which the characters forming his name are placed, or the character Shan, which implies all gods; and these and the altars below are seen from the street."

"As there are streets of shops and trades, so there are streets of dwelling-houses; but even the finest of these present a miserable appearance to the passers-by, for all

**Private houses.** one can see is a lofty and dimly-lighted stone vestibule, furnished with carved ebony chairs with marble seats and backs, and not infrequently with gigantic coffins placed on end, the gift of pious juniors to their seniors. Many Chinese mansions contain six or seven courtyards, each with its colonnade, drawing, dining, and reception rooms; and at the back of all there is a flower-garden adorned with rockeries, fish-ponds, dwarf trees, and miniature pagodas and bridges."

We have said little of the dominant class in China—the Manchu Tartars; but their supremacy is still real,

**The Manchus.** because of their physical vigour. In many ways the Chinese mandarins, with their intellectual cultivation, have influenced them; but they keep firm hold of power, being far more determined and capable soldiers than Chinese proper, and forming a great part of the imperial armies. It is a strange instance of the change of circumstances, that the Chinese now occupy Manchuria, from which their conquerors came, and that the Tartars scarcely have any part in it. The separation

A CHINESE SCHOOL.

between the peoples is still so marked that most Chinese cities have a separate Tartar quarter, strictly closed at night, and often walled round.

Although our very natural idea is, that the Chinese

constitute a very distinct and homogeneous people, the fact is, that we might almost regard them as a group of nations, presenting more diversity than the varied populations of the United States of America. The southern Chinese not only do not mingle freely with the inhabitants of the northern provinces; they actually show considerable hostility to them. It is not an uncommon thing for the mandarins in power in a given province to require interpreters in intercourse with the provincials. In fact, the Chinese nation consists of a mixture of peoples in which every neighbouring Mongoloid nation or stock is included; and the mixture is in varying proportions in different regions. The whole is kept together by the official dialect, the uniform education of the educated classes, and the strong hand of the Manchus.

**Diversity among Chinese.**

Much remains to be known of the hill-tribes who abound in different parts of China and in the islands of Hainan and Formosa, more isolated than many of the hill-tribes of India, and governed in much the same miscellaneous way. It cannot be safely stated that all these people are of the Mongoloid stock, though many are probably related to them; but we believe no specimens of them have been carefully examined by European men of science. They do not intermarry with the Chinese, who hold them in contempt and abhorrence. For the most part they present a striking contrast to the conventionality and ceremonial of the Chinese, being lively, noisy, fond of the open air, passionate, and convivial.

**The hill tribes.**

The aborigines of the province of Kwei-chow have the curious custom of the *couvade;* the mother gets up at once after the birth of a child, and performs her usual work, while the father takes to bed for a month with the baby, thus giving expression to the idea that the life of a father is inseparably bound up with that of the child.

Formosa is inhabited in the western regions by Chinese, who steadily but slowly augment their territory; but nearly all the mountainous tract of the east and south is occupied by aborigines, or rather

**The Formosans.**

natives sprung from Malay stock, for it is doubtful whether these may not be successors of a race now extinct. Their languages belong to the Malayo-Polynesian group. A small proportion of these tribes are settled, and acknowledge the authority of the Chinese, and both intermarry with them and adopt their customs. These are known as Pepo-hoan (savages of the plain). But by far the larger proportion of the natives remain wild and intractable, instantly slaughtering any stranger. For the most part they are of small proportions, with long limbs and short bodies; but taller and finer men are not wanting, and it is possible that two races may be here mixed. Some of the women in the settled villages are of a clear

CHINESE CHEST.

olive colour, while others are as dark and coarse as Malays. Their eyes are large, round, and full. The cheek-bones are all high; but some have thick and others very thin lips. The hair is long, straight, and jet black. The women's ears are pierced in five places for rings worn on ceremonial occasions. Both men and women wear the tunic and short loose trousers of the Chinese.

The savages proper, or "sheng-fan," include the smaller people, who intermarry very closely and are very inferior in physique. Very low foreheads predominate, and the whole expression is unintelligent, with a peculiar sinister dogged look. The men wear ear-rings a quarter of an inch thick, and the women wear two in each ear, of hollow bamboo tubes, through which strings of beads are hung. The women are very short and thick-set, accustomed to carry heavy burdens. Their being tattooed with dark blue lines with indigo adds greatly to their ugliness; the men are tattooed in the same way, to a more moderate extent.

The men wear usually only a long piece of cloth wound about the loins; but the chiefs are more fully dressed, and adorned with disks of bone and tassels of beads. The women have, as a peculiar indispensable garment, a small piece of cloth tied around the leg just below the knee. Many of the men wear a profusion of brass wire rings on their fingers and bracelets on their arms. The canine teeth are knocked out of all children, with the idea of strengthening speed and wind in hunting.

**Hunting.** These savages live chiefly by hunting small deer with spears, bows and arrows, knives, etc. Their spear and knife sheaths are usually ornamented with tassels of hair from the heads of Chinese they have killed.[1] On their hunting expeditions they bivouac at night round a fire, lying head to head and feet to feet in a circle, on bundles of grass, sometimes building rude huts as a shelter. Some of the savages also cultivate sweet potatoes, yams, etc., and weave good mats. They barter a good deal of their produce to the Chinese for knife-blades, powder and shot, pans, cloth, etc.

**Huts.** Their huts are constructed by fixing two upright poles in the ground, and laying others sloping from the tops of these, then others again lengthwise over these, and covering the whole with coarse dry grass. A few stones in the middle of the hut form the fireplace. Grass spread on the ground serves for beds. The most acceptable present to these people is a pig, which they cook whole for about a quarter of an hour only; then it is cut up, and many save their shares for special occasions. They are very prone to intoxication; and the Chinese frequently take advantage of this to get from them whatever they wish.

[1] See Mr. E. C. Taintor's paper on "The Aborigines of Northern Formosa," in the Journal of the North China Branch of the Royal Asiatic Society. No. IX. Shanghai, 1875.

Blood revenge is in full force among these savages. The murder of a relative is bound to be avenged by his kindred. This adds zest to the pursuit of Chinese who have killed Formosans; but, independently of this, a savage who has not killed and beheaded a Chinaman is not respected, and he rises in position with the number of Chinese heads he can count. They are said to have no idea of the year or of the seasons, and to be unable to tell their own ages. They bury their dead standing upright without coffins, and their weapons and utensils with them. They pledge friendship by each man putting his arm round the other's neck and then, placing their heads and mouths close together, they both drink at the same time from one cup.

FORMOSAN (PEPO-HOAN) WOMAN AND CHILD.

Chinese ideas about these troublesome subjects may be gathered from the following extract from an official account of the island, "To govern them is impossible; to exterminate them not to be thought of; and so nothing can be done with them. The only thing left is to establish troops with cannon at all the passes through which they issue on their raids, and so overawe them by military display, from coming out of their fastnesses. The savage tracks lie only through the dense forests, thick with underbrush, where hiding is

**An official view.**

easy. When they cut off a head, they boil it to separate the flesh, adorn the skull with various ornaments, and hang it up in their huts as evidence of their valour. Even if any attempts were made to keep them within bounds, it must sooner or later end in failure. If it is asked, then, What shall be done? the reply is, Murders must be punished in kind, and friendly aborigines must be used to gradually reclaim and civilise them. They must be conquered, to make them fear, and then they can be controlled, to make them obedient. Their country must be opened up and Chinese settlers introduced, and then the harm done by them will gradually cease. Later they will become tamed, and finally they may be enrolled as subjects, and pay tribute."

The Coreans.

The peninsula of Corea, to the north-east of China, is occupied by a race in several respects intermediate between the Chinese and the Japanese, both having frequently invaded it, and compelled its kings to pay tribute and do homage. For a long time they have been greatly isolated from the rest of the world, and have had very little intercourse with Europeans. In 1883 the old barriers were at last broken through, and European diplomatists and consuls were admitted.

The Coreans have the usual Mongolian characteristics, black coarse hair, oblique eyes, flat faces, broad cheekbones, yellow to tawny complexion, and slight beard. They are of a vigorous muscular type. In language they resemble the Japanese more than the Chinese, having, however, their own peculiar vocabulary, but writing in Chinese characters.

From the seventh to the thirteenth centuries of our era was the period of Corea's prime. It was about this time that Buddhism was introduced; and the remains of Buddhist temples of that date are still found. Corea was then in communication with Arabia and Persia, and many Persian ornaments have been found as relics of this period, during which the ceramic art was supposed to be introduced into Corea from these countries. Few antiquarian or historical remains are to be found in the

NATIVES OF COREA.

peninsula; the great Japanese invasion destroyed almost every vestige of art in the country.

**Character of the people.** The people are exceedingly peaceful and civil to strangers. The women are kept in strict confinement all day, and are only allowed to walk abroad in the evening, when all the men retire indoors, and go out after nightfall under penalty of imprisonment. All classes are decent and orderly in their dress and demeanour. The country is so primitive that the people have almost no wants; and the difficulty of trading with them is, that they have nothing to supply, for the reason that they want nothing. The houses have no furniture except a mat, a pillow, and a screen. There is no great desire to make money, beyond what will last through the winter; there is nothing to invest money in, and if a man has more than he urgently needs, it is generally taken from him by the officials. The men are greatly addicted to drink; and it is a common thing to see them rolling helplessly drunk about the streets, and nobody appears to take the least notice of them. The prevailing colour of the dress is white. The proper names are nearly all Chinese, pure and simple. The country is about the size of England, Wales, and Scotland, while the population is about one-third of that of Great Britain.

**The government.** The government is monarchical, and the king keeps up great state. All the people have to work for the king three months a year. Every king receives his title from the emperor of China, to whom his ambassadors have to ko-tow. The land is all held to be the king's property, and the nobles hold it of him by feudal tenure. Great regard is paid to learning, which, however, consists chiefly of Confucianism. Learned men have a special rank and precedence assigned to them. Buddhism is prevalent, but Taoism is also much in vogue.

Tobacco is to Corea what opium is to China. The Corean goes about with his pipe, about three feet long, held in one hand, while with the other he tries to do whatever work he is at, whether it is digging with a spade or any other employment. The result is, that fifteen men can only do the work of three; for nothing will induce a Corean to relinquish his pipe for a moment. Another great impediment to work is their dress, on account of their long, loose sleeves, into which they cram everything they want to carry. This has been recognised as such a nuisance by the king, that he issued a proclamation against long sleeves, ordering his subjects to adopt short, tight sleeves, which he wore himself; but the order was utterly disregarded, and the people still keep their long pipes and their long sleeves. The people are said to have an intense admiration for the natural beauties of their country, which are very great.

**Long sleeves and long pipes.**

Just recently Corea has been again coming more under Japanese influence, and making efforts to be completely independent of China. The Chinese resident has had a very unpleasant time of it for some years. The Corean king has decided to send representatives to several European courts. If this be successfully done, Corean independence is asserted; but at present the whole foreign trade of the country would not support five envoys abroad. Such independent action is a fitting consequence of the long vacillation of China about Corea.

CHINESE ORNAMENTS.

# CHAPTER XI.

## The Japanese.

**Japan compared with Great Britain—Early history—The Mikado—Rise of the Shoguns—Mongol invasion—Development of feudal system—The revolution of 1868—The new constitution—Early European visitors—Recent treaties with foreigners—Modern changes—Japanese physical features—Mental capacity and character—Imitation of Europeans—The happy despatch—Japanese ladies—Muscular peasantry—Acrobats—Tattooing—Dress—The kimono—Hair-dressing—The chignon—Powder and paint—Rough country dress—Wedding ceremonies—Delight in children—Their obedience, good temper, and docility—Schools—Teaching of girls—The public baths—Houses and furniture—Religion—The Ainos of Japan—Distinct from Mongol type—Hairiness—Physical character—Aino women's looks—Children—Clothing—Jewellery—Houses—Food—Saké—Curios—Hunting—Notions of religion—Marriage—Good qualities—The Loo-choo islanders—Physical characters.**

**Japan compared with Great Britain.**

EVEN more than China, Japan bespeaks and commands our interest. She occupies in several respects a parallel position to Great Britain—as an insular power, as having developed to her present condition through an elaborate feudal system, as having great mineral wealth and manufacturing skill, as including the flower of the Mongoloid people, and especially as having lately thrown off ancient traditions to a very large extent, and adopted many features of the civilisation of western Europe.

Japanese history cannot be relied on so far back as Chinese. This is perhaps due to the insular position, and to the succession of destructive invasions to which islands, especially fertile and rich ones, are mostly exposed. We can look back to a period when tribes resembling the remaining Ainos of Yezo, inhabited such parts of the islands as were redeemed from forests. These were graduallv driven northwards by the ancestors of the present Japanese. That these were in part of **Early History.**

JAPANESE WELL-TO-DO FAMILY.

Chinese origin cannot be doubted; but how far the Manchus, Coreans, Malays, and Papuans may have a claim to share in the Japanese ancestry, cannot yet be settled.

Kioto was early the capital and chief seat of Japanese power. The emperor has long been termed the Mikado, a word meaning much the same as "Sublime Porte," the emperor being too sublime a being to be spoken of directly or in other than a figurative way. He became surrounded by a noble class, chiefly descended from the imperial family, called "Kuge." Gradually, in order to repress the aborigines, or to expel invaders from the mainland, a military system was organised, and placed under a *Shogun*, or general. This office in time became hereditary; and around the Shogun a military caste arose, quite distinct from the peasantry. As the Shogun increased in power, the Mikado was of less practical importance. In the tenth and eleventh centuries the office of Shogun was alternately held by members of two powerful clans, the Taira and Minamoto, who between them ruled the whole country. After fierce civil wars they succeeded in annihilating each other; and several other families in succession held the Shogunate, not without many civil wars, till the accession in 1603 of the Tokugawa family, which held power till 1867. The chief event in Japanese history during the earlier period of the Shogunate was the repulse of the great Mongol invasion in 1281, in the time of Kubla Khan.

**The Mikado.**

**Rise of the Shoguns.**

**Mongol invasion.**

The first Shogun of the Tokugawa dynasty, Iyeyasu, and his grandson, Iyemitsu, must be credited with the full development of the remarkable feudal system which lasted till 1868. Under them, too, Yedo grew to great political and manufacturing importance. They subjected and grouped around them all the *daimios* or territorial nobles, and the military clan by which Iyeyasu gained his power, and whom he created a nobility known as *hatamoto*. The daimios ruled over the eighteen provinces of Japan, and within their territories were practically supreme, each having a *han*, or governing clan, under him. Usages, laws, currency, etc., differed in adjacent provinces, and rendered intermixture of the population very difficult. Altogether, though the nation as a whole was at peace, the peasantry suffered greatly under the exactions of the han. The shoguns kept up a strict authority over the daimios, and

**Development of feudal system.**

JAPANESE GIRLS WITH MUSICAL INSTRUMENTS.

when they were not at Yedo, detained their wives and families there.

Meanwhile the Mikado was always the titular sovereign, invested each Shogun with his office, and kept his court of nobles at Kioto, though retaining no real power; but the Shogun never assumed to be supreme sovereign. The title of Tycoon (or taikun), formerly supposed by Europeans to be that of the "temporal ruler" of Japan, is a Chinese word, meaning "great Lord," and was often used by the Japanese.

HARUKO, EMPRESS OF JAPAN.

The revolution of 1868.

During later periods of Japanese history, instead of the earlier maritime enterprises being repeated, the people were forbidden to leave the country without express permission; and very few foreigners were permitted to enter it. The peasantry grew impatient of the yoke of the daimios, while the latter equally resented the yoke of the Shoguns. Finally, the people's minds turned towards the revival of the Mikado as sole sovereign, as offering a hope of an improved state of things. The last Shogun resigned in 1867, and in 1868 the Mikado's authority was fully re-established, after comparatively little fighting. The Mikado removed his court from Kioto to Yedo in 1869, and changed the name of Yedo to Tokio (meaning eastern capital). Thus quietly was brought about a more important revolution than our own of 1688.

In 1873 the Mikado granted his subjects a representative constitution; and in 1875 a senate was appointed, as well as a supreme council and college of ministers. In 1878 assemblies were constituted for the provinces and departments, and the representative

**The new constitution.**

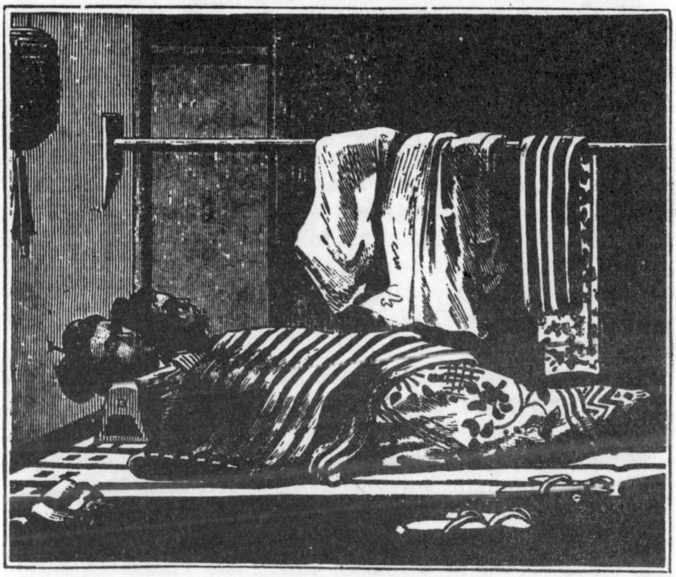

JAPANESE BEDROOM.

system is to be completed by a national assembly, which will meet for the first time in 1890.

In the sixteenth century Portuguese traders visited Japan; and Portuguese missionaries under St. Francis Xavier landed about the middle of the century at Kagosima. But in consequence, it would seem, of the possibility of their attempting the subjugation of Japan, the Portuguese were expelled in 1639. The Dutch arrived in 1610, and though strictly

**Early European visitors.**

limited to Nagasaki, maintained almost a monopoly of Japanese foreign trade till recent times. An Englishman named William Adams, from Kent, reached Japan early in the seventeenth century, as pilot to a Dutch vessel, and gave the Japanese instruction in ship-building. But no English factories were established in consequence. The United States, as represented by Commodore Perry, must be credited with having broken the ice between the Anglo-Saxons and the Japanese, although in a somewhat high-handed manner. Several ports were thenceforth opened to American trade. England soon followed suit; and now, eighteen foreign nations have treaties with Japan, obtained by persevering insistence. Before 1868, all foreign powers treated with the Shogun or Tycoon; but in that year the British, French, and Dutch ministers went to Kioto and obtained the Mikado's direct sanction to the treaties already concluded. It must not be imagined that foreigners brought about the revolution of 1868; it had been long in preparation, and they have simply reaped many of its advantages.

**Recent treaties with foreigners.**

Since 1868 Japan has made more rapid progress than perhaps any other country in ancient or modern times. Universities, railways, telegraphs, light-houses, dockyards, steamship lines, postal communication, machine manufactures, newspapers, and other European and American notions have been introduced; and even the picturesque and appropriate native costume bids fair to disappear in favour of much less charming European fashions.

**Modern changes.**

Although considerably modified from the typical Mongoloid form, the Japanese show plainly their relationship by their yellow or yellowish complexion, prominent cheekbones, black hair and eyes, small nose, scanty beard, and slightly oblique eyes. The nobles and military caste are fairer, with longer heads and higher foreheads, an aquiline nose, thin lips. The peasantry are much more Asiatic in appearance, more muscular, flat and broad in face, low-browed, thicker-lipped.

**Japanese physical features.**

**Mental capacity and character.**

There is no question that the higher classes in Japan have high mental capacity and are quick to learn. They love knowledge and are enthusiastic for progress. Yet they can scarcely be

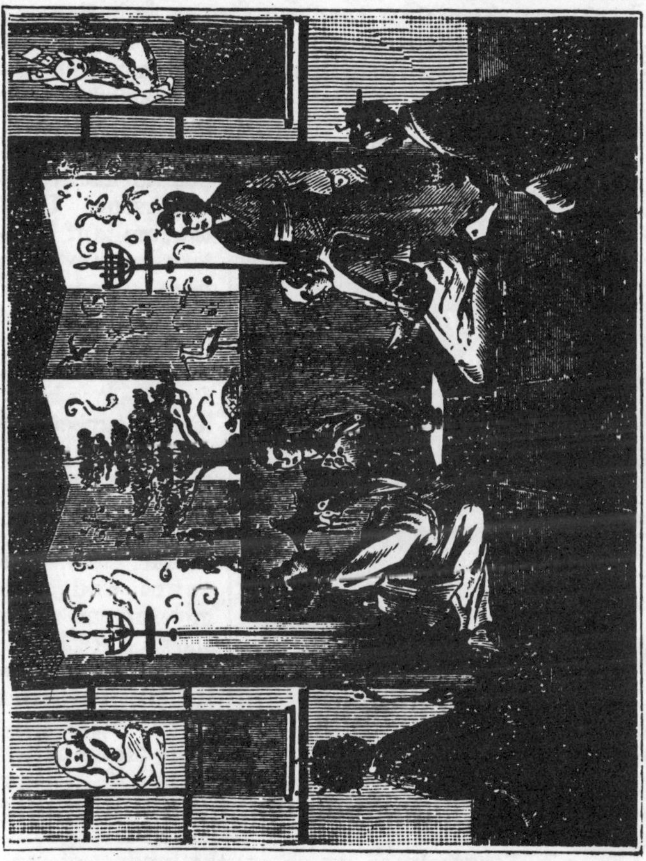

JAPANESE WEDDING CEREMONY.

denominated philanthropists. Keenly appreciating the advantages of that intercourse with the rest of the world which has so long been denied to them, and realising that wealth, importance, elevation in the mental and material scale, have come to Europeans in consequence of their wide intercourse and broad education, they are eager to secure for themselves a good share of all advantages to be obtained by following their example; and they have thrown themselves headlong into an imitative and

Imitation of Europeans.

assimilative career, which may not be the most fruitful they could pursue. Yet they must not be blamed if they make mistakes or meet with disappointments in this endeavour. Until the results of Western culture have been tested, they cannot find out its defects, or know what to avoid. Perhaps it is hopeless to expect the Japanese as yet to attain a healthy independence of thought and action; still, the court and the government have shown a resolution to take rank as independent and equal with the European powers, which argues well for the future of the country. It will be greatly to be regretted if, in their haste to become Europeanised, the Japanese throw aside elements of their own, either in dress or thought, in habits or in manufactures, which are the product of centuries of adaptation to their surroundings. We must hope that, as in other cases, nature will be too strong for the Japanese, and will recur under new conditions, pre-

JAPANESE LACE-MAKER.

serving the best features of the past and carrying them to new perfection. Japanese art deserves much detailed notice, for which we cannot find space. In textile fabrics, in bronzes and inlaid and lacquered work, in pottery, porcelain, and wood-carving, the native Japanese work is as distinctive and special as that of any country ever was. Decorative work is their speciality, for their designs are always treated flatly.

JAPANESE GIRL AT HER TOILET.

The Japanese on the whole must be described as highly courteous and anxious to please, brave and warlike, having a sense of personal honour almost like that prevailing among the French. Indeed, duels are not infrequent among them; and the *harakiri*, or "happy despatch," is another form of sacrifice to the same sentiment of honour. The happy despatch used to be in vogue, to avoid imperial censure or condemnation, the unfortunate offender assembling his friends to witness his own action of cutting himself in the lower part of the stomach, followed by his decapitation by a skilled executant.

The happy despatch.

Japanese ladies must be acknowledged to have numerous charms, if the possession of beauty can hardly be granted them, according to Western ideas. They have much grace, ingenuousness, simplicity, naive curiosity, and sweetness of smile and expression; and in some cases their complexion approaches not

**Japanese ladies.**

JAPAN: PRESENTING NEW-BORN BABE IN SHINTO TEMPLE.
*(The archway in front is the general symbol of Shinto.)*

a little to a European style, and the lips alone, the artificially blackened teeth, and the peculiar style of the head-dress, remain to remind us of the contrast of types. Then their small slight figures seem puny in comparison with the robuster Europeans. Even the men are of quite low stature, seldom rising beyond five feet four inches.

The muscularity of the peasantry is in strong contrast to the slightness of the aristocracy. They can endure a surprising amount of fatigue, bearing heavy burdens. And as for skill in muscular actions, those who have seen Japanese acrobats do not need to be reminded of their extraordinary agility and suppleness of limb. With all this, old age comes on early in Japan, to women as well as men. At thirty both sexes are often wrinkled and worn. Of course the hideous fashion of blackening the women's teeth aids in producing this appearance of age.

**Muscular peasantry.**

**Acrobats.**

It is hardly safe to say from year to year what is the prevailing costume of parts of Japan, since European modes have been introduced. It is likely that tattooing will become more and more uncommon, but in the past it prevailed extensively, even among high-class women. Now-a-days the "runners" who act the part of cab-horses exhibit some of the showiest patterns, extending over almost their entire body, and displaying not unfrequently great richness of design. Birds, dragons, and flowers in red, white, and blue, elaborately arranged, supply the main ideas.

**Tattooing.**

Notwithstanding the spread of European clothing, which needs no description, the mass of the Japanese, especially at a distance from the capital and the trade routes, have by no means as yet discarded their old vestments. Formerly every rank had its appropriate cut and colour; but the universal garment for both sexes was the *kimono*, commonly of cotton, among the rich of silk. This is an untrimmed narrow tunic reaching to the feet, with huge baggy sleeves, often used as pockets, and containing, among other necessaries, rolls of paper which serve as pocket-handkerchiefs and table-napkins. The better classes wear an under skirt, the poorer wear trousers. For cold weather, additional garments of similar type are worn; in rain, straw mantles, and waterproofs made of layers of waxed or oiled paper. A great girdle surrounds

**Dress.**

**The kimono.**

the waist. High wooden sabots complete the costume.

JAPANESE LADY.

A peculiar kind of straw slippers, often needing to be renewed, is worn by porters and runners.

Hair-dressing is an elaborate piece of work. Men shave the front of their scalps, and coil the remainder of their hair at the back. Women wear all their hair, which is partly raised in front, and partly dressed in an elaborate chignon, secured by great pins, and made smooth by bandoline. There are two uniform partings on the right and left. The women's head is never covered out of doors, and the hair remains dressed for a week or more, being preserved at night by using a wooden pillow, not to lay the head on, but the neck, leaving the hair and skull projecting behind (fig. p. 203). Married women at once, or soon after marriage, remove every hair of the eyebrows, as well as blacken the teeth with a sort of ink. The face, ears, and neck are literally covered with white powder; and the lips being artificially reddened, a Japanese married woman becomes most unpleasing in countenance. It is very remarkable that jewellery is not worn by Japanese women.

**Hair-dressing.**

**The chignon.**

**Powder and paint.**

Elaborate and good costume is not, however, to be found everywhere in Japan; and Miss Bird in particular found many localities where the men commonly wear scarcely anything, and the women only put on a short, tight petticoat, or wretched tight blue cotton trousers, with a loose vest of the same material tucked into the band. In these cases it was often difficult to distinguish men from women, except by the eyebrows and teeth. The women usually carry naked babies on their backs.

**Rough country dress.**

Marriages take place early, but by no means in infancy; bridegrooms are usually from twenty to twenty-one years old, brides sixteen or seventeen. It is only in modern times that the couple are allowed to meet before marriage. On the wedding day the bride's trousseau is laid out for inspection in her new home, where the wedding is celebrated at an improvised altar decked with flowers, and with images of the gods in front. The bride is veiled in white, which also is the colour of the wedding robe; and she arrives at her new home led by her two bridesmaids and a richly-dressed assembly of rela-

**Wedding ceremonies.**

tives and friends. The bridesmaids, who are supposed to represent the male and female butterfly, the favourite patterns for married life, have a number of important functions. Several of the ceremonies represent a sort of solemn eating together by the bride and bridegroom, who also drink alternately, out of a vessel with two mouths, nine small cups of saké, the Japanese favourite liquor (fig. p. 205). The bride now puts on the dress she has received from the bridegroom, who in his turn puts on a special dress given him by the bride, and a full meal is

JAPANESE CHILDREN AT PLAY.

taken. Various ceremonies between the newly-wedded couple and the visitors follow, including the drinking of nine cups of saké by every one present.

Their attention to and affection for their children is a striking feature among the Japanese. "I never saw people take so much delight in their offspring," says Miss Bird in "Unbeaten Tracks in Japan," "carrying them about, or holding their hands in walking, watching and entering into their games, supplying them constantly with new toys, taking them to picnics and festivals, never being content to be without them, and

**Delight in children.**

treating other people's children also with a suitable measure of affection and attention. Both fathers and mothers take a pride in their children. It is most amusing, about six every morning, to see twelve or fourteen men sitting on a low wall, each with a child under two years in his arms—fondling and playing with it, and showing off its physique and intelligence. At night, after the houses are shut up, looking through the long fringe of rope or rattan which conceals the sliding door, you see the father, who wears nothing but a *maro* (loin-

JAPANESE CHILDREN AT PLAY.

cloth), in the bosom of his family, bending his ugly, kindly face over a gentle-looking baby, and the mother, who more often than not has dropped the *kimono* from her shoulders, enfolding two children, destitute of clothing, in her arms. For some reason they prefer boys; but certainly girls are equally petted and loved.

**Their obedience, good temper, and docility.**

The children, though for our ideas too gentle and formal, are very prepossessing in looks and behaviour. They are so perfectly docile and obedient, so ready to help their parents, so good to the little ones; and in the many hours which I have spent in watching them at play, I have never heard an angry word or seen a sour look or act. But they are little men and women rather than children, and their old-fashioned

JAPANESE SINGING GIRL.

appearance is greatly aided by their dress, which is the same as that of adults." The children perhaps gain excessive gravity owing to sitting up with their parents and constantly being with them.

Boys up to three years old have their heads shaved

alogether, giving them an appearance of abnormal size. Then the hair is allowed to grow in three tufts—one over each ear, the other at the back of the neck. At ten, the crown alone is shaved; at fifteen, boys assume the manly fashion of hair; girls, though their hair grows long and

JAPANESE LADY OF RANK.

is elaborately dressed, have minor peculiarities according to their age.

Even village schools are now being modified after the European pattern. The schools have good apparatus, maps, etc. The pupils are taught by excellent object-lessons; and, in fact, "the usual branches of a modern education" are imparted. Some of the Chi- **Schools.**

nese classics are studied, in order that Chinese writing may be acquired. So intense is the regard for parents and teachers, that punishments are rarely needed, and are not severe. Much of the children's play is of a grave nature; but it interests them greatly, especially the variety of mechanical devices applied to running water.

**Teaching of girls.** Girls are carefully taught household accomplishments, embroidery, cooking, etc., and all learn to make their own clothes—a really simple task. For recreation there are circulating libraries, well supplied with Japanese love-stories or histories of heroes. The arrangement of flowers and of rooms is part of every girl's education, and is really exquisitely done.

**The public baths.** The bath is greatly in vogue in Japan; but, contrary to our ideas, it is taken very much in public, the sexes being usually not separated. The people have no idea of shame at the custom, and are astonished that we should be shocked at it. As Sir Rutherford Alcock says: "It is a custom of the country. Fathers, mothers, and husbands all sanction it; and from childhood the feeling must grow up, as effectually shielding them from self-reproach or shame as their sisters in Europe in adopting low dresses in the ballroom."

**Houses and furniture.** Japanese houses are almost invariably of one storey—or at most of two, and built of wood—usually bamboo. The roofs are high-peaked, and project beyond the walls. The rooms are often large, and only divided by movable partitions of wood or paper. Mica and oiled paper are largely used for windows, and paper is also the only protection for lamps and lanterns, which accounts for the frequent fires in Japanese towns. Furniture is of the simplest, mats and quilts being the principal items. How easy it is to set up housekeeping, where chairs, tables, sofas, and bedsteads are not wanted! A few mats and quilts, a box of clothes, a pan to cook rice, a few cups and trays, a bath tub,—there you have a household almost equipped. To go to bed, it is simply necessary to put on a bulky, wadded garment of full length, and lie down under a quilt, the head resting on a box covered with a paper pillow.

Religion.

The religions of Japan are somewhat peculiar, inasmuch as it is possible to profess several without inconsistency. The primitive religion, possibly native in origin, is Shintoism, meaning "the way of the gods." It has no code of doctrines, but includes a vague belief in a universal deity, too distant from mortals to be prayed to; a sort of ancestor- and hero-worship; and a nature-worship, which sees spirits in all natural phenomena, and reckons their number at eight millions. The salient fact of political importance is, that the Mikado is held to be a descendant of the Sun-goddess, and that he must therefore be implicitly obeyed. No further moral system is laid down, except the necessity of purity of mind and soul. Offerings are made to the spirits at simple shrines throughout the country, not containing images to be worshipped, although there is usually some object in them in which a spirit is believed to reside. Formerly there were great human sacrifices at the burial of princes and nobles. The dead are either buried or their ashes deposited in cemeteries distinguished for natural beauty.

Confucianism was introduced from China about the sixth century, and gained a great influence over the social and political systems; but at present it is rather a philosophy than a religion, and its largest hall at Tokio is a library of European, Chinese, and Japanese works. This philosophy has however largely given way in recent years before the so-called "English philosophy" of Mill, Darwin, and Herbert Spencer, many of whose works have been translated into Japanese.

Buddhism found its way to Japan in the sixth century also, but gained no great influence until the ninth, when the priest Kukai, or Kobo Daishi, showed how to adapt Shintoism to Buddhism by asserting that the Shinto deities were transmigrations of the Buddhistic ones. Thus explained, Buddhism gained great ascendency. In the seventeenth century a philosophical awakening took place, under which every man was taught to long for perfection, to believe in successive transmigrations of souls, and to look forward to the perfect reward of absorption into Buddha. A very great number of Buddhist

JAPANESE LADY.

shrines and temples exist, vastly more ornate and wealthy than those of the Shinto, containing images of extraordinary variety for adoration, supporting till lately a numerous priesthood, who took care to attract the people in every possible way, by spectacles, games, lotteries, and even shooting galleries. The recent revolution, however, has been attended with a great spoliation of Buddhism, suppression of temples and monasteries, melting of bells for coinage, etc.; and the religion now only exists on sufferance, and has already put forth renewed efforts to gain spiritual influence over the people. It now has to meet the additional competition of missionaries of various Christian Churches—Protestant, Roman Catholic, and Greek, who, especially the last, are making a fair amount of progress.

JAPANESE.

The Japanese language has a certain amount of affinity to the Chinese, but the most important features of resemblance have been borrowed from Chinese in recent centuries. The people speak in a musical tone, which is as pleasing as Italian pronunciation. There are forty-seven primary syllables, which by certain modifications become seventy-two. As in Chinese, slight shades of pronunciation are very important. There are no ordinary inflexions, these being indicated by prefixed or affixed particles. There are different modes of speech for addressing equals, superiors, and inferiors. One of the great difficulties of the language, is the difference of the inflexion particles in written and in spoken language. It is written with Chinese ideographic symbols combined with two varieties of the phonetic system. It is a question whether English may not ultimately supplant Japanese, so many of the people have in late years learnt it.

JAPANESE FURNITURE.

Japanese, like Chinese, books begin where ours end; the lines of writing and print are perpendicular, the first being to the right. Owing to the former use of wooden blocks for printing, old books are very few, and are largely in the form of ancient histories, local geographies and guide books, and books of short poems, none of high rank. Novels, fairy tales, and children's toy books are abundant; newspapers are becoming numerous, subject, however, to severe government restrictions, one of them being, that if any one complains of a false statement being made about him, his denial shall be published in full, in the same column and type as the original statement.

## THE AINOS OF JAPAN.

One of the most interesting aboriginal races anywhere to be found, is that known as the Aino—literally, "the men," or "the people," in their own language. They formerly spread over the whole of the Japanese and Kurile Islands, and Saghalien. The Japanese and Manchus have for many centuries been restricting their range, till they are now only to be found in Northern Yezo, Southern Saghalien, and some of the Kurile Islands. What renders them so interesting is, that their physical characters are very different from

**Distinct from Mongol type.**

JAPANESE MUSICAL INSTRUMENTS.

those of the Mongoloid peoples, and their language is fundamentally distinct.

**Hairiness.**

Miss Bird, in "Unbeaten Tracks in Japan," describes the Ainos as "about the middle height, broad-chested, broad-shouldered, thick-set, very strongly built, the arms and legs short, thick, and muscular, the hands and feet large. The bodies, and especially the limbs, of many are covered with short bristly hair. I have seen two boys whose backs are covered with fur as fine and soft as that of a cat. The heads and faces are very striking. The foreheads are very high, broad, and prominent, and at first sight give one the impression of an unusual capacity for intellectual development; the ears are small and set low, the noses are

AINOS OF JAPAN.

*(In official state dress when visiting the Japanese Governor of Hakodaiti, Yezo, 1867.)*
*(From a photograph lent by* DR. BEDDOE, F.R.S.)

straight but short, and broad at the nostrils; the mouths

are wide, but well-formed; and the lips rarely show a tendency to fulness. The neck is short, the cranium rounded, the cheek-bones low. . . . The eyebrows are full, and form a straight line nearly across the face. The eyes are large, tolerably deeply set, and very beautiful, the colour a rich liquid brown, the expression singularly soft, and the eyelashes long, silky, and abundant. The skin has the Italian olive tint, but in most cases is thin, and light enough to show the changes of colour in the cheeks. The teeth are small, regular, and very white; the incisors and 'eye-teeth' are not disproportionately large, as is usually the case among the Japanese; there is no tendency to prognathism. The features, expression, and aspect are European rather than Asiatic."

**Physical characters.**

Other accounts describe the forehead as low, the brow ridges prominent, the nose thick and rounded at the end, the eyes not oblique, and intensely black. The abundant development of the hair and beard is their most conspicuous character. It is black, coarse, straight, and shaggy, that on the head worn long, down to the shoulders and mingling with the beard. The women are much inferior in looks to the men, ageing soon, owing to the hard work they have to do, and to their heavy tattooing. This is done on the forearm, lips, and cheeks, of an ugly light blue hue. Miss Bird was of opinion that their ugliness was due to art and dirt. They are seldom more than five feet and half an inch high, but are well formed and lithe, with small feet and hands, well-arched insteps, well-developed busts, and a firm gait. They have superb teeth, and use them liberally in smiling. Miss Bird says, "that one girl whom she saw, who had not been tattooed, was the most beautiful creature in features, colouring, and natural grace of form she had seen for a long time."

**Aino women's looks.**

Tattooing is performed in childhood, in successive stages from five years of age till marriage. The Japanese government has now forbidden the practice, at which the Ainos are greatly distressed, saying that tattooing of girls is part of their religion; they can't be married without it.

The children are much loved and caressed. They do not receive names till they are four or five years old. They are carried on journeys on the mother's back in a net or loose garment, supported by a band round the forehead. No clothing is worn till eight years old, and the younger children's hair is completely shaven; from five to fifteen the boys are partially shaven, while the girls grow their hair.

**Children.**

In winter the Ainos wear one or more coats of skins, with hoods. Their summer garb is a sort of kimono, or loose coat of cloth, which they weave from bark. Both sexes wear tight leggings of bark-cloth or skin, without shoes or sandals. The women will not change one garment for another except alone or in the dark. "Lately," says Miss Bird, "a Japanese woman took an Aino woman into her house, and insisted on her taking a bath, which she absolutely refused to do till the bath-house had been made quite private by means of screens. On the Japanese going back a little later to see what had become of her, she found her sitting in the water in her clothes, and on being remonstrated with, she said that the gods would be angry if they saw her without clothes!" Their holiday garments are handsome, with geometrical patterns in blue cotton with scarlet and white braiding. The women wear a good deal of jewellery, including large silver or pewter ear-rings, hoop-shaped neck-ornaments, etc., and they are passionately fond of anything red-coloured.

**Clothing.**

**Jewellery.**

The Aino houses are simple but interesting, having doorways, windows, central fireplaces, and raised sleeping benches, unlike the Japanese, and more like primitive Europeans. They are built of a framework of posts, neatly covered with reeds in close bundles, and are very capacious, sometimes forty feet square, but with low walls and a high-pitched roof. Long poles, crossing from wall to wall, serve as shelves. Mats carefully made of reeds supply bedding, and small stiff bolsters are also used. The oblong fireplace has hanging over it a black mat, from which the soot is collected for tattooing, and which diffuses the smoke

**Houses.**

over the house. The great cooking-pot hangs from the same framework as the mat.

Food and drink. Aino food is very varied and not dainty, including all kinds of fish, seaweed, slugs, wild vegetables and berries, and venison and bear's flesh. They have wooden spoons for stirring, and use chop-sticks in eating. Saké is their great drink, to which they are immoderately and banefully addicted. For it they will sell anything but the Japanese curios they have acquired by inheritance or gift. These are sometimes richly covered with gold, or fine specimens of Japanese art.

Curios.

Hunting. The men spend all the year except summer in hunting deer and bears, which they obtain by arrows, arrowtraps poisoned with monkshood, and pitfalls, but the Japanese have lately forbidden the use of poison and traps, as dangerous to travellers.

Notions of religion. The Ainos have a very simple kind of worship, without temples or priests, a sort of vague nature worship. They pay reverence as gods to wands and posts of peeled wood with the curled shavings attached. The only act of sacrifice they perform is to place a dead bird near one of their gods till it decays. "Drinking for the god" is their chief religious act, so that drunkenness is part of their religion such as it is. They also have a crude reverence for the bear. They have a great dread of snakes and of death.

Marriage. The Aino women are very faithful; girls marry at seventeen, men at twenty-one. Miss Bird says, "When a man wishes to marry, he thinks of some particular girl, and asks the chief if he may ask for her. If leave is given, either through a go-between or personally, he asks her father for her, and if he consents, the bridegroom gives him a present, usually a Japanese curio. This constitutes betrothal; and the marriage, which immediately follows, is celebrated by carousals and the drinking of much saké. The bride receives as her dowry her ear-rings and a highly ornamented kimono. It is an essential that the husband provides a house to which to take his wife. Each couple live separately," only the chief may have three wives, each in a separate house. A very few, with childless wives, take a second wife.

These people live in village communities, and are very simply governed, each by its own chief, whose power is permanent. Miss Bird concludes, from her experience, that the Aino must be ranked high among uncivilised peoples, being charming in many ways, especially for their courtesy. They have some real idea of home, and a word for husband which comes very near to "house-band." They value truth, revere and treat kindly the aged, and infanticide is unknown. Yet they seem to show no capacity for elevation at present, and as regards education, are stupid and apathetic. Their good physique is in favour of their continuing to exist; and it is to be hoped that some way may be found of raising them to a higher state. Probably there are not more than ten thousand of them now surviving, and unless some change occurs, they may be extinct in another century.

Good qualities.

## THE LOO-CHOO OR LIU-KIU ISLANDERS.

The Loo-choo islands, stretching between Formosa and Japan, were long subject to China, to whom the Loo-choo king paid tribute. Gradually, in late years, the hold of China relaxed and that of Japan grew; and in 1879, the Japanese deposed the Loo-choo king, and set up their own government. This change has been rendered easy by the manifest relationship of the people to the Japanese, though they are easily distinguishable from them, having less flattened faces, more deeply-set eyes, and noses more prominent at the base. The forehead is also high, and the cheek-bones less prominent than in the Japanese, and they are shorter but better proportioned. Those who work in the fields are nearly as dark as Malays; but the upper classes are much fairer, and without the yellow tinge of the Chinaman. They have long, black, rather thin beards, sometimes plaited. All the people, of both sexes, have a space shaven on the

Physical characters.

crown of the head; and the rest of the long hair is gathered up and twisted into a knot over the bald spot, and transfixed with two peculiar pins the metal of which varies with rank. The women have the backs of their hands tattooed. The expression of the people is almost always gentle and pleasing, though somewhat sad.

Napha-kiang, the seat of government, is peculiar in structure, the houses being built in little enclosures, separated from the street and one another by massive limestone walls from eight to fourteen feet high; but in other respects it is like a Japanese town. The climate is almost tropical, though the chief vegetation is of a temperate character. Rice, wheat, and sweet-potatoes are the principal crops; and tobacco is largely grown. A more happy and laughter-loving people, says a recent visitor, Dr. Guillemard, can scarcely be found.

KALMUCK TARTARS.

# CHAPTER XII.

## The Mongolians, Kashgarians, etc.

The Mongol empire—Jenghiz Khan—Ogdai—Kubla Khan—The Modern Mongolians—Marco Polo's account—Scattered tribes—The Khalkas—Introduced customs—Chinese rule—Mongol religion—Language—The Tanguts—Chinese Turkestan—Great mixture of races.

GEOGRAPHICALLY limited at the present day to the northern portion of the Chinese empire, and of comparatively small importance, the Mongols in the middle ages ruled a great empire, and produced remarkable leaders. The greatest of these was Genghis or Jenghiz Khan, born, in 1162, in a tent on the banks of the river Onon, being the son of Yesukai, who ruled over a considerable kingdom in Mongolia. At first his name was Temuchin. He succeeded his father at the age of thirteen, and early showed his prowess. By the year 1206 his power was widely established, and he took the name of Jenghiz Khan (meaning perfect warrior). He never ceased his conquering career,—subduing all Mongolia, China, north of the Yellow River or Hoang-ho, Turkestan, Herat, the

**The Mongol empire.**

**Jenghiz Khan.**

Punjab, Georgia, and Circassia,—even routing the Russians on the banks of the Dnieper in 1222.

When Jenghiz died, in 1227, his kingdom was divided among his sons—Ogdai, the second surviving son, being named chief Khan. Ogdai completed the ruin of the Kin, or Golden dynasty of North China, in 1234, and then, destroying Jelal-al-din, the subject ruler of Kharezm, on his way, overran Mesopotamia, Khelat, Georgia, Armenia, and other districts of Western Asia, committing frightful cruelties. In 1235 his power was so great that he was able to despatch three great expeditions—one into Corea, another against the Sung empire (South China), and a third into Eastern Europe. The latter conquered the early Bulgarian state on the Volga, destroyed Riazan, Moscow, and Kief, and then reached Pesth and conquered the Magyars, pursuing them to the Adriatic in 1241. Another army conquered and devastated Poland. But at this time Ogdai died of a disease due to drink and licentiousness. Under his successor Asia Minor and Syria were brought under subjection.

**Ogdai.**

For another century the Mongol emperors continued supreme in war throughout Asia, performing such exploits as the capture of Bagdad, in 1263, followed by the capture and sack of Aleppo and Damascus, and the conquest of South China. Kubla Khan was the first Mongol emperor of China; and in 1264 he founded Pekin to be the capital of his empire. It was not till 1276 that the Sung dynasty in South China was conquered; and in 1279 Kublai was ruler over all China. He was much more advanced in ideas than any of his predecessors: he forbade massacres,—till then inseparable from Mongol conquests,—encouraged literature, science, Christianity, and Buddhism. His expeditions against Japan, Cochin China, Burmah, and Java were unsuccessful; but others to Southern India, Eastern Africa, and Madagascar brought back at least professions of homage. His long reign ended in 1294, and no great man followed him on his throne. Although some of his successors were tolerant and enlightened, and made some progress in

**Kubla Khan.**

TURKISH GUARD AT KASHGAR.

administration, as a rule they were incapable of consolidating their empire, or gaining the allegiance of conquered peoples. The Mongol troops became enervated in the softer climate of China; and in 1355-58 the Buddhist priest, Choo Yuen-Chang, was able to drive them out, and become the first Chinese emperor of the Ming dynasty, under the title Hung-Woo.

After this period the Mongols ceased to have a powerful centre, and they gradually became merely a number of scattered tribes, and a considerable number of them yielded submission to the (Manchu) Chinese empire. They became, to a large extent, Buddhists. Their many changes of grouping and wandering expeditions are so complex that we cannot here detail them.

**The modern Mongolians.** The Mongolians of the present day, occupying Mongolia from Siberia to the great wall of China, from Manchuria to the Altai mountains, and extending southwards over the great wall to the Blue Lake (Kuku-nor), and over the northern border of Tibet, are characterised by an agglutinative form of language like the Finns and Magyars. The order of words in sentences is almost the reverse of our own. A single sentence sometimes fills several pages.

**Marco Polo's account.** The account of the Mongols given by Marco Polo is one of the best, and shows that six hundred years ago they lived very much as at present. "The Tartar (*i.e.* Mongol) custom," he says, according to Col. Yule's translation, "is to spend the winter in warm plains, where they find good pasture for their cattle, whilst in summer they betake themselves to a cool climate among the mountains and valleys where water is to be found as well as woods and pastures. Their houses are circular, and are made of wands covered with felts. These are carried along with them whithersoever they go. . . . They also have waggons, covered with black felt so efficaciously that no rain can get in. These are drawn by oxen and camels, and the women and children travel in them. The women do the buying and selling, and whatever is necessary to provide for the husband and household; for the men all lead the life of gentlemen, troubling themselves about nothing but hunting and hawking, and looking after their goshawks and falcons, unless it be the practice of warlike exercises. They live on the milk and meat which their herds supply, and on the produce of the chase; and they eat all kinds of flesh, including that of horses and dogs, and 'Pharaoh's rats' (*i.e.* jerboas), of which last there are great numbers in burrows on those plains. Their drink is mare's milk. . . . Any man may take a hundred wives an he so please, and if he be able to keep them. But the first wife is ever held most in honour, and as the most legitimate. The husband gives a marriage payment to his wife's mother, and the wife brings nothing to her husband. They have more children than other people, because they hav so many wives. They may marry their cousins; and if a father dies, his son may take any of the wives, his own mother always excepted; that is to say,—the eldest son may do this, but no other. A man may also take the wife of his own brother after the latter's death. Their weddings are celebrated with great ado."

**Scattered tribes.**

At present their condition may be summed up in one sentence: they are subject to and divided between the Russian and tho Chinese empires. They are without any national cohesion, being divided into scattered tribes. The Khalkas inhabit the northern steppes, not far from the Buriats, a kindred people now under Russian rule. The Chakars, or Khakars, occupy the southern steppes, nearer to China. The Ordos, much diminished in numbers, dwell within the northern bend of the Hoang-ho. The Eleuts (Kalmucks) occupy Western Mongolia, forming the Altai and Thian-Shan hordes.

**The Khalkas.**

The Khalkas, who claim to be the purest Mongols of the present day, are rather brown than yellow in complexion, and have not oblique eyes. The face, however, is wide and flat, the cheek-bones are prominent, the hair is black, and the beard scanty. Of medium height, but vigorous physique, the Mongols are framed to endure hardship and resist fatigue, and will perform wonders of horse or camel riding, though not good at marching. The horse is their favourite mount, over which they have a complete mastery; their skill in managing their steeds is surprising, yet they have now very little of their ancient valour and audacity. Their virtues are those of feebleness. They treat strangers with hospitality, but they are idle,—except in regard to riding—dirty, and gluttonous. As far as possible, they get slaves to look after their flocks, which are their chief property. The women look after the well-being of the animals, while they talk about and admire them. Every manufactured article they buy from the Russians or Chinese, the latter furnishing them with the indispensable tea, to which they often add brandy. Their diet is almost exclusively animal, but they dislike birds and fish.

The customs of the Mongols reflect in various ways the foreign influences to which they have been subjected.

**Introduced customs.**

Thus, the men shave their heads, excepting the pig-tail. The Manchus likewise introduced monogamy in the seventeenth century. Parents arrange the marriages of their children by the aid of astrologers; but a price is paid, as among the Kirghiz, and a form of capture is gone through, as among the Turcomans. The bodies of chiefs and their wives are buried in tombs, before which the family offer sacrifices at fixed intervals. The bodies of superior priests are burnt, and their ashes covered with heaps of stones, while the common people are simply exposed to be devoured by beasts and birds. Dogs follow the burial processions, and crows are always in attendance on Mongol settlements.

The Chinese government has known how to keep the Mongols well in subjection by dividing them carefully

**Chinese rule.**

into hostile tribes and assigning them military functions. Their chiefs, pensioned, honoured with titles and by marriages into the imperial Chinese family, are but shadows, having to refer every important matter to Pekin. More important still, the industrious Chinese population is penetrating gradually into every fertile part of Mongolia, though only slowly assimilating the Mongols themselves. But, like so many other peoples, they seem doomed to assimilation or extinction.

Most of the Mongols are devoted Buddhists, deriving their sacred books from Tibet, and reverencing the grand Lama most highly, though they have a Lama of their own, whose seat is Ourga, in Northern Mongolia; but the government of Pekin takes care to have a voice in the selection of the Lama. Other divinities of the Mongolians are Yamandaga, or the Ox-face, wearing a crown of human skulls, and various domestic spirits, often mere wooden images. The Mongolians are exceedingly zealous in their religious performances, being almost equal to the Tibetans in that respect.

**Mongolian religion.**

The Mongolian languages are distinct forms of the Ural-Altaic or Finno-Tartar group. Each main group speaks a different dialect not understood by the others, but they are really closely related. Many Manchu, Chinese, Tibetan, and Turkish words have been adopted. For over two thousand years the Mongolian language has been a written one, having first borrowed the Chinese characters. Later a Turkish alphabet was taken up, and afterwards supplanted by a native alphabet of peculiar construction.

**Language.**

Further west, in Kansu and Kuku-nor, the Mongols are oppressed by a more powerful, fierce, and hardy people of Tibetan race, the Tanguts, who are black-eyed, oval-faced, without prominent cheeks, black-bearded, and with straight or aquiline noses. They are withal a trading, bargaining people, but do not hesitate to rob and plunder. Their wives are purchased, but the men go through a form of capture; polygamy is practised by those who can afford it. Herds of Yak are kept by the Tanguts, who cover their tents with their skins. They are zealous Buddhists.

**The Tanguts.**

Chinese Turkestan includes a mixture of peoples, some being Galchas, allied to those to be described subsequently in the chapter on the Afghans. Many fair people are met with in Yarkand, of typical Aryan appearance, recalling the features of Englishmen. Besides these, Persians, Arabs, Tibetans, Kirghiz, Kalmucks, Mongols and Turks, Hindus and Chinese are represented in this central tract of country.

**Chinese Turkestan.**

**Great mixture of races.**

The settled agriculturists of the plains are very different from the pastoral and often bandit tribes of the hills, who are mostly Kirghiz or Kalmucks. The townspeople call themselves after their place of residence, Khotani, Yarkandi, Kashgari, Tarimtze, etc. Urumtzi is the present seat of (Chinese) government, though Yarkand is still the largest centre of trade and population. Owing to the abundance of blinding dust, blind people, or those with bad eyes, are numerous. One out of every three in Yarkand has a goitre. Most of the people are Mahometans, and speak a Turkish language like that of Russian Turkestan, although numerous Chinese and Tartar words are used. The houses are of beaten earth, and dust is everywhere. The streets open on to small squares containing open tanks, the only water supply.

A few extracts from Surgeon-Major Bellew's narrative of his visit to Yarkand during the last Mussulman rebellion against China, will give an idea of a city of Chinese Tartary. "To the traveller coming from India, and mixing in the scene, the change is complete, and he almost fancies himself in some country town of Eastern Europe. In place of the dark skins, lithe forms, and airy drapery on the south of the passes, he finds a people of so light a complexion that an Indian in their crowd shows like a black sheep in the fold; he sees bulky frames that do not lose in height what they gain in breadth; and his eyes meet, in place of the delicate folds of muslin and gauze, or the close shapes of calico and print, the loose robes of buckram and frieze, or the capacious wraps of bold-coloured silks and heavy fur." The restaurants contain familiar dishes at a low price. The shops are crowded and varied. There are as many persons mounted as on foot. In the cattle market one may see horses exchanged for cows, or cows for sheep, or a Kalmuck youth for a fur coat, or a girl for a silk robe. Minstrels, fortune-tellers, and dancing dervishes abound. Tanning is very successfully carried on, and Yarkand boots and shoes, furs and hats, are famous in all the adjacent territories.

# CHAPTER XIII.

## The Inhabitants of Siberia.

**Modern immigration from Russia—Former inhabitants—The Khagasses—The Mongol empire—Russian conquests—Exiles—Colonists—Agriculture and hunting—Modification of Siberian Russians—Abundance of food—The Buriats—The Tunguses—The Yakuts—Expert artisans and traders—Their good qualities—The Samoyedes—Primitive habits—The Ostiaks—Religion and morals—Musical instruments—The Voguls—The Tchukchi—The Koriaks—A happy release—The Kamchadales—Picturesque villages—The Giliaks—Aspect and character—Decaying types.**

TUNGUS.

**Modern immigration from Russia.**

SIBERIA is a great example of the converse process to the old one of Asiatic immigration into Europe, for the present population is nearly six-sevenths of European (Russian) descent. But this is a phenomenon which two centuries have sufficed to bring about. Changes of population have been comparatively rapid in Siberia. Many remains on the borders of the lakes show that a busy population occupied the country in the neolithic or polished stone period; and it appears probable that successive populations, worsted in the strife for dominance, were driven constantly northward; and more than one race of the past may have wasted and perished in the inhospitable regions of Northern Siberia.

**Former inhabitants.** The name of Yeniseans has been given to an early race of Siberians; but little is known of them. The Ugro-Samoyedes apparently followed them north, some time before the Christian era, and established a bronze

BURIATS.

period and a much higher grade of civilisation than that of the preceding race.

**The Khagasses.** From about the fifth to the thirteenth centuries a Turkish stock (the Khagasses) migrated into the same region, subjugating the native population, introducing iron, employing bronze for artistic purposes, and manufacturing pottery of very good design. Many remains of them are preserved in the Hermitage Museum at St. Petersburg. In the 13th century the advancing Mongolian empire, under Jenghiz Khan, conquered these Turkish people, and in destroying their civilisation did not bring in anything better.

**The Mongol Empire.**

The country underwent continuous decline, until the Russians, in the sixteenth century, having established their empire in Europe firmly, began to turn their attention eastwards. Various Tartar invaders gained an ascendency over the tribes east of the Urals, and there came into collision with the Russian colonists. In 1555, Khan Ediger promised to send to Moscow every year a thousand sables as tribute. A tendency to form invading expeditions into Siberia now began; and soldiers, hunters, and other adventurers advanced in various directions, built forts, and organised supplies. They easily conquered the Tartar and Turkish populations, and by 1650 they had reached the Pacific and the River Amur.

**Russian conquests.**

The surplus population of Russia has since been gradually settling in Siberia; and in addition, the system of severe repression which the empire has always maintained has served to people many districts with political exiles as well as convicts. In many years the exiles have approached or exceeded 20,000 in number. Of course many have died, owing to the hardships they have endured, and it is not probable that the exiles in Siberia exceed 200,000. To a large extent the Russian government has also peopled Siberia by sending Cossacks to occupy the frontiers, and by subsidising colonists of various descriptions. Yet, after such great attempts at colonisation by government, it is by unaided immigration that far the greater part of the Siberian population has arrived. Fur hunting, escape from serfdom, from religious persecutions, and from conscription have been the main incentives to this great exodus. It has been not unusual for entire villages to migrate; and it is estimated that something like 40,000 persons per annum thus seek a new land. Such an uninterrupted stream indicates that something not to be

**Exiles.**

**Colonists.**

despised may be found in Siberia; and truly there are large tracts in Southern Siberia whose climate is good and soil fertile; there are also vast forests and gold-mining districts of no slight value.

Agriculture is the main occupation, and cereals afford

TUNGUSES.

the chief crops; in many regions also there are large herds of cattle, sheep, and horses. Fur animals are still hunted with profit in some districts, though man has here, as elsewhere, rendered scarce that which he values, but does not take measures to preserve in good supply. But everything is backward, and might be improved by good administration. At present business is still largely conducted at great fairs, as that of Irbit,

**Agriculture and hunting.**

where more than five millions sterling are annually turned over.

Residence in Siberia has affected Russians considerably in some parts, though not so much by intermixture with the natives as by the influence of changed habits and climate. The natural increase of population has not yet become nearly equal to that of Russia, owing to the great loss of child life. Several of the towns and districts on the outskirts show striking variations from the ordinary Russian type. At

**Modification of Siberian Russians.**

YAKUT MAN AND WOMAN.

Irkutsk, the Tunguses and Buriats have exercised a strong influence over the Russian settlers, leading them largely to adopt their language. Yakutsk has similarly a strong native population, and the Russians have married freely with the Yakuts. In some parts also the Tartar influence still predominates.

The Rev. H. Lansdell, a well-known Siberian traveller, found in the southern Yenisei district in 1879 a state of things almost paradise-like in the abundance of provisions. He was offered "live ducks for

**Abundance of food.**

five farthings each, large fish, called *yass*, for 1½*d.* a pair, and pike for a farthing each. Milk cost 2½*d.* a bottle, but young calves in remote villages could be purchased for 6*d.* each. The belt of rich black earth in the region immediately north of the Altai lets for 3½*d.* per acre, and from it wheat may be purchased for about one-twentieth its cost in England. Still farther north, in the forest region, rich in excellent timber and fur-bearing animals, meat was bought up wholesale in 1877 at less than a halfpenny a pound; whilst in the Tundras the rivers are so full of fish that one of the ordinary difficulties of the natives is to avoid breaking their nets with the weight of the draught."

We will now deal in turn with the principal non-Russian peoples and tribes of Siberia, the first being of Mongolian stock. The Buriats now existing around Lake Baikal are variously estimated at from 125,000 to 250,000. They are a dull, lazy, phlegmatic people, markedly Mongolian in type, and their want of vigorous qualities is shown by their readiness to change their religion. Part of them still retain the old Shamanistic religion, or wizardry; but many have become Buddhists, while others have joined the Greek Church. It cannot be said that their Christianity has penetrated very deeply. Drink and tobacco are their great delights. In other respects they are fairly good and peaceful subjects of the Russians, who interfere little with them. They have been advancing in agriculture in late years. In the south-eastern districts they are largely under Chinese and Tartar influence, and the men wear the pig-tail, the rest of their heads being shaven. More to the west they have become Russianised, and speak a Russian dialect.

**The Buriats.**

The Tunguses, although fewer than the Buriats, are much more widely spread and a much more energetic people. In race they are closely allied to the Manchu Tartars. They occupy a great territory north and east of the Buriats, extending north to the Arctic Ocean and east to the Amur. They also show Chinese influence, especially in dress, houses, and agri-

**The Tunguses.**

culture. The various tribes occupy themselves, as the locality may favour, in fishing, hunting, agriculture, some being named Horse, Reindeer, or Dog tribes, according to the animal of which they make most use. Where they have not been lowered by contact with cheating and lying Russians, Yakuts, and other merchants, they display many noble characteristics. Their cheerfulness, perseverance, good faith,

SAMOYEDE OF LOWER YENISEI.

courage, and independence are lauded by every one who

has come in contact with them. They avoid the Russians, and refuse to enter their service. Many of them, like the Buriats, have conformed to the Greek Church, but are still at heart Shamanists. They are very fond of animals, and even keep bears, wolves, and foxes, eagles, and other creatures in captivity. The stone age has not long ceased to exist among these peoples.

The affinity of the Yakuts of the Lena basin is mainly with the Turki branch of the Mongoloids, though they have so considerably mingled with the Tunguses and the Russians that their type is much modified. Many of them have features of a very Mongolian type. Probably it is owing to this intermixture that they are the most thriving of the Siberian natives. They have been called the Jews of Siberia, being extremely persevering and clever traders when they like, duping even the Cossacks; but frequently they give up work for pleasure, till forced by want. They have a very hardy constitution, which enables them to endure extreme cold with very little clothing. By their adaptability they have thriven remarkably of late, and the Russians have eagerly sought their daughters in marriage. They shine as industrious artisans, making excellent tools plated with gold and silver; they also extract iron from its ores with great skill. At Yakutsk they beat the Russians out of the field in many occupations. They take Russian, Polish, or German names. Most of them are baptized into the Greek Church, but Shamanism is still largely believed in, many additions to their evil spirits being made from the Greek Church lists. They may be taken as numbering about 200,000.

**The Yakuts.**

**Expert artisans and traders.**

In many ways the Yakuts possess good qualities. Their women are modest and chaste, and never allow the head or feet to be seen uncovered; they honour their parents, who choose wives for their children, and are implicitly obeyed. Hospitality is greatly practised among them. They make their own boats of planks or birch bark, and are expert in navigating the numerous rivers. On land they use the horse,

**Their good qualities.**

SAMOYEDE WOMAN OF LOWER YENISEI.

reindeer, and dog for draught. Planks and bark form the material of their houses. As to burial, they seem divided between simple intermen , with some of their property, and elevating the coffin on upright posts, and leaving it merely covered with ox hides.

The Samoyedes of Northern and Western Siberia bring us to quite a different stock of the Mongoloid peoples,—the Ural-Altaic or Finnish-Ugrian, Ugria having been formerly the name of a tract on both sides of the Ural Mountains. They are a dwindling people at present, not more than 25,000, dispersed in small groups or tribes from the Altai Mountains along the basins of the Obi and Yenisei, and from the Khatanga River to the White Sea. In the south they have intermingled with Tartars to some extent; in the east with Ostiaks.

**The Samoyedes.**

SAMOYEDE WOMAN.

The Samoyedes have a flatter face than most of the Finnish groups, most approaching the Mongolian. They have narrower eyes and darker complexions than the Finns; thick lips, little beard, and black stiff hair. They probably emigrated northward from the Altai Mountains, and this process still continues. They were no doubt once much more numerous, and still

**Primitive habits.**

OSTIAK.

appear to live in a condition like that of the age of stone and bone weapons, hunting and eating beasts of prey, and clothing themselves in skins. Smallpox and spirits, introduced by the Russians, are fast lessening their numbers. Many good qualities are attributed to them by some travellers, especially honesty, courage, independence, and hospitality. Some of them who can accumulate their captures, take reindeer and other skins to the Russian towns in winter, and buy meal, powder, shot, etc. Their tents are made of great poles and birch bark, and in many cases they are kept very clean. The people, however, look sad and depressed. Shamanism is their religion, mixed with some degree of Fetishism, although some have been baptized. They imagine that their gods are flesh-eaters, and raw flesh is periodically placed between their teeth

OSTIAKS.

The language of the Samoyedes is pleasant-sounding and sonorous, and has several dialects and sub-dialects through its wide range. It is agglutinative, like the Finnish languages generally, but has numerous peculiarities.

It is difficult to say whether the Ostiaks of the Obi basin are more closely allied to the Finns than to the Samoyedes. They were formerly much more numerous,

**The Ostiaks.**

and at any rate inhabited a considerable part of the old "Ugria" of the Russians. They are now reduced to about 20,000. Many of them are still quite nomadic, readily removing from place to place with their herds of reindeer. They are rather below the middle size, with small feet and hands, and are round-headed. Some describe them as red-haired, but such individuals are rare, dark features predominating; the hair is dark, but soft, the women wearing it in two long plaits down the back. A flat and broad nose, large mouth, thick lips, and scanty beard are further Mongoloid features. In some parts they are very much Russianised, and live chiefly by fishing. They can carve well in wood or bone, tan skins, make implements from birch bark, etc. They still use bows and arrows, only a few having guns. They eat raw flesh of carnivora, as well as other animals.

**Religion and morals.**

They are more or less Christianised, but Shamanism has more power over them, and they have not done much more than borrow St. Nicholas from the Russians, as so many Siberian natives have done. They only show degradation of morals where corrupted by Russians; they hate theft and disturbances, and are both kind and gentle. If they are dirty, according to our ideas, they are like most of the less civilised and some

**Musical instruments.**

of the so-called civilised peoples. Their stringed musical instruments are worthy of notice. One of them, the *dombra*, is boat-like and has five strings. The Hungarian Magyars, it will be remembered, have just such an instrument, the *tombora*, in itself a powerful confirmation of the relationship of the peoples. Their language too is, of all Finnish forms, that which approaches most closely the Magyar. Their inordinate consumption of spirits seems likely soon to make an end of the Ostiaks.

The Voguls of the Ural ridges, who are closely allied in race to the Ostiaks, perhaps represent the primitive stock from which the Magyars sprang. They are an undersized hunting people, not more than 5,000 in number. "With their thick furs," says M. Reclus, the "hoods decked to right and left with animals' ears, they at a distance look like wild animals; but their countenance is timid, even frightened." They shave off their hair and moustaches. They have conformed to the Greek Church and been baptized, but they still have their family totems,—bows and arrows, circles, etc.,—tattooed on their heads, arms, and legs. Their tribes are very isolated, reduced almost to families, and they are but little united. Wives are left on very slight provocation; and instances are known of the hunter living solitary after such a divorce, with only his reindeer and his dog for company. Their burials are very simple; a hole dug in the ground when a member died suffices, in which is placed, with the deceased's weapons, some tobacco and spirits.

The Voguls.

The Voguls are peculiar in not using salt. The meat which they do not eat at once, they dry in strips in the air. They are very slight vegetable eaters, living chiefly upon the flesh of the elk. The fur of the sable is one of their principal objects of trade; but they pay their tribute by means of elk skins.

Coming now to the north-eastern part of Siberia, we find a few remnants of ancient peoples whose relationship it is by no means easy to settle, and who are probably doomed to extinction. A large tract of the north-east is occupied by the Tchukchi, whom some consider merely a branch of the Esquimaux, while others regard them as more nearly related to the Koriaks, who occupy the country between them and the Kamchadales. The Tchukchi are a hardy race, who long successfully withstood the Russians, and still number twelve thousand. They formerly depended chiefly upon reindeer, of which they still possess large herds; but many of them are expert whale and seal-fishers and walrus-hunters. They are, on the whole, of Mongolian type, round-headed.

The Tchukchi.

wide and flat-faced, with sunk noses and thick lips. They are muscular and thick-necked, and in many points resemble the Esquimaux. In disposition they are peaceful and good-humoured, with much family affection. Many have been to some extent Christianised, but they still burn their dead or expose them on piles to the crows, and

TCHUKCHI.

sacrifice to numerous nature-gods. They marry more than one wife when they are rich enough; and their wives are faithful, industrious, and in many ways skilful. In language they differ considerably from the Tartar, Turki, or Finnish groups of Mongoloids. Many of the women are tattooed like the Tunguses. Formerly the men passed a walrus's tooth through a hole in their cheeks; now they who have been baptized have a black cross painted on the cheek. If it were not for brandy introduced by American traders, with whom they deal most, the Tchukchi might hope to last long, from their evident fitness for their inhospitable climate.

The Koriaks occupy the Eastern country intervening between the peninsula of Behring and Southern Kamtschatka, and appear to be both less numerous and less hardy and respectable in character. In fact, travellers give them quite a bad character for

**The Koriaks.**

KORIAKS.

drunkenness, lying, and thieving. This is more the case with those who have lost their reindeer from one cause or another, and have only fishing and hunting to depend on. Those who are still nomadic, with large herds of reindeer, retain much dignity and independence, a few families only living in company. Mr. Kennan, the author of "Tent Life in Siberia," during a residence of two years and a half among them, never saw a nomad Koriak strike his wife or children. They will not sell a reindeer alive at any price, such is their attachment to them.

The Shamans are in full force among the Koriaks,

sacrificing to evil spirits, and executing remarkable feats of wizardry. It is perhaps among these tribes that the practice of killing old and infirm people is most in vogue. The hardships of the nomadic life get to be unendurable, and the infirm readily consent to this mode of putting them out of their misery. In fact, it is considered a part of filial duty to expedite their release in this way, and it is a sort of official ceremony. Immediately after death the corpse is burnt and the ashes are scattered. Wives are purchased by one or more year's labour of the bridegroom for the girl's father, and meanwhile the girl is carefully guarded, and the youth kept off, if necessary, by whips and sticks. The marriage ceremony is a form of capture.

**"A happy release."**

The Kamchadales present a similar combination to the Koriaks, of Mongoloid features, with a distinct language. They are of short stature, have prominent cheeks, small sunken eyes, flat noses, black hair, and a tawny complexion. Their language is of different grammatical structure from that of the Koriaks, and has unchanging roots modified by various prefixes. In some parts the people have become Russianised, and have adopted the Greek faith. Under the influence of spirits and disease they have diminished to three thousand. They become violently intoxicated by eating a dried fungus—a species of mushroom. A trifle, says the traveller Steller, will make them go mad or commit suicide.

**The Kamchadales.**

Despite their excitability, they have a reputation for honesty and truthfulness, and are very hospitable. They are rather weak-minded than vicious, and have little of the heroic temperament of the Koriaks. They have some popular poetry, dealing with love, hunting, and travelling, the plaintive chanting of which is mixed with wild animals' cries, and imitations of their movements and actions.

In the winter these people are dressed in furs, in the summer in shirts of calico, and the women have adopted the Russian head-dress. They do not learn to accumulate wealth. Their draught-dogs, much resembling wolves, are of the first importance to them, but they have recently been suffering greatly from disease. Some of the Kamchadales have learnt a little agriculture, and have settled down and built comfortable dwellings. Mr. Kennan says: "The village is permeated with a peculiar, ancient, and fish-like smell, eloquent of the occupation of the villagers and the food on which they subsist. High square frames of horizontal poles stand beside every house, filled with thousands of drying salmon, and on the beach dug-out canoes lie bottom upwards, covered with large, neatly tied seines; two or three long narrow dog-sledges stand upon their ends against every house, and a hundred or more sharp-eared, wolfish dogs, tied at intervals to long heavy poles, lie panting in the sun, snapping viciously at the flies and mosquitoes which disturb their rest. But what is most characteristic of such a hamlet is the Greek church, glorious in red paint and glittering dome, contrasting strangely with the rude log-houses over which it extends the spiritual protection of its resplendent gilded cross. If you can imagine a rough American backwoods settlement of low log-houses, clustered round a gaily coloured Turkish mosque; half a dozen small haystacks mounted on high vertical posts; fifteen or twenty titanic wooden gridirons similarly elevated, and hung full of drying fish; a few dog-sledges and canoes lying carelessly around, and a hundred or more grey wolves tied here and there between the houses to long heavy poles, you will have a general but tolerably accurate idea of a Kamchadale settlement of the better class."

**Picturesque villages.**

The Giliaks, now restricted to the southern shores of the Okhotsk Sea and the northern part of Saghalien, are by some thought to be related to the Ainos of Japan; but there can be little doubt that they are Mongoloids of a primitive type, and are the last relics of a people who once overspread a much larger territory. They long resisted civilising influences, and showed many savage qualities. Yet they have some skilled artisans. They have generally proved treacherous and revengeful; but this may spring chiefly from their great love of their own freedom, and dislike of submitting to any civilised

**The Giliaks.**

restraints. Among them wives are bought at an early age, and brought up in the house of their future father-in-law. The dead are either burnt or exposed on scaffoldings. The favourite dog, fattened, is sacrificed on his master's tomb, it being imagined that the soul of the latter has taken refuge in the body of the dog.

GILIAKS.

Fire is among the most sacred objects to the Giliak. It must never be carried from one hut to another, or be removed from the hearth. The bear is worshipped as well as eaten, being fattened in captivity, and killed on a feast-day with much ceremony. The Giliaks also keep eagles in cages, but they do not hunt the wolf.

M. Niemojowski, a Polish traveller, was much impressed

by the Giliak countenance and physical appearance. **Aspect and character.** "Tall and thin," he writes, "there is something diabolical in the aspect of their slanting eyes, shaded by bushy eyebrows. No smile of mirth ever breaks over their lips, and on their features appears only a sneer. Seeing them walk, one fancies they are ghosts; their smothered voices have a hollow, unearthly sound. In the most ordinary relations with them one does not know how to act or what to do. The shrewdest man, seeing their long, stiff, bony, almost inhuman forms, is lost in speculation, and unable to solve this living sphinx riddle." Patriarchal government prevails among them; communities can scarcely be said to exist. Some of the elders are more influential than others, and are appealed to on important occasions. It is said that the imperturbability of these stony elders is so great that a father has been known to receive a chance visitor with the most perfect coolness when his own son has just suffered death at his hands, and lies at his feet still warm, though covered from view.

Such are the principal types of people whom Russian influence in Siberia will certainly extinguish before long, **Decaying types.** peoples who have failed in the struggle for existence, and have succumbed to vices, to wars, to pestilences, to the lack of moral stamina. Less fortunate than the hill-tribes of India, perhaps, they must pass out of existence, doomed by the contact of stronger races. Let us never think of them with contempt or levity; let us respect human nature, even in its lowest types, recollecting that the least human among them shows a higher than human handiwork, even though much marred by evil.

# CHAPTER XIV.

## The Inhabitants of Turkestan.

**The true Turks of Turkestan—Their subjugation—The Usbegs—Costume—The Kirghiz—The Turcomans—A Kirghiz nomad family—Encamping—Houses—Food—Pilau—A meal with Turcomans—The height of politeness—Jewellery and ornaments—Betrothal and marriage—The jester—Birth and youth—Burial—Turcoman tribes.**

KIRGHIZ.

**The true Turks of Turkestan.**

WE are too apt to think of the Turks of Constantinople as the typical Turks; but they are in reality very much modified from the original stock, chiefly by inter-marriage with Circassians, Georgians, Greeks, Albanians, etc., until some authorities incline to the view that they are now more Caucasian than Mongoloid. In Europe, too, the Turk has gained a polish and a *savoir-faire* which make him, in the eyes of many, the finest gentleman in Europe—that is, when viewed in good specimens. But still we may say of many a Turk what has been applied to Russians also, "Scratch a Turk, and you find a Tartar underneath." And if we want to know the kind of people from whom the Turks sprang originally, we must go to their home in Turkestan, and study the Turcoman or true Turk. The term Tartar, which has been applied so widely and vaguely, is perhaps best dropped, or only applied to the more eastern group—the Mongol and Manchu Tartars. From Lake Baikal to Southern Russia, from South-Western Siberia to south

USBEGS.

of the Oxus, Turks are to be found, and are generally predominant. The greater part of them now acknowledge the supremacy of Russia; some are feudatories of China. Thus the powerful race which once threatened to subjugate all Europe has lost the political sceptre, except so far as that is wielded by the decaying power of the Porte.

**Their subjugation.**

The chief Turkish people of Turkestan may be divided into Usbegs, Kirghiz, and Turcomans. The Usbegs are regarded as the most civilised; and, perhaps owing to their intermixture with the Mongols and other Tartars, they gained and kept the predomi-

**The Usbegs.**

nance on the break-up of Jenghiz Khan's empire. They gradually abandoned a wandering life, and became settled and flourishing agriculturists in Khiva and Bokhara, and formed a centre round which Tajiks, Galchas, and other Iranian and Aryan people were attracted. In process of time these have largely intermingled with and modified the race. They are Mahometans of the Sunni division, although some heathen and Parsee observances are retained. They have a literary language or dialect—the Jaghatai. The Usbegs, wherever settled, are almost as proud of their nationality and tribes as the Jews, although their mixed origin is testified by their flat faces and oblique eyes, combined with long flowing beards like the Persians. Their nomad and predatory ancestry still manifests itself in the habits of not a few, who prefer the brigand life of the hills to the settled life of the plains and oases; and it is a saying that almost all the brigands, as well as the saints of the country, are Usbegs.

Costume.

Prof. Vambéry, the unrivalled student of these races, in his "Travels in Central Asia," describes the Usbeg as walking about in summer, clad, as to the body, merely in a long skirt, although wearing a high round fur hat on his head, and great thick leather boots. The women wear lofty globular turbans, made of nearly a score of Russian kerchiefs, large heavy gowns and coarse boots; and in this hot garb they drag to their houses heavy pitchers of water.

The Kirghiz.

The Kirghiz are a much more numerous division of the Turks, being found all over the Steppes from Lake Balkash to the Volga; but they are divided into a very large number of tribes or hordes. Like the Usbegs, they have some affinity to the Mongolian Tartars; but their language is purely Turkish. Acknowledging no superiors among themselves, every Kirghiz horseman is an aristocrat. When two Kirghiz meet, their first question is, "Who are thy seven ancestors?" and not a tribesman will be found who cannot recite his lineage. They are of a somewhat sullen, morose, and fierce disposition, and incredibly idle. The women, on the contrary, have to toil unceasingly, although they are not without their holidays, when they decorate themselves with rouge and white powder, and abundance of jewellery and false hair. They are less strictly kept in seclusion

KIRGHIZ, WITH DROMEDARIES.

than the Usbeg women, for the Mahometan yoke, though nominally adopted, sits lightly on the Kirghiz. Agriculture and pasturing cattle are the chief occupations, and koumiss, or fermented mare's milk, is the principal drink. What the Kirghiz will do now that their diversion of brigandage is checked by the Russians cannot yet be foreseen. They may die out from inanition, or they may develop new qualities under settled and peaceful conditions.

The Turcomans make up the remainder of the Turkish stock in Turkestan. They are divided into as numerous

KIRGHIZ WOMEN MILKING MARES.

tribes as the rest; and when they are not agriculturists or brigands, they are nothing; the women do all the work. They are remarkable for their bright, sparkling, fiery eyes, but are much fairer than the Mongoloid type usually is; and the women are frequently good-looking, and almost European-like when young. But the majority have the wide flat face, small oblique eyes, small firm nose, large lips, outstanding ears, and thick, short, black hair of the Mongoloids.

**The Turcomans.**

The Persians, Tajiks, and Galcha tribes, who, to the number of at least a million, permeate Turkestan, will be left to be described with the Persians and Afghans, to whom they have affinity.

Prof. Vambery, penetrating into the inmost life of Turkestan before it had yielded to Russian influence, has

KALMUCK WOMEN IN TENT.

given us the most graphic descriptions of the people a few years ago, under conditions which can never be repeated. Take his description of a Kirghiz family in its wanderings ("Sketches of Central Asia"): "A Kirghiz family, which has packed house and household furniture on the backs of a few camels,

**A Kirghiz nomad family.**

moves slowly over the desert towards a spot indicated to them by the raised lance of a distant horseman. The caravan rests, according to nomad notions of rest, while thus on the march, to become lively and busy when they settle themselves down to repose according to our ideas. Nevertheless, the elder women seated on the humps of

TURCOMAN WEDDING.

camels (for the younger ones travel on foot) grudge themselves repose even then, and occupy their time in spinning a sort of yarn for sacks out of the coarser camels' hair. Only the marriageable daughter of the family enjoys the privilege of being completely at leisure on her shambling beast. She is polishing her necklace of coins—Russian, ancient Bactrian, Mongolian, or Chinese—which hangs down to her waist. So engrossed is she in her employment, that a European numismatist might take her for a fellow-connoisseur; nevertheless, not a movement of the young Kirghizes, who seek to distinguish themselves by all manner of equestrian gymnastics, as they caracole around the caravan, escapes her notice."

When the group has arrived at its camping-place, the utmost order is observed. "While the paterfamilias unsaddles his cooled horse and lets him loose on the pasture, the younger lads collect, with frightful clamour, the sheep and the camels, which are only too disposed to wander. They must stay to be milked. Meanwhile the tent has been taken down. The old matron seizes on the latticed framework and fixes it in its place, spitting wildly right and left as she does so. Another makes fast the bent rods which form the vaulting of the roof. A third sets on the top of all a sort of round cover or lid, which serves the double purpose of chimney and window. While they are covering the woodwork with curtains of felt, the children inside have already hung up the provision-sacks, and placed the enormous tripod on the crackling fire. This is all done in a few moments. Magical is the erection, and as magical is the disappearance of the nomads' habitation." Women here, as throughout Turkestan, perform every fragment of menial or domestic duty.

Encamping

Accustomed to this free life, it is not to be wondered at that the Turks who build fixed houses are in a minority, and that houses are looked upon as gloomy places. The Usbegs have more houses than the rest. Mud forms the floor, and the walls are built of clay or stone and wooden laths. The ceiling is of closely-fitted planks; small holes are left for windows, closed by oiled paper in winter. The number of rooms (on one floor only) varies with wealth. Carpets, felt coverlets, chests, and pots and pans form the chief furniture.

Houses.

Meal is the principal food, mutton, goat, beef, and horse and camel's flesh being valued in the order in which they are named. Horseflesh, boiled soft with carrots, onions, and dumplings, is very popular. Pilau **Food.**

TURCOMAN WOMEN IN TENT.

is, however, the favourite dish—pieces of meat boiled in fat, with pepper, carrots, and rice in abundance. It is the almost universal dish; but numerous others are to be met with in Turkish houses, most of them being highly seasoned. These are usually served up in a huge dish laid on the floor. Describing a meal with Turcomans, Mr. O'Donovan, in his "Merv Oasis," says: "The entire company sat round, and fished out each a handful. Contrary to ordinary Mussulman habits, there was no preparatory washing of hands, and especially in the case of our acting host, 'the hand that mingled in the meal' might have been more scrupulously clean. Each person boldly grasped a handful of rice, squeezed it into a ball in the palm of his hand, and then clapped it into his mouth by a movement similar to that of a conjuror swallowing a table knife. Our host, who seemed to have taken an especial liking to me, from time to time scraped pieces of mutton off the bones with his dirty thumb-nail, and threw them into my part of the dish, expressing his wonder at my small appetite for animal food. After dinner there was no more washing than before it. The guests stuck their fingers one after the other into their mouths, thus removing the excess

Pilau.

A meal with the Turcomans.

KALMUCK SHAMANESS.

of rice and grease adhering to them. The meal concluded, tea was served again. As is usual all over this part of the East, the tea was served in porcelain bowls or glass tumblers. It is drunk in prodigious quantities, very weak, over-sweetened, and without milk or cream. My attentive host, noticing that half a dozen flies were swimming in my tea, immediately plunged two of his great unwashed fingers up to the knuckles into my glass to fish out the intruders, and on each similar and oft-repeated bath on the part of the insects, it was only my own prompt action that prevented a repetition of the attention. On his part it was meant in the kindliest possible spirit, and the act was one of genuine politeness."

**The height of politeness.**

KOKHAND WOMAN.

Nearly the entire capital of a Turcoman family is invested in jewellery and ornaments for the women. Here is a description of a woman of about forty, according to Mr. O'Donovan. "Her only garments were a dark purple silk one, which we can only describe as a shirt reaching nearly to the ankles, and close-fitting trousers drawn tightly round the ankles. On her head was a bright crimson silk handkerchief arranged turban-like, and one end falling on her left shoulder. But her ornaments were sufficient

**Jewellery and ornaments.**

in quantity to deck a shop-window. On her neck was a massive silver collar about an inch and a half deep, and a third of an inch thick. At intervals around it were set flat oval cornelians and lozenge-shaped panels of embossed gold. From its front there hung a score of silver chains, halfway down which were lozenge-shaped pieces of silver embossed with gold, supporting a silver cylinder hanging down below the waist, and containing talismanic writings for defence against evil spirits. On either side of her bosom hung so many silver coins, Russian and Persian, as to resemble a cuirass. Each shoulder bore a flat silver box, a cylinder of four inches diameter, with a cornelian in the centre. Her long, coarse hair, plaited in two tails reaching below her waist, was also richly studded with silver coins. On her wrists were enormous silver bracelets with more gold panels and cornelians."

**Betrothal and marriage.**

Contrary to the practice of many other Moslem countries, the people of Turkestan are ardent lovers before marriage; and the young people themselves inform their parents when they have formed an attachment. Female go-betweens are then employed to arrange the affair and discuss the marriage portion. The question always is, how many times nine sheep, cows, camels, horses, or ducats the father of the bride is to receive for her. The price ranges from once nine, to nine times nine, which the Khan alone pays. The future bridegroom also has to present a complete set of ornaments to the bride, including eight rings, a tiara and a semi-tiara, a bracelet, ear-rings, nose-rings, and neck ornaments, of gold or silver. After these proceedings, the betrothal festivities last several days, with music, dancing, and horse-racing, an inseparable accompaniment. The bridegroom even provides the food for the wedding festivities, in enormous quantities; and during the preparatory cooking the young men carry on lively flirtations with the girls. "Men and women gather round the fire-place in groups, laughing, talking, joking, and shrieking, whilst musicians play and sing and children shout and yell. These noises are mingled with the bleating of sheep, barking of dogs, neighing of horses, and braying of donkeys; while loud above the general hubbub is heard the clown's stentorian voice in coarse sallies of Usbeg wit and humour. . . . Now he mimics this person or that, now he tells of some droll prank or merry adventure, or whistles like a bird and mews like a cat; and thus he has to continue without interruption, although from sheer exertion the perspiration runs down his face in streams" (Vambery). During the last few days before the wedding, the young man is not allowed to leave his tent. The marriage ceremony is performed by a mollah, neither party appearing in person, both being represented by two witnesses. After it is over, the bridegroom appears, but only approaches a few steps from the door. After much feasting, the bride leaves her home for that of the bridegroom, in a procession protracted by a circuitous route.

The jester.

FEMALE SLAVE IN BOKHARA.

The birth of children, especially boys, is celebrated by much feasting and amusement. During early years they are carefully guarded against evil

Birth and youth.

spirits by talismans of various kinds hung round the head. Girls are early taught to be useful in the household; while boys take to horseback at five, and are skilled jockeys at ten. The corpses of the dead are only kept about twelve or fifteen hours, and are then buried in cemeteries in settled parts, and singly in the desert among the nomads. A large mound is raised over the grave if the deceased was an important personage. Numerous funeral feasts follow a burial at stated intervals.

**Burial.**

The Salor Turcomans are the oldest tribe, as far as records go, and formerly possessed Merv, until displaced by the Tekke. They, as well as the Sariks, are renowned for their bravery. The latter are the well-known marauders of Pendjeh. The Tekke, till their subjugation by the Russians, were the most important and powerful tribe, divided into the Akhal, east of Tejend, and the Mervi. Their marauding life now finds itself under severe restraint, much to the comfort of the neighbouring Persians, Afghans, etc. A considerable number of Turcoman tribes yield subjection to the Shah of Persia, such as the Goklen of the Gurgan region, etc.

**Turcoman tribes.**

As far as the picturesqueness of life is concerned, we cannot but regret the conquest of Turkestan by the Russians; but peace, order, and prosperity are indefinitely promoted by the rule of the new masters of these fiercest, most intractable, most hostile (to strangers) of Asiatic races. A vivid account of a great portion of Turkestan will be found in Dr. Lansdell's "Russian Central Asia," 1885. At Aulie-Aba, where Kirghiz predominate, he was much struck by the habits and manners of the people. "Here was a man striving to allay the dust, not with a water-cart, but by carrying a skin of water, and sputtering it out of the aperture. Behind the charcoal fire of a Kirghiz smith sat an unfortunate individual, whose calling in life was to blow the bellows, consisting of two leather bags he had to press alternately for twelve hours a day, for which he was paid 2*s.* a week. At many of the stalls they exhibited in cages, for 8*d.* each, quails or other small birds caught by hawks. They teach them to sing and to fight.

"Everything had to be purchased, of course, by haggling, fixed prices being unknown; and I observed in the course of my purchases an illustration of a custom as old as the time of Job—that of 'striking hands' in connection with suretyship or agreement. A man had asked me too much for an article; and the Russian officer who accompanied me offered a second price, and then, after the Kirghiz custom, held out his hand, whereupon the salesman, hesitating a moment, raised his hand, and, in token that he agreed to the bargain, brought it down with a slap on the officer's palm."

TURCOMAN ORNAMENTS.

# CHAPTER XV.

## The Persians.

**Persia and Iran—The great monarchies—The Median kingdom—The conquests of Cyrus—Darius the Great—Alexander and the Seleucids—The Parthian empire—The Sassanian dynasty—The Eastern Caliphate—The Mongols and Turcomans—The Sufi dynasty—Shah Abbas—Nadir Shah—Aga Muhammad—Persia a great battle-ground—Various races—Caucasians and Mongoloids—Physical characters of Persians—Moral character--Slavery—Vices and virtues—Men's clothing—Women's faces—Painting—Hair—Women's dress—Marriage—Astrology—The bazaar manufactures—Food—Houses—Dervishes—Future of Persia—Iranian languages—Firdosi and epic poetry—Omar ben Khayyam—Sadi—Hafiz—The Guebres—The Kurds and Luris—Arabs, Armenians, and Jews—Nestorians—Turcomans—Iliats.**

PERSIAN.

**Persia and Iran.**

COMING to the South-west of Asia, we find ourselves again in contact with the Caucasian peoples, or "whites." A section of them possess sufficiently marked characteristics to be set apart as a group, known as Iranian, distinct in language and to some extent in physical features from the Aryans and the Semites; but they originally shared with the Brahman race the name of Aryans. The name Persia, which originally belonged only to the limited district now known as Fars, or Farsistan, is now extended over a great territory properly known as Iran, the term still used by the Persians for their country.

The history of Persia is bewildering from its extent and

PERSIAN DERVISH.

importance, as well as from the uncertainty surrounding much of it. The great Achæmenian and Sassanian empires, the rule of Alexander and his successors, the

Parthian empire, the Eastern caliphate, the Mogul domination, the modern empire, include a great variety of dramatic incident, and belong to important periods and movements of the world's history. It is manifestly impossible even to sketch these great monarchies here.

**The great monarchies.**

The authentic history of Persia begins with a period of domination by rulers issuing from the high lands of Media, north of Persia proper. Their capital was Ecbatana (now Hamadan). Deioces is the first king of whom we have any certainty; he reigned at the end of the eighth and well into the seventh century B.C. His son Phaortes appears to have extended his sway over Persia proper, but was slain in attacking Nineveh. His son Cyaxares, at the end of the seventh century, raised the empire to great power, being successful both against the Assyrians and the Scythians, and carrying his arms into Armenia and Cappadocia, which he subjugated by the aid of an opportune total eclipse on the 28th of May, B.C. 585.

**The Median kingdom.**

PERSIAN. TURCOMAN.

This Median empire attained a considerable degree of civilisation, such indeed as to impress its institutions, both political and military, upon the succeeding Persian empire. Already the Zoroastrian religion was probably adopted as the state religion, for the Magi, the priestly caste, are stated by Herodotus to have been a Median tribe. The Persian empire, founded by Cyrus, the descendant of Achæmenes, was rather the

**The conquests of Cyrus.**

successor than the supplanter of the Median. A genuine inscribed cylinder of Cyrus, found at Babylon, gives an account of his ancestry and conquests. He was the heir of the provincial rulers of Persia proper, who, under Cyrus, revolted from the control of Media, and took Ecbatana, about B.C. 550. His conquest of Crœsus king of Lydia, and of the Greek cities of Ionia, of Babylon (about 539 B.C.), of Syria, and of much of Turkestan and Afghanistan, mark him as one of the greatest conquerors. He died in B.C. 529. His tyrannical and blood-thirsty son Cambyses added Tyre, Cyprus, and Egypt to the Persian dominions; but he put an end to himself in B.C. 521, while marching against the usurper the false Smerdis.

**Darius the Great.**

The great Darius (the son of Hystaspes), a leader of the conspiracy which destroyed the false Smerdis, was a descendant of a younger branch of the Achæmenians. He conquered Thrace and Macedonia, and attempted the conquest of Greece; but his army was defeated at Marathon in 490 B.C. He even conquered a portion of north-western India; but Darius's distinction is derived as much from his government as his arms. He developed the system of satrapies or provincial governments, reducing them to proper control and limiting taxation. Every one knows of the great army assembled by Darius's son Xerxes for the conquest of Greece, and of his defeat at Salamis and Platææ. These events led to the gradual advance of the Greeks eastward, culminating in Alexander the Great's conquest of Persia in 331-330. Some years after his death Persia became a dependency of Syria under the Seleucid dynasty. Many Greek settlements were founded by the Seleucid kings in Media and other parts of Persia.

**Alexander and the Seleucidæ.**

About 250 B.C. the Parthian kingdom was founded in north-east Persia by Arsaces, with a band of still more northern Scythian horsemen. This kingdom became predominant in Iran under the remarkable King Mithridates I. (171-138) who conquered Media and Babylonia. Mithridates II. (the Great), conquered Mesopotamia, and was the first Parthian king to come in

**The Parthian empire.**

contact with Rome, which, after long contests, almost destroyed the Parthian power, although at first Parthia inflicted numerous defeats on Rome. The end of the Parthians however came from the rising dynasty of the Sassanians in Persia proper, about 228 A.D., having gradually thrown off their allegiance to the northern kingdom.

The Sassanian empire (supporting the Zoroastrian religion) lasted till it was overthrown by the Moslems. Among the great kings of this dynasty was Khosrau I., or Chosroes, 531–579, who made great conquests in the East, West, and North. The defeat of the Persians by the Arabs in 636 was the commencement of the celebrated rule of the Eastern Caliphate, which lasted till 1258, centred at Bagdad, near Ctesiphon, the former capital of the Sassanians. Haroun-al-Raschid (786–809) was the most celebrated Caliph, his grand vizier being Giafar. The "Thousand and One Nights" have immortalised their names in literature; but it must be remembered that the opinion of the best scholars is, that the stories refer to a much later period, and describe mainly Egyptian scenes. But Haroun deserves his fame.

**The Sassanian dynasty.**

**The Eastern Caliphate.**

The Mongols then gained sway over Persia, under Jenghiz Khan; and later, Timur (Tamerlane) harried and subdued the land towards the end of the fourteenth century. In the next century the Turcomans gained empire over parts of Persia, but the general condition was one of anarchy.

**The Mongols and Turcomans.**

In 1499 the Sufi dynasty was founded by Ismail I., signalising the rise to power of the Shiite sect of Mahometans. Other great rulers of this dynasty have been Abbas (1586–1628), who made Ispahan his capital, and who had much intercourse with European kings through ambassadors. The Afghan Mahmoud conquered and devastated Persia, in 1722: and the Afghans ruled till they were overthrown by Nadir, originally a Turcoman robber chief in 1727–30. Nadir was proclaimed Shah of Persia in 1736, and proceeded to conquer Cabul in 1738, and Northern India in 1739; but contented

**The Sufi dynasty.**

**Shah Abbas.**

**Nadir Shah.**

himself with marrying his son to the granddaughter of Aurungzebe and restoring the crown to the dethroned emperor.

The modern rulers of Persia belong to yet another dynasty, the Kajar, founded by the Turcoman chief Aga Muhammad, in 1795, after he had already ruled over a part of Persia for many years. He fixed the capital at Teheran, where it remains. The contests of his successors with Russia and England have ended in giving Persia quiet possession of her present territory, by renouncing all ambition to recover old possessions of the empire. The visit of the present Shah (Nasr-ul-Din) to England in 1873 is fresh in many people's memory.

**Aga Muhammad.**

### THE MODERN PERSIANS.

Persia, it is evident, has been a great battleground of the nations, who have come from all quarters to contest supremacy there. One might imagine that Persia contained things eminently worth having; and certainly the well-watered provinces of Persia are very fertile; but two-thirds of the land is barren from lack of water, and Persia seems to owe its great importance rather to its situation on the main line between India and Europe, Turkestan and Egypt. Northern freebooting conquerors found the plains of Ispahan and Shiraz and other Persian provinces paradises compared with their steppes, and sought to win them and to make them stepping-stones to greater things.

**Persia a great battleground.**

When the East had sought to conquer the West, the West in turn attacked the East; and Alexander, the Romans, and the Mahometans successively penetrated Persia, and the latter truly established themselves and impressed their religion deeply upon the people. Thus the Persians are to this day among the most devoted Mahometans, and pride themselves on the number of sacred cities within their kingdom.

The Persians are even more mixed than the succession of conquests would indicate. Not merely is Persia a meeting-ground of Caucasians and Mongoloids, but it includes considerable tribes of several

**Various races.**

principal branches of these stocks. Thus the Aryans are represented by the Iranians, including the dominant

**Caucasians and Mongoloids.**

Persians and Tajiks, the Kurds, the Luri of Luristan, the Laks, and a hundred thousand Baluchis in the east, by a considerable number of Gipsies and Jats, of Hindu stock, and by 150,000 Armenians, who may be reckoned as allied both to the Circassians and the Semites; while the Semitic stock is represented by Arabs, Jews, and Nestorians (Chaldeans). The Mongoloids include the Turki Iliats, numbering half-a-million, an indefinite but not very large number of Turcomans, together with 250,000 Aymaks of Mongol origin.

PERSIAN LADY.

There is no doubt of the predominance of the Persians or Tajiks; and they bear themselves as a ruling race. They are tall, handsome, rather fair people, with black hair, and large

**Physical characters of Persians.**

brown eyes. Their bearing is noble and composed, and their tall head-gear of lambskin or hair adds much to their appearance. The nose is almost straight, slightly aquiline; the lips and chin of medium size, the latter covered in men by a luxuriant black silky beard. The skull is long and narrow, and the cranial capacity considerable. Their limbs are slender and flexible, capable of marching long distances and with grace.

Although the Persian courtier is reviled as possessing all the vices of the most corrupt diplomatist, he is not to be taken as the type of the people. Those who know

PERSIAN WEDDING DANCE.

the Persians well, credit them with many virtues, including hospitality, generosity, kindliness, reverence towards parents, great affection for children. Although black slaves are largely held, —an Abyssinian fetching about £40, while negroes from the interior of Africa fetch much less,—

**Moral character.**

**Slavery,**

they are rarely ill-treated, and in fact are both trusted and made comfortable.

Dissimulation and peculation are however so common in Persia as to be regarded as strictly legitimate. The lie is given without offence; and exaggeration and "buncombe" are natural to the Persian. "To-morrow" is an oft-repeated day for the fulfilment of promises; and written contracts are much disliked. Persians, however, are clean in person, washing both themselves and their garments frequently. Abstinence from alcohol is the rule, except among the upper classes and the townspeople; and morals in the country are perhaps above a European standard, though the towns harbour quite enough vice.

DAUGHTER OF A PERSIAN NOBLEMAN.

**Vices and virtues.**

**Men's clothing.**

The men wear short cotton shirts, loose trousers, of cloth among the higher classes, of white, blue, or red cotton among the rest. Another garment of print covers both these, and then comes the tunic, of various fabrics from calico to velvet, but as rich and costly as the wearer can procure. The looseness of the trousers specially suits the general habit of sitting upon the heels, chairs being only used by those who conform to European fashions. For outdoor and winter wear and for ceremonial occasions many other garments are worn, dress being a leading idea of the Persians. Long and ample sleeves are very much in vogue. The villagers wear thick felt coats in winter. The belt is a very important article of attire, its materials varying with the class. Its folds are used as pockets, knives or rolls of paper, and pencases being among the

TAJIK WOMAN.

contents. A great turban is worn by priests, but all others wear the great hat of cloth or sheepskin on a frame of pasteboard; the fashions of hats change yearly among the upper classes. Socks and shoes or slippers are worn by both sexes.

The Persian women are many of them naturally good-looking, especially the harem women, who are generally of Circassian or Armenian descent. Their brown or black languishing eyes and fair complexions would make them attractive anywhere, if they did not spoil themselves by painting their faces as extravagantly as a clown's on all important occasions. "The eyebrows," says Dr. Wills ("Land of the Lion and Sun"), "are widened and painted till they appear to meet, while sham moles and stars are painted on the chin and cheek; even spangles are stuck at times on the chin and forehead." Tattooing is common among the poor villagers, and is at times seen among the upper classes. The hair is usually abundant, and often plaited into many long tails. If it is deficient, an artificial supply is used; although naturally black, it is frequently dyed red with henna. After bearing children, the women rapidly lose beauty and figure, nothing in the nature of a corset being worn.

**Women's faces.**

**Painting.**

**Hair.**

Out of doors all women of respectable families are most strictly veiled, and indeed enveloped in the most unsightly and ungainly garment imaginable, almost like a bag. At home they pass to the other extreme of unveiling, wearing voluminous skirts much shorter than ballet-girls', and nothing else but short socks, a transparent gauze chemise not reaching to the skirts, and a very open jacket. Jewellery in abundance is superadded. The court is now introducing trousers, each leg being covered by full skirts, sometimes a dozen pairs being worn, the result being rather ludicrous to our eyes.

**Women's dress.**

Much cannot be expected of women whose only career is in the harem, and in whom sensuality is cultivated. They are ignorant, and pass their time in frivolity and smoking, gossip and quarrelling. The women of the lower classes are hard-working and care much for their children.

Marriage is an elaborate business; and men of wealth have as many wives and concubines as they can procure. Girls are not unfrequently betrothed while infants, though they can in some circumstances refuse to complete the contract. Great feasts are given at every wedding, sometimes lasting forty days. The completion of the ceremony is marked by the husband seeing his wife's face for the first time, and giving her a piece of sugar candy from which he has himself bitten half. Divorce is practically rather frequent, even for bad temper and extravagance; but the wife's dowry has to be returned. In case of unfaithfulness, a wife is generally put to death, without resort to law.

**Marriage.**

Astrology flourishes in Persia, every village having its diviner, who predicts fortunate hours or days, tells fortunes, and recovers stolen property. Sticks are given to the suspected, and they are told the guilty man's will grow. In fear, the guilty man will often break a piece off his, and so detect himself. Frequently the suspects are sworn to innocence in the name of a local saint, and are told that his vengeance will fall on the guilty man if the property is not returned; it frequently is restored before the morning.

**Astrology.**

Most of the business is transacted in the bazaar; which in Teheran is a series of vaulted arcades extending in half-a-dozen different directions. The shops are open, in which the merchant, seated in the interior behind his goods, awaits his customers. Every trade has its separate avenue, but they are somewhat mixed in the main thoroughfares. "The salient feature of the place," says O'Donovan in his "Merv Oasis," speaking of the Teheran bazaar, "is the confused and overwhelming babel of sounds which strike the ear. In one avenue there arises the din of a hundred coppersmiths, sledging away at their anvils while manufacturing pots, kettles, and other utensils. In the next, perhaps, an equal number of persons are yelling out, extolling the excellence of their wares, or trying to converse with one

**The bazaar.**

another from their shops on opposite sides of the way, pitching their voices to the utmost to dominate the hubbub around and the din of the passers-by. . . . In the narrow way between the sh ps a motley multitude hurries by, each one jostling the other, without the least regard for mutual convenience. Any one having a brass plate on his hat, or being in the slightest way connected with an official personage, seems to believe it his privilege to run amuck at full speed. All through the bazaar there is a general rush. Sometimes a whole flight of diminutive grey asses comes charging through the narrow thoroughfares, laden with bricks and tiles scarcely cold. Occasionally the foot-passengers are obliged to take refuge within the shops, as a mule or gigantic ass, laden on each side with enormous bundles of hay, comes trotting through, filling up the passage; and sometimes a train of sardonically smiling camels stalk past, appropriating all the road to themselves."

Cereals and sugar, tobacco and opium, madder, henna, and other dyes are among the favourite agricultural products of Persia. In some parts silk is largely produced; and the wines, especially that of Shiraz, enjoy considerable repute. Flowers and fruits of the choicest description and greatest variety are produced in the fertile parts. Various manufactures, especially metal work, wood carving, enamelling, jewellery, embroidery, carpets and shawls, are carried to great perfection; and Kurd rugs, Khorassan carpets, and Persian shawls are well known in European markets.

**Manufactures.**

A great variety of bread is eaten by the Persians. The favourite kind is called "flap-jack" by European residents—a sort of sheet of bread three feet by one foot, and less than an inch thick, baked rapidly on heated stones. It is eaten hot with butter, and is pronounced first-rate. An unleavened bread is used in marching, made of a paste rolled as thin as a wafer and of great size. It is damped before use, and is said to keep well for a couple of months. Many forms of biscuits and buns are also used. In fact, bread in various forms is the staple diet of the Persians; eggs, curds, and

**Food.**

cheese being the relishes. Meat is almost restricted to the well-to-do classes, whose appetite for pilaus and highly seasoned dishes is equal to that of the Turcomans.

**Houses.**

Persian houses are far less attractive than Persian clothes. There are very few which are really comfortable, except those built by Europeans and the nobles who imitate them. The streets are very mean; and the houses, though they have a fair amount of space, are very unfurnished. In many villages the houses are made entirely of mud.

NESTORIAN WOMAN OF HAKIARI.

**Dervishes.**

The crowd of dervishes who infest the country are one of its greatest plagues. Their chief tenet is, to do no work and to be well rewarded for it. "Many are clothed all in white, having taken a vow to that effect; and most of them refrain from shaving or from cutting the hair. All, or nearly all, wear a tall cap of felt or cloth, shaped like a sugar-loaf, and ornamented by inscriptions of texts from the Koran. Most of them carry a carved alms-holder, which is generally composed of a huge nut elaborately carved, and suspended by brass or silver chains from the waistband. A striking appearance is attained at all hazards;

often the clothing being merely a pair of short drawers, an antelope, panther, or tiger skin being slung across the shoulder, and an axe or huge club, often armed with spikes, being almost invariably carried. When a dervish meets a horseman or any one of condition, he offers him in the politest manner a flower, or even a leaf or blade of grass; as a rule it is accepted and a trifle given. At other times the dervish will simply stretch out his hand or his alms-holder, and favour the passer-by with a steady stare, the word 'hue' (my right) being suddenly ejaculated."—(Wills.) Many are drunkards, confirmed opium-eaters, debauchers of women, and they are nothing but a plague.

**Future of Persia.** Whether Persia is likely to rise in the scale of nations while independent, is doubtful. The present Shah is desirous of introducing many European improvements, but finds his people do not readily respond. The fact is, Oriental ideas of courtesy and ceremony, of idleness and rights of rank, cannot easily be made to give way. It is to be feared that Persia will oppose no very effective obstacle to the march of Russia to the Indian Ocean.

**Iranian languages.** The Persian language, as indeed all the cognate Iranian family, is distinguished from the Sanscrit group by the great development of the aspirate *h*, instead of the letter *s*, and the insertion of other aspirates, together with the abundance of soft sibilants. Zend is the language of the Avesta, or sacred book of the Zoroastrian religion; this language is almost as old as Sanscrit and of a very primitive type, approximating much more closely to the language of the Veda than modern Persian. The latter began with the great poet Firdosi; but since his time the language has been greatly influenced by Arabic, from which it has adopted many words. Among modern Iranian languages distinct from Persian must be named Kurdish, Baluch, Afghan, and perhaps Ossetian and Armenian.

**Firdosi and epic poetry.** Firdosi wrote about the end of the tenth and beginning of the eleventh centuries. His great work was a sort of epic poem of Persian history, the Shahnama, which Sir William Jones termed a "glorious monument of Eastern genius and learning," rivalling the Iliad in invention. It was largely imitated, and followed by many poetic novels and tales. Other poets described the events of recent history; and Persian poets at the courts of the Mogul Emperors excelled in this species of composition. Persian literature also excels in love stories of romantic interest, in panegyric and satirical poetry, in philosophic verse, and in lyrics. The Sufic doctrines of pantheism and mysticism were given forth in the aphorisms of the celebrated Omar ben Khayyam, and the didactic poetry of Nasir ben Khosrau and others. But the greatest moral teacher of Persia is Sadi (died 1292), whose Bustan (Fruit garden) and Gulistan (Rose garden) are far-famed. Hafiz (died 1389), the incomparable lyric writer, is the greatest poet of Persia. Since his time, Persian literature has declined, although a new kind of drama has sprung up in this century, developed from a religious ceremony lamenting the fate of the caliph Ali, the hero of the Shiites. Histories of India and of the world, works on geography and travel, biographies, mathematical and astronomical works, however, by no means exhaust the copious list of ancient and modern Persian books.

**Omar ben Khayyam.**

**Sadi.**

**Hafiz.**

The old fire-worshippers are now only represented by a small and decreasing sect, the Guebres, chiefly congregated at Yezd, in addition to the Parsees of India, to whom we have already referred. They are much persecuted, being fleeced on every possible excuse, and placed at many legal disadvantages, compared with the Mahometans.

**The Guebres.**

The Kurds, of Kurdistan, being only one-third or one-fourth subject to Persia, we shall defer speaking of them till we deal with the inhabitants of Asiatic Turkey. They are at daggers drawn with the Persians in religion, most of them being Sunnite Mahometans, others heathens. The Luris, of Luristan, are a group exceeding half a million, not far removed in race from the Kurds, but speaking a different language, and having much earlier accepted Mahometanism. The Baktiari

**The Kurds and Luris.**

Luris are a distinct group, speaking a language more like Persian, and having the shortest and roundest skulls among the Iranians. They are robust, fine-looking people, of brown complexions and black, wavy hair, with thick eyebrows, long, aquiline noses, square chin, and projecting cheek-bones. In summer they are pastoral nomads; in winter they dwell in villages in the plains. The Baluchis, on the south-east, overlap into Persian territory, but will be described in the next chapter.

The Semitic group is represented by several hundred thousand Arabs in the south-west, and spread more or less through the country. The Armenians are in considerable numbers in the territories bordering on Armenia; while Jews are found plentifully at most of the principal trading centres. In each town they are compelled to live in a separate quarter, and much contemned, though very useful. A score of thousands of Nestorian Christians (Chaldeans) maintain themselves near Lake Urmia, and are much under the influence of American Protestant missionaries.

**Arabs, Armenians, and Jews.**

**Nestorians.**

The Turcomans we have already sufficiently described. It is remarkable how completely they have contrived, like the Manchus in China, to seize on power and retain it, still supplying the greater part of the army; equally remarkable is the way in which the Persians, like the Chinese, have influenced their conquerors. They have acquired even more than a Persian hatred of the Osmanli Turks. In every way heavier and more massive, they are less cunning, but more fierce than the Persians.

**Turcomans.**

The wandering tribes of Persia, who occupy a great part of the country, are generally designated Iliats. Many of them are Iranians, but a very large number are truly Turcomans or Tartars, and still maintain allegiance to their hereditary tribal chiefs, who pay the Persian taxes for all. These people wander as pasture serves, and live in typical Turcoman tents in the North; in the South, in tents with flat roofs, or but slightly sloping.

**Turki Iliats.**

# CHAPTER XVI.

## The Afghans, Baluchis, etc.

**The Afghans, or Pathans—The Bactrian kingdom—Sultan Mahmoud—Various conquests—Dost Mahommed—British supremacy—Numerous tribes—Physical characters—Moral character—The Ameer and chiefs—Spirit of freedom—Women and marriage—Clothing—Occupations—Food—Religion—The Tajiks—The Hindki—Turkish tribes—The Hazaras and Aymaks—The Siah Posh Kafirs—Hatred to Mahometans—The Galcha stock—Habits and customs—Religion—Kafir dances—Clothing—Horses—The Brahuis—The Baluchis—Dress and Language—Government.**

KHATAK (WEST AFGHAN FRONTIER TRIBE).

EVEN more complex racially than the Persians, are the inhabitants of Afghanistan. With more Hindu or Brahman blood, they have a large number of Iranian tribes, and others recently recognised as distinct from them, the Galchas, including the Kafirs of the Hindu-Kush, and Kohistanis, north of Cabul. Afghanistan also has a large number of Usbegs, Turcomans, and Kizil Bashis, Hazaras, and Aymaks, all more or less Mongoloid and Turkish by race.

The Afghans, or Pathans.

The Afghans call their country Pukhtun-Kwa, and their language is the Pushtu or Poukhtu, an Iranian language with a large infusion of Hindu (Aryan) words. The Hindus term the Afghans Pathans. Many of the Afghan people speak Persian; others use Hindu dialects. The Afghan chroniclers call their people

A GHILZAI OF CANDAHAR.

Beni-Israel, and trace their descent from King Saul. We hear of Afghanistan as early as Darius's reign over Persia, in which it was then included. Alexander marched through it in his career of conquest; and Strabo mentions it under the term Ariana. After Alexander's time, some of his soldiers founded a Greek kingdom in Bactria (Balkh), now Afghan Turkestan; and this afterwards extended its dominion over Afghanistan, and later, under

SIRDAR WALI MOHAMMED KHAN.
(*Half-brother to the Ameer Shere Ali.*)

Demetrius, made extensive conquests in India. But it gradually yielded to invasions of Scythian hordes (probably not unli e the Turcomans), and is not heard of after about 126 B.C. Already Buddhism had spread to this kingdom of Bactria, and some of the barbarian invaders adopted it. Kanishka, one of the monarchs of the new power, was a great conqueror, and ruled over a wide extent of Afghanistan and India. He was long celebrated in Buddhist legends.

**The Bactrian kingdom.**

From this time for many centuries we hear in turn of Hindu and Turkish rulers in Afghanistan, often contemporary, warring against each other. The Mahometans did not finally conquer Cabul from the Hindus till the end of the tenth century. A Turkish dynasty after this time produced the famous Sultan Mahmoud (eighteenth century), whose capital was Ghazni. Like his successors, the Ghor dynasty, he ruled over a large part of North India; and they may be regarded as the means of establishing Mahometan power in Northern India.

**Sultan Mahmoud.**

DOST MAHOMMED.

Timor conquered all Afghanistan, and the Mongols ruled the country for centuries. Sultan Baber took Cabul in 1504, and Candahar in 1522, and Cabul remained under the Mogul empire till 1738. Herat was meanwhile annexed to Persia. During this time the Afghan (Pathan) tribes proper were rising into

**Various conquests.**

prominence, and in 1708 the Ghilzais expelled the Persians from Candahar, which they then held, and even temporarily conquered Ispahan, but did not keep the mastery for many years. In 1737 Nadir Shah recovered both Candahar and Cabul. After his assassination (1747) a stable Afghan dominion was formed by Ahmed Shah,

DURANI OF CABUL.

who at his death (1773) ruled the Punjab and Cashmere, as well as Afghanistan.

**Dost Mahommed.**

It was not till this century that the British had any dealings with the Afghans. It would be profitless to narrate the unfortunate events which led to and attended the successive Afghan wars against Dost Mahommed, who died in 1863, and Shere Ali, his successor. Suffice it to say, that British influence is now established in Afghanistan, so far as the intractable character of the people will permit; and that we have taken charge of the foreign relations of the country, and obtained a settlement of the boundary towards Russian Turkestan in a sense very favourable to the Afghans, whose hold on some of the Turcoman territory left to them is certainly very modern, dating only from 1850–59 as regards Balkh and the western khanates, while Badakshan submitted in 1859.

British supremacy.

The Afghans can hardly be said to form a nation. They are rather a collection of tribes, tribally governed; and the difficulties which perpetually recur are due largely to the fact that they do not regard with a sense of reverence any but their own tribal chief. Thus the predominant ruler, or Ameer, is chiefly supported by his own tribe. The Ghilzais are perhaps the bravest of these tribes. They live north of Candahar, extending east to the Suliman mountains, and north to the Cabul river. The Duranis live in the south and south-west, between Herat and Candahar. The Yuzufzais, north of Peshawur, maintain their independence of Cabul, as do the Kakars of the south-east. All the tribes are much subdivided into clans and minor branches; and their cohesion is further hindered by the number of other races intermixed with them and speaking different languages.

Numerous tribes.

Col. Yule speaks with considerable respect of the tradition which connects the Afghans with the Jews; and certainly, if both Arabs and Jews have migrated west and east, it is not at all unlikely that there should be some ethnical relation between the Iranian and the Semitic stocks. Certainly not a few Afghans, as well as other Iranians, have the high prominent forehead, aquiline nose, thick lips and abundant beard of many Jews. In general, the Afghans are remarkably massive in build, and very muscular and hardy. They are long-headed, with prominent cheek-bones and noses, thick eyebrows, and thick black hair and beard. In colour they vary from an olive to a brown tint. Their aspect is fierce, brusque, and haughty, indicating a tem-

Physical characters.

per of great cruelty when roused. At first, and if all goes favourably, an Afghan appears most hospitable and magnanimous; but in war he is savage and revengeful, treacherous, and greedy of plunder. "God protect you from the vengeance of an elephant, a cobra, or an Afghan!" is a Hindu saying. **Moral character.**

Every tribal division and subdivision among the Afghans has a chief usually hereditary; but the chiefs of tribes are either nominated by the Ameer of Cabul or chosen by the tribe. Each chief is controlled by the assembly of subordinate chiefs over which he presides. Even the Ameer is regarded only as the principal chief among other chiefs his equals in standing. This is the weakness of the Afghans as a nation—their tribal sentiment is stronger than their patriotism. "We are all free," they love to think and say; and hence arise many local feuds, many and varying alliances and discords. One good point about this free spirit is, that the Afghans have no slaves; they may kill their enemies, but they do not reduce them to that abject condition of being "portable property." Something like a vendetta still exists in Afghanistan, and this occasions much bloodshed. The tribal councils often endeavour to compose these quarrels, by enjoining the marriage of one or more women belonging to the party in fault to members of the antagonistic family. **The Ameer and chiefs.** **Spirit of freedom.**

The Afghan women are handsome, somewhat Jewish-looking, of fair complexions, wearing their hair in two long plaits behind. They are strictly secluded in the towns, but have more liberty in the country. Marriage is usually by purchase, but elopements are not unknown in case the parents' consent cannot be obtained. In some tribes the would-be bridegroom enters the service of his wife's father and waits years for her. In many respects the marriage customs are the same as in other Mahometan countries. **Women and marriage.**

The Afghans mostly wear a sort of frock reaching below the knees, a cap or turban, and loose trousers, with laced boots. A sheepskin cloak is worn over all, if the weather is cold. The women wear **Clothing.**

ADAL, A HAZARA.

a long tunic dress, often gaily embroidered, coloured trousers, and a coloured silk cap, often embroidered with gold thread; a sort of cotton sheet is thrown over the head when a stranger is present. Ear-rings, nose-rings, and finger-rings are abundantly worn, together with gold and silver chains and strings of coins. Sometimes they imitate Persian modes of dyeing the hair and adorning the face.

War and pasture may be defined as the chief occupations of the Afghans. They are not prone to cultivate the soil; and they have a great objection to the settled life of the artisan or the shopkeeper. If they have business to do, they do it by deputy; and the intelligent Persian or Hindu is always "willing to oblige."

**Occupations.**

Notwithstanding the want of variety in their occupations, the Afghans manage to feed well. Even the poor can obtain mutton or goat or camel's flesh, as well as pottage and pulse. Milk, curds, tea, and tobacco are largely used by all classes. Cleanliness is not one of their virtues: love of home is; and they will, if possible, be buried with their fathers. If they die at a distance from their ancestral burial-place, their bodies are most carefully embalmed and taken home.

**Food.**

On the whole, however, we cannot express a high opinion of the Afghans. An old man told Elphinstone: "We are content with discord, we are content with alarms, we are content with blood, but we will never be content with a master." Sir H. Edwardes says, "Nothing is finer than their physique, or worse than their morale." Being Sunnite or orthodox Mahometans, they are in antagonism to the Persians, whom they hate worse than unbelievers. They are much under the influence of their religious teachers, but yet retain much belief in charms, omens, astrology, and local saints. Indeed, the shrines of the latter are found on every hill top. Thus it is evident that Mahometanism is but a veneer in many cases.

**Religion.**

The Iranians are perhaps more truly represented in Afghanistan by the Tajiks, or Parsiwan, as they call themselves, who are very numerously settled in the towns. Their settled habits are however their chief distinction from the Afghans. They are either agriculturists, artisans, or traders, and are unlike the Persians in being Sunnite Mahometans.

**The Tajiks.**

The Aryans of Afghanistan include many people termed Hindki, of Hindu descent, besides many natives of India. Much of the trade, exchange, etc., of the towns is in their hands; and they flourish in spite of the high taxes levied upon them. There are many Jats too in Afghanistan, fine dark handsome people, occupied as farm servants, barbers, musicians, etc.

**The Hindki.**

The Mongoloid stock of the Turkish branch are represented by the numerous Usbegs of Afghan Turkestan, the Turcomans of Herat and Maimana, and the Kizil-Bashis (or Red-heads) around Cabul. The latter are much Persianised, and indeed came from Persia with Nadir Shah (1737). They are Shiite Mahometans, but in spite of their heresy have managed to gain many influential posts in the Afghan service, many being skilful scribes, physicians, merchants, etc. As secretaries and confidential servants, they are both complaisant and useful to their employers, and suitably dictatorial to the inferior people, who accuse them of insolence and cruelty.

**Turkish tribes.**

More akin to the Mongols are the Hazaras and Aymaks, of the Paropamisus Mountains, western extension of the Hindu-Kush. The Hazaras are markedly Mongoloid in features, and are probably descended from the tribes who followed Jenghiz Khan and his successors. However, they mostly speak a Persian dialect. They maintain a very great independence of the Afghan Ameers, only paying tribute when compelled; they are good horsemen in their craggy homes, and excellent shots, being able to make their own gunpowder. They are Shiites, and obey a number of absolute chieftains, who often war against each other. Recently, however, many of them have spread through Afghanistan, and even Northern India, in search of domestic work. The Aymaks are tribes akin to the Hazaras, dwelling somewhat west of them, Sunnites in religion and still nomadic in habits.

**The Hazaras and Aymaks.**

## THE SIAH-POSH KAFIRS.

The mountainous districts north and north-west of Cabul, including the northern and southern slopes of the Hindu-Kush, form a region almost unknown to Europeans, and indeed largely unknown to Mahometans, and still pagan. Consequently a large part of the district has obtained the name of Kafiristan, country of the Kafirs or infidels. No Kafir is thought much of among his people, unless he has killed one or more Mahometan. It was only as lately as 1883 that the first European (Mr. W. W. McNair) penetrated the country to some distance in disguise as a native doctor; so that our knowledge of it is still very uncertain. The people have been lately grouped as Galchas, a sort of intermediate stock between Iranian and Aryan. Some have believed they are the nearest representatives in Asia of the original Celts. Others call them variously Arabs, Indian aboriginal refugees, descendants of Alexander's Greeks; whence it is plain that we do not yet know much about them. They have somewhat European features, with blue mixed with dark eyes, and somewhat light hair; but mixed with them are darker people, very like Hindus. They are hardy, strong, and daring, but overmuch given to wine and pleasure. Mr. McNair says the women do all the field work. They have no blood-feuds among themselves, and thus are able to hold their ground against the Mahometans, with whom they are always fighting. "Towards the British," says Mr. McNair, "they are extremely well-disposed. Slavery exists to a certain extent among them. Polygamy is rare; mild corporal punishment is inflicted on a wife for adultery, while the male offender is fined so many heads of cattle. The dead are coffined, but never buried. One Supreme Being—Imbra—is universally acknowledged. Priests preside at their temples, in which sacred stones are set up; but to neither priests nor idols is excessive reverence paid. In evil spirits, authors of ill-luck, the Kafirs firmly

**Hatred to Mahometans.**

**The Galcha stock.**

**Habits and customs.**

**Religion.**

believe. Their arms are bows and arrows. Wealth is reckoned by heads of cattle. There are eighteen chiefs in all, chosen for bravery mainly, but with some regard to hereditary claims."

The Kafirs hold themselves firmly bound by their oath; and the best way of visiting the country is to obtain a promise of safety from some Kafir. When once a guest has been received in a Kafir house, the master alone waits on him. It is said that the most bitter quarrel among them may be settled by one of the parties kissing the nipple of his antagonist's breast, as signifying drinking the milk of friendship. Women go uncovered, but do not eat at the same table with men. Bread is the staple food; but all kinds of meat are eaten, except fish. It would be profitless to repeat more of the accounts given by hearsay from Mahometans, who themselves can only have reached the outskirts of the country. Mr. McNair's account before the Royal Geographical Society (see "Proceedings," 1884) is the only authentic one. He says, there are three main tribes, each inhabiting a separate valley, speaking a different dialect from the rest, and having little to do with each other.

**Kafir dances.**

Both sexes are passionately fond of dancing. Mr. McNair says, "The dancing was invariably begun by a single female performer appearing on the scene, and, after going through a few graceful movements, a shrill whistle (caused by inserting two fingers into the mouth), given by one of the men, is the signal for a change. Several performers then come forward, advancing and retiring on either side of a huge bonfire, at one end of which were the musicians; their instruments a large drum, two kettle-drums, and a couple of flutes. To this music, more particularly to the beating of the drums, good time is kept. The whistle sounds again, when immediately the performers set to partners, if I may use the expression; after a while they disengage, and begin circling round the fire singly, men and women alternately. The dance ended by again setting to partners; each couple, holding a stick between them, their feet firmly planted on the ground, and close together, spin round at a great pace, first from right to left, and then from left to right."

The men shave the whole of the head, except a circular patch on the crown, where the hair is allowed to grow. Indian cotton clothes are worn by the men; for shoes, they have strips of hide tied on with strings of the same. The women wear only one loose garment, gathered in at the waist. Their long hair is plaited, and covered with a broad cap.

**Clothing.**

The Siah Posh live in houses of which the lower storey, built of stone, is only used for storage of timber and dung (used as fuel). The house for living is raised on the roof of this, and has only one or two rooms, the door and frames being rudely carved with figures and scrolls. The furniture is scanty, low wooden chairs and wicker stools being used to sit upon, thus markedly distinguishing the people from Mahometans. A pure, unfermented grape wine is drunk.

**Houses.**

The subdivisions of the Hindu-Kush peoples,—now believed to form a stock of Aryans distinct from the Iranians and Hindus,—it is not desirable here to enter into, as they are so little known. The Siah-Posh Kafirs must be taken as representing them.

Inhabiting the poor and ill-developed country known as Baluchistan, the Brahuis and Baluchis are neither a very numerous nor a very prosperous people, perhaps not numbering 400,000. The Brahuis are the dominant people, to whom the Khan of Khelat, the ruler of the country, belongs; their origin is unknown, but they are most abundant in the east, and may have come from Sind. Their language, the Brahuike, is not allied to Persian, but contains a great many Hindu words. They have short, thick figures, round faces, with flat features; and their hair and beard are frequently brown. They wear calico shirts, buttoned round the neck, bound in by a waist-sash, and reaching below the knee; trousers drawn in round the ankles, and small silk or cotton caps. The women dress similarly, with very wide trousers. Both Brahuis and Baluchis are Sunnite Mahometans.

**The Brahuis.**

The Baluchis are taller than the Brahuis, with longer

faces and more prominent features. They are generally brown in complexion, and look a good deal like Arabs. Their hair and beard are abundant. They are quick and active in their movements, athletic and hardy, and combine pastoral pursuits with predatory variations, in which they are not by any means scrupulous. General Green, who long resided in the country, says: "They will protect and kindly entertain a stranger while their guest, but feel no scruple in robbing and murdering him as soon as he has left their precincts. They are indolent, and, unless excited by amusement or war, spend their time in idleness, rude dissipation and gambling, smoking tobacco or hemp, and chewing opium." They are temperate as to intoxicating drinks, but eat incredible quantities of flesh, strongly seasoned with capsicum, onions, and garlic. They have as many slaves as they can get, and numerous wives and concubines, even among the lower classes; these are obtained by purchase. Their dress is much like that of the Brahuis, but they wear a turban. In winter the poorer classes wear great surtouts of mixed goat's hair and woollen cloth. Their language is distinctly Persian in origin, though the pronunciation differs widely from Persian. It appears probable that the Baluchis have at various times been recruited by stragglers from the various ravaging armies and hordes going to and from India.

**The Baluchis.**

**Dress and language.**

At various times under the control of Persia and Afghanistan, at intervals independent, the Khans of Khelat have been partly induced, partly compelled, to acknowledge the supremacy of the British Government, to admit a British agent, and not to enter into negotiations with other States without the consent of the British. For preventing plundering by his subjects in or near British territory, and for protecting merchants, the Khan receives a subsidy. In the late war in Afghanistan, the Khan rendered the British army substantial aid; and recently the districts of Pishin, Thal, Chotiali, and Sibi, have been annexed to British India, under the title of British Baluchistan, Quetta being the capital.

**Government.**

# CHAPTER XVII.

## The Caucasians, Georgians, Lesghians, etc.

**Boundary between Europe and Asia — Valour and independence of Caucasians — Schamyl — Russian conquest — Wholesale emigration — The Tcherkess — National costume — Family feuds — Sale or capture of girls — Foster fathers — Fraternity — Nature-worship — The Abkasians — The Kabardians — The Tchetchens — The Lesghians — The Georgians — The Georgian kingdom — Physical characters — Singing and dancing — The Mingrelians — So-called princes — The Imeritians — The Khevsurians — The Ossetians — Mixture of types — Tartar civilisation.**

CAUCASIAN AND GEORGIAN.

SEPARATING, yet uniting the two continents, are the interesting peoples here described. We include the inhabitants of Caucasia as a whole in Asia. There is a very intelligible reason for this. The mountains of Caucasia do not furnish a satisfactory division, and similar races inhabit both sides of the Caucasus. Moreover, the steppe river Manich occupies a deep depression indicating a former strait be-

**Boundary between Europe and Asia.**

tween the Caspian and the Black Seas, which would have left Caucasia entirely in Asia. The great Caucasus range, stretching in an oblique line no less than 720 miles, from Kertch to Baku, divides Caucasia into two parts, Cis-Caucasia, north and east, and Trans-Caucasia, south and west.

TCHERKESS BRIDE'S RIDE.

**Valour and independence of Caucasians.**

This district has long been the home of many diverse races. Pliny relates that 130 different interpreters were required to deal with them all in his time. The Greeks had early founded the colony of Dioscurias, whose name is still preserved in that of Cape Iskuria, north of Batoum. Mithridates the Great subdued the tribes up to the foot of the mountains. No Roman army ever penetrated so far. The hardy tribes preserved their independence both of Russia and Turkey till this century, although not infrequently overrun by invaders such as Timor and Nadir Shah. After having annexed Georgia, in 1801, the Russians always aimed at the complete subjugation of Caucasia. In 1829 the Turks ceded to them their nominal suzerainty over the Caucasus tribes, and from that time till 1859 the Russians were unremitting in their efforts to break down the hardy mountaineers. They sacrificed immense numbers of lives in conquering small portions of the Caucasus; and when they hoped that their efforts were nearly successful, the celebrated Schamyl (born 1797) arose and roused the Lesghians to new feats of resistance. His own marvellous successes and escapes long baffled the Russians. The Lesghians, however, were completely subdued in 1859, when Schamyl was made prisoner. The last of the Caucasian tribes was subjugated in 1864; but the people, rather than remain under their conquerors, emigrated almost wholesale, to different provinces of Turkey. The total number of emigrants approached half a million, and they left a territory of nearly 200 miles, between the Caucasus and the Black Sea, almost uninhabited; a significant proof of bitter racial antagonism between the Russians and their victims.

**Schamyl.**

**Russian conquest.**

This, one of the most remarkable emigrations of modern times, deserves more than a passing notice. As Reclus well says, the chain of history has been roughly snapped; traditions, languages, dialects, have been irrevocably lost, for the majority of the emigrants are dead, and it is not among scattered groups of demoralised fugitives that the assemblage of ideas and customs which constitute the soul of a country will be found. The conqueror commanded the Circassians to leave their mountain fastnesses and settle along the shore and in the plains. Rather than obey, they left their native country for ever. The sufferings they underwent in their voyages and journeys, often without food, heaped upon the decks

**Wholesale emigration.**

of vessels, and the difficulties they met with among the strange tribes by which they found themselves surrounded in the lands granted to them by the Turks, caused the death of large numbers in a very short time. Many of them found war was the only profession they could exercise in their new abodes, and became brigands. Their extinction from their native land is a calamity to ethnology and even to civilisation, for so brave a race certainly had something in them worthy of assimilation or of toleration by their neighbours.

**The Tcherkess.** The Tcherkess—which name we have translated into "Circassian"—called themselves Adighe; and it is best to regard them as a type of a distinct group of the Caucasian stock (in its largest sense). The Tcherkess were handsome tall people, with slender figures and broad shoulders, fair complexions, oval faces, and usually black hair. Obesity, or any other disfigurement due to indolence and vice, they regarded as a disgrace. Their favourite costume has become habitual among all the peoples of Caucasia, even the Cossacks and Tartars and Russian officials, so we will give a brief description of it, from Baron von Thielmann's "Journey in the Caucasus," translated by C. Heneage, 1875.

**National costume.** "The most important portions of this dress are the *tcherkesska* and the *beschmet*, two lengthy garments, worn one above the other. The beschmet is a coat with sleeves hanging down half over the thigh; fastened in front up to the neck by a row of hooks and eyes, with a low straight collar and capacious pockets on either side, embroidered the whole way down. The beschmet is composed of striped or printed cotton, and in the case of wealthy persons, the portions around the neck and on the sleeves, which show, are made of silk. The tcherkesska is worn over the beschmet, being broader and longer, with sleeves hanging down so far that they require to be turned up; in front it is fastened across the chest by a row of microscopically small buttons woven of thread, and joined together by means of eyes, a labour entailing much time and trouble; it hangs loose round the neck, showing the beschmet underneath. On both sides of the breast are sewn some seven, eight, or ten

TCHERKESS BEAUTY.

rows of cartridge-pouches, frequently adorned with silver

and gold, and, amongst the notables, often containing boxes of ivory or horn with silver lids, holding ammunition." This garment has no pockets, but has slits

CAUCASIAN VESSELS.

by which the pockets in the beschmet can be reached. It is usually made of stout woollen material. Another garment worn in rainy weather is the *bruka*, a great felt cape with the shaggy side out. Tight trousers, covered with leather or cloth gaiters, often richly embroidered, are worn, with half shoes or even sandals. The predominant headgear is the sheepskin cap, known as the papach, but made in very varied shapes; often round, with a cloth top.

MOUNTAIN-FOREST DWELLING, CAUCASUS.

**Family feuds.** The Circassians were by no means a people at unity among themselves. Split up into disunited tribes, with families often at variance with neighbouring families, the law of blood revenge was supreme among them; yet it was never carried out in the presence of women. Wives were obtained by capture, real or pretended; but a large number of the girls were sold at an early age for exportation to Turkish and Persian harems, usually commanding a high price, and being indulgently treated in consequence of their beauty, their polished manners, and the poetry of their language. Boys were usually, from fear of spoiling them by parental partiality, not brought up at home, but by a sort of foster-father, chosen for his physical and mental qualities, his courage, politeness, and skill in arms. But, true to the spirit of their customs, the foster-father took possession of the child a few days after birth by a kind of capture, yet in presence of seven witnesses who could after-

**Sale or capture of girls.**

**Foster-fathers.**

CAUCASIAN MUSICAL INSTRUMENTS AND ORNAMENTS.

wards attest the identity of the child. Not till grown up did the child return home, trained in all the manly and polite arts of his people.

Under their tribal chiefs, the Tcherkess were all grouped into fraternities, united to one another till death; these gave strength to their resistance to conquest. There were besides many slaves, captives or refugees. The popular assemblies decided questions that arose; the chiefs were simply executors of the popular will.

**Fraternities.**

The Tcherkess, though long nominally Christianised, retained many pagan beliefs, many of them reverencing Chiblé, the god of thunder, war, and justice, and propitiating the spirits of the air, water, forests, etc. In later days Mahometanism made great

**Nature worship.**

progress among them, especially through its antagonism to the Christianity professed by their enemies the Russians.

The Abkhasians, a related tribe, much reduced by emi-

CAUCASIAN GIRL RIDING IN MALE COSTUME.

The Abkhasians.

gration, occupy a tract on the coast of the Black Sea, between Pitzunda and the river Ingur. They are shorter, browner-complexioned, and black-haired, wilder in aspect, and with more irregular features.

Many of them were hardy sailors and pirates, and were formerly to be found in the service of the Khedives of Egypt as mercenary soldiers. Some of them still remained without money, and the cow was their standard of exchange, when the Russians first came among them. In religion they are much like the last people, mingling much nature worship with Mahometan practices.

LESGHIAN WOMEN.

**The Kabardians.**

The Kabardians, another allied tribe, occupying the northern slopes of central Caucasus, who have at length accepted the Russian rule, and have been pacified by being allowed to retain their local customs, are a handsome race, speaking a different dialect from the Tcherkess. They have many horses and sheep, which they pasture in the undivided mountains and forests. Theft is honourable, so long as it is practised outside the native village or tribe, and the robber escapes capture; similarly the bride is still often captured and carried away by stealth. Many fine men of this nation have become "Circassians" in the Russian Imperial guard.

The Tchetchens are a group of tribes on the northern slopes of the Eastern Caucasus (or Western Daghestan), not numbering more than 15,000, but yet having something like a score of different languages, or at least very marked dialects. They are ardent (Sunnite) Mahometans, and were among the most devoted of Schamyl's followers. After his downfall, very many of them emigrated to Turkish Armenia. In physical qualities they are the equals of the Circassians, while surpassing them in generosity and pride. These qualities made them the most redoubtable foes of the Russians. A variety

The Tchetchens.

CAUCASIANS.

of modes of government prevailed among them previous to their conquest; some tribes were purely republican, everything being settled by popular government, others having hereditary chiefs. Their fine garments are equally remarkable with their simple, even rude dwellings. It is said that blood vengeance has still its old sway among them.

The native tribes inhabiting most of Daghestan (Eastern Caucasus) are grouped together as Lesghians, the diversity of languages among them being almost as great as the number of tribes. Altogether they may number half a million, though many of them have emi-

The Lesghians.

grated since their countryman Schamyl failed in his efforts to preserve their independence. Their dialects, approaching thirty in number, are full of guttural sounds, and are very difficult for Europeans to pronounce. In order to communicate with one another, Lesghians of different tribes use an Arabic or a Turkish patois. The most celebrated tribe for valour is that of the Avars.

The Lesghians are better agriculturists than the rest of the tribes of the Caucasus, and even have beautiful fruit and vegetable gardens. But they are by nature addicted to plunder, and often turn their arms against one another. Most of them are Sunnite Mahometans, retaining some Christian and Pagan customs. However, they drink much wine and smoke to excess. Their wives do most of the work, and are readily divorced.

**The Georgians.**

The Georgians are a group of tribes forming something much more like a nation than the other tribes we have spoken of, although even they include more than a score of allied peoples. The Georgians are by far the most numerous (about a million), inhabiting the lowlands south of the Caucasus and east of the Suram mountains. All the peoples of their kinship are collectively known as Kartvelian, their languages being termed Kartli.

**The Georgian kingdom.**

A Georgian kingdom was founded in the time of Alexander the Great, and existed for over two thousand years. Early in the fourth century, the Georgians adopted Christianity, and at the end of the sixth, joined the Greek Church. In the seventh, eighth, and ninth centuries, they were frequently under the domination of the conquering Mahometans, who at various times enforced their religion upon them. Almost the whole history of Georgia is occupied with wars, and the resistance of invasions. The Mongols were among the most ruthless of their conquerors. Finally both Turks and Persians became such formidable enemies of this little people that the protection of the Russians was sought in the sixteenth and seventeenth centuries. They passed at various subsequent periods under the sway of the Persians and Turks; but the country was finally annexed to Russia in 1801; Imeritia was annexed in 1810; and Gouria in 1829. Georgia is now included in the Russian governments of Tiflis and Kutais.

Physical characters.

The Georgians fully deserve their reputation for beauty. Abundant black hair, large eyes, clear skin, white teeth, supple figures, and small hands are among their characteristics. Their bright, often almost scarlet complexion is due to their immoderate use of wine. The women cannot be said to be as good-looking as the men, partly because of their unintellectual character. They are somewhat cold and unattractive-looking, notwithstanding their good features. On the whole, the Georgians are rather slovenly and dirty, but have considerable gaiety and sociability. They are passionately fond of singing and dancing. Although their gutturals and sibilants are by no means pleasing in song to Western ears, they sing all day long at their work, and in concerted arrangements. Fêtes are numerous, and largely attended, some having a religious object and others a social one; but all being equally accompanied by music and dancing.

GURIAN (GEORGIA).

Singing and dancing.

The Mingrelians.

The Mingrelians and Imeritians are allied races, occupying the western side of the Suram mountains and the basins of the Rion and Ingur, inhabiting a rich and fertile country, with first-rate cattle; but the Mingrelian people, dwelling in the best regions, are the most indolent and unprosperous. They are very finely made, and include people of both dark and fair complexions, the former due to Arab and even negro intermixture. The Mingrelians long suffered under a despotic land system, the lords possessing both soil and workers, and even claiming the priests as serfs. Tyranny of the worst kind was habitually exercised by them, although naturally there were frequent revolts. It was little less than an insult for Russia to propose as a prince for Bulgaria, the descendant of one of the old tyrant lords of Mingrelia. Although serfdom is abolished, the people are not yet greatly elevated. Their diet is largely a kind of porridge; and their clothing is often little but a plain outer garment drawn in by a cord.

**So-called princes.**

The Imeritians are the people occupying the more elevated regions above the Mingrelians. They are a hardier, more industrious, and more prosperous stock; and since their submission to the Russians, have made considerable progress. Having unfavourable conditions to contend with, they meet them vigorously.

**The Imeritians.**

CAUCASIAN.

The Khevsurians, a tribe of a few thousands, seated near the peak of Mount Borbalo, are a curiously mixed people, still savage in no little degree. They include a great variety of feature and figure, and are extremely lean, with large feet and hands, adapted to scaling their mountains, which they do very skilfully, even with heavy burdens. Many of their customs, as regards marriage, childbirth, burial, etc., recall some of the rudest Indian tribes. Although they have adopted Christianity, these people have introduced into it numerous heathen customs, worshipping the god of war, the mother of earth, the angel of the oak, etc. They keep Friday like the Mahometans, do not eat pork, worship sacred trees, and make offerings to the spirits of the earth

**The Khevsurians.**

and the air. Certain priests among them have duties like

A MINGRELIAN.

(*From a Photograph lent by Dr. Beddoe, F.R.S.*)

those of medicine men, exorcists, and witch-doctors, who

do not fail to reap a rich harvest of reward. They are fond of rich garments, and still wear coats of mail and helmets, and a complete apparatus of protection, as well

AN OSSETIAN WARRIOR.
*(From a Photograph lent by Dr. Beddoe, F.R.S.)*

as guns and sabres for attack; this is due to the prevalence of blood revenge, and the constant danger of surprise.

Such is a brief account of some groups of tribes in and

around the Caucasus; but it must be understood, that though the most important have been named, there are many others worthy of notice, which it has been impossible to include. But separate mention must be given to one other group,—the Oss, or Ossetians, of the central Caucasus,—who appear to be an isolated Aryan race, which long ago immigrated into these mountain tracts, and have maintained their individuality ever

**The Ossetians.**

GEORGIAN WOMEN.

since. Some have even compared them to Germans in appearance; being fair, muscular, sluggish, and somewhat ungraceful. They have been ascribed to many different Aryan families; and we shall not detail the many theories started about them. It is certain that they are far inferior in looks to the Circassians. Their language is Aryan in type, but they call themselves Iron, which recalls the Iranian group. Unlike the other mountain tribes near them, the Ossetians use beds, tables, and chairs, shake hands, and salute in European fashion, and brew beer from barley. Many of them have in past times served as mercenary soldiers under neighbouring powers. They did not contest for liberty with the Russians; but submitted to them, and made the most of the change, becoming Greek Christians to please the Russians, though

PEASANT SCENE IN GEORGIA.

they had long been Mahometans. Yet they retain polygamy, and not a few heathen practices.

Caucasia is a true meeting-point of races, and perhaps includes at present more types than ever. Russians from various quarters, Bulgarians, Bohemians, and Cossacks are among the modern settlers, num- **Mixture of types.**

bering about a million and a half. Tartars and Mongols, such as Nogais, Turcomans, Koumiks, Kirghiz, Turks, and Kalmucks, now amount to as many, and are mostly Sunnite Mahometans. The Nogais and other Tartars live in Northern Caucasia, and many still live in tents; but

MAHOMETAN WOMEN OF TIFLIS, HOME AND STREET COSTUME.

there is a large Tartar contingent in South-east Caucasia, who are skilled agriculturists. In the South are many Armenians, Kurds, Persians, and allied "Tats," and Jews of Persian descent; while other Jews are descended from residents for two thousand years.

It is perhaps in the Southern Caucasus that the Tartars are seen to greatest advantage. Indeed, they have been termed the civilisers of the Caucasus. They are active, industrious, serious, and well-conducted, and they are spoken of as showing true integrity and delicate hospitality. They include the best artisans, agriculturists, and shepherds of the country; and in numerous cases have profited by education even beyond the Russians, some being expert linguists. Their language,—the Turkish dialect of Adarbaijan,—is used by all the tribes of the country for intercommunication, and the Tartars act as interpreters. Were it not for the usurious control which many Armenians have acquired over them, they would occupy a commanding influence. They are tolerant, rarely practise polygamy, and allow their wives much freedom, even permitting them to work with uncovered faces. Sunnites and Shiites live in peace together, and do not show animosity to Christians.

**Tartar civilisation.**

GEORGIAN WOMAN.

In some districts the Tartars so skilfully utilise the mountain streams for irrigation that they transform the desert into a garden; and tracts which were formerly populous and fertile, have now been restored to fertility, by the old irrigation canals being redug, but some still remain waste, owing probably to change of climate.

The mountainous districts of Lenkoran, near Baku, which Russia has seized, are subject to earthquakes, which have often wrought damage in Chemaka; and explosions of burning naphtha sometimes occur. The peninsula of Apcheron, on which Baku stands, is a seat of incessant volcanic activity, and contains the famous springs of mineral oil which have made the district so valuable in recent years. Some of the petroleum springs have been so abundant that they had to be allowed to flow away into the Caspian, because no adequate reservoirs were ready to receive them.

Some Suabian colonies from Wurtemberg established themselves around Tiflis and elsewhere about 1817, and have been very successful in agriculture. Although they have not mingled with the surrounding people, the climate appears to have influenced their physique remarkably; they now have dark hair, black eyes, oval and regular features, and they present little resemblance to their kinsfolk at home.

# CHAPTER XVIII.

## The Inhabitants of Turkey in Asia.—I.

**Asia Minor the meeting-place of races—Early Greek colonies—Famous Ionians—Lydian empire—Crœsus—The Lydians Aryans—Syrian domination—The Romans in Asia Minor—The Arabs—The Seljuk Turks—The empire of Roum—The Crusaders—The Mongols—The Osmanli, or Ottoman Turks—Sultan Bajazet—Capture of Constantinople—Armenian history—Gregory the Illuminator—The Anatolian Turks—The Yuruks—Turkish agriculturists—Hospitality and tolerance—Wives—Sufferings and patience of Anatolians—Mixed population—The Greeks of Asia Minor—Success in business—Primitive communities—Levantines—Lingua Franca—The Armenians—Language—Christianity—Armenian Scriptures—Armenian Church—Character of people—Features of women—Women's dress—Marriage—The Kurds—Costume—Religion—Character.**

TURKISH WOMAN FEEDING BIRDS.
*(At window of inner court.)*

AS the great meeting-place of East and West, Asia Minor necessarily includes many people of diverse races. There Mongoloid Turks are face to face with Semitic Arabs; the Aryan Greek meets the Circassian, the Armenian, and the Kurd. It is not surprising then that this territory should in the past have seldom been united under one rule. It has either been parcelled out among a number of small states, or has come under the domination of foreign powers, such as the Roman, the Byzantine, and the Turkish. Still more remarkable has been the history of the southern portion of the Turkish dominions in Asia. The representative of Mahomet to-day controls the remnants of more famous cities than almost any other monarch. Pergamus, Smyrna, Miletus, Halicarnassus, Cæsarea, Iconium, Nineveh, Bagdad, Babylon, Damascus, Palmyra, Tyre, Jerusalem—these names, while man exists, must call up some of the most potent thoughts and feelings. We shall deal first with the northern, and then with the southern portions of Asiatic Turkey.

**Asia Minor the meeting-place of races.**

It can scarcely be asserted that we find anywhere the descendants of the primitive inhabitants of Asia Minor; and it is little more feasible to say who they were. When we first hear of them in history, Greek-colonies had settled in many places on the coasts of Asia Minor; and it is quite certain that the Asiatic Greeks were not less advanced than their western brethren; and, if no Greek city of the East has such a renown as Athens, the group of cities which produced Homer, Thales, Pythagoras, and Herodotus can compare with almost any other.

**Early Greek colonies.**

**Famous Ionians.**

But Greek civilisation had little influence on Asia Minor generally until the rise of the kingdom of Lydia, which emerges from myths and undatable records into history with Gyges (Gugu, or Gog), about 690 B.C. A century later, the Lydian empire included the Asiatic Greek cities and nearly all Asia Minor; and the last king, Crœsus (560–546 B.C.), was the richest monarch of his time. But Cyrus, King of Persia, defeated him, and established Persian preponderance in Asia Minor until Alexander's invasion.

**Lydian empire.**

**Crœsus.**

The old Lydians appear to have been an Aryan people,

although probably including people of more primitive races. They were remarkable for industrial arts and inventions. The oldest known coins belong to them, and they are believed to have invented dice and other games. Herodotus says they were the

**The Lydians Aryans.**

A TURKISH SULTANA'S BEDROOM.

first to establish inns; and they were skilled in sculpture, music, and gymnastic exercises.

After Alexander's death, Asia Minor passed, not without many contentions, under the dominion of Seleucus, and remained a considerable period attached to Syria.

A small kingdom, with Pergamus as centre, remained independent in the North-west, and was enlarged by the Romans after their defeat of Antiochus III., at the battle of Magnesia (B.C. 190).

**Syrian domination.**

**The Romans in Asia Minor.**

Sixty years later, the Romans annexed this kingdom, and it formed their province of Asia. Meanwhile the kingdoms of Bithynia and Pontus, in the northern region, had grown and preserved their independence; and Mithridates of Pontus gave the Romans some of their toughest fighting before he could be conquered. After this, the Roman empire, and their successors in the Byzantine empire, ruled Asia Minor for many centuries. Although the Arab Mahometans frequently made successful inroads, and repeatedly marched through Asia Minor, they did not annex it; and it was reserved for another Mahometan power, that of the Seljuk Turks, to break down the power of the Greek empire in Asia, in A.D. 1071-84.

**The Arabs.**

TURKISH WOMEN IN OUTDOOR COSTUME.

The Seljuks were a family belonging to the Turkish tribe of the Ghuzz, which had attained predominance in Turkestan. They and their allies became Mahometans while settled to the north of the Oxus (Amu-Daria of modern geography). Early in the eleventh century they began a conquering career, first setting up their power at Merv, under Toghrul Beg, then spreading over much of Persia and Armenia, Palestine and Syria, and finally, in 1071, Alp Arslan, nephew of Toghrul, took prisoner the Greek emperor, Romanus Diogenes, and founded the Seljuk empire of Roum in Asia Minor. The Seljuks constituted themselves the defenders of the orthodox Mahometan faith and of the Abbasid Caliphate seated at Bagdad, against the Egyptian Fatimites. A sort of feudal system was established by them, even Christian princes being admitted to it on condition of paying tribute and serving in the Seljuk armies; this system, however, paved the way for the break-up of the Seljuk power, which became divided into several smaller and independent ones. The conqueror Soliman, or Sulaiman, reached the Hellespont, and actually assisted one of the rival claimants to Romanus's throne to gain Constantinople.

**The Seljuk Turks.**

**The empire of Roum.**

Antioch was taken by the Seljuks in 1084, and Nicæa became the seat of their empire; but the first crusaders, under Godfrey de Bouillon, took the new capital in 1097, and defeated and drove out the Turks from much of Asia Minor. The Seljuk sultans retired to Iconium (Konieh), leaving the Greeks in possession of the whole of the coast. Even Iconium was taken in 1190 by Frederick Barbarossa, on his way to Jerusalem. Later, the Seljuks had a fresh lease of power, conquering the Armenian princes of Trebizond and various Mahometan armies of hostile factions, and building fine mosques and other buildings at Iconium and elsewhere. The Mongols now came in contact with them, and succeeded in subduing them in the middle of the thirteenth century.

**The Crusaders.**

**The Mongols.**

All this time the Turks had been growing in numbers in Asia Minor; and the Mongol supremacy did not check this tendency. Towards the end of the 13th century the existing era of Turkish domination commenced with the arrival in Asia Minor of

**The Osmanli or Ottoman Turks.**

GREEKS QUITTING SCIOS (CHIO) IN 1822.

Osman or Othman, a Turk who had been driven westward from Khorasan by Jenghiz Khan, and who first entered the Greek territory of Nicomedia in 1299. His son, Orchan, crossed into Europe and took Gallipoli. His son Amurath conquered all Thrace, and thus the Turkish empire in Europe was securely founded.

**Sultan Bajazet.**

Sultan Bajazet (1389–1402) entirely subdued the Seljuk empire in Asia Minor, and conquered much of Armenia and Mesopotamia, besides making great conquests in Europe. In 1402, however, the great defeat of Angora humbled the Turks beneath the power of Timor. But under Mohammed and Amurath II. the Turkish power again reached a great height, while Mohammed II. in 1453, consummated it by the capture of Constantinople. Selim, early in the sixteenth century, extended the Turkish power over Egypt and Syria. Soliman the Magnificent, besides his great conquests in Europe, augmented his empire in the East at the expense of Persia. From this period Asia Minor has been uninterruptedly held by the Turks, and having become very largely peopled by them, has supplied continual draughts of fine soldiers for Turkish hostilities elsewhere. These furnish the bulk of the Turkish army to-day, the former standing army of janissaries (established in 1360, and composed largely of Christian captives, who became proselytes more fanatical than the Turks, and often deposing and murdering Sultans) having been destroyed by Sultan Mahmoud II. in 1826.

**Capture of Constantinople.**

**Armenian history.**

Passing now to the history of Armenia, so closely connected with Asia Minor, it emerges into clear light only when Alexander the Great conquered it; and subsequently it came under the dominion of the Seleucid dynasty of Syria. About B.C. 190, a Seleucid governor of Eastern Armenia, Artaxias, proclaimed his independence. About the middle of the second century B.C., the great Parthian king, Mithridates I., set his brother Arbaces on the throne of Armenia and his great-grandson, Tigranes II., added Syria, Western Armenia, and many other provinces to his kingdom. But having joined his father-in-law, Mithridates of Pontus, against Rome, he had ultimately to submit to Pompey, and was allowed to keep most of Armenia. His son, Artavasdes, attempting to assert his independence of Rome, was taken prisoner by Antony, and beheaded by Cleopatra, in Alexandria, B.C. 30.

Henceforward for a long time Armenia was in anarchy. In the third century the Christian religion was completely established by the conversion of Prince Gregory, known as the Illuminator; but soon afterwards Armenia was partitioned between the Persian and Roman empires.

**Gregory the Illuminator.** The Greek empire, succeeding the Roman, held sway over Armenia, and fought with Persia, and later with the Turks and Mongols; and at times an independent line of princes ruled part of the country. In modern times Armenia has been shared between Russia, Persia, and Turkey, by far the greater number of the people being under the latter.

**The Anatolian Turks.** Leaving out of question the primitive populations of Asia Minor, we know of Greek, Arab, Turkish, Gaulish (Celtic), Persian, Armenian, Kurdish and Circassian immigrants; but there is no question that the Turk at the present day claims the first place, in numbers at any rate. As a migration in masses, followed by settlement and multiplication, the Turkish is the last great one prior to that which has planted the European races so firmly in America. One reason for its success is said to be the fact, that the elevated plateau forming the inland portion of the country, with its salt lakes and morasses, afforded a sufficient resemblance to the wild steppes of Turkestan from which the invaders came, and thus it was possible for them to lead much the same kind of nomad life. But the modern Turk of Anatolia is no longer proud of his national name, which has almost degenerated into a term of reproach, as if the word Turk or Anatolian signified a clown. The term "Yerli" is much more to his taste.

**The Yuruks.** The Yuruks of western and south-western Asia Minor, the descendants of some of the earliest Turkish immigrants, still lead a nomad life, and for the most part live in

ARMENIAN WOMAN.

tents covered with goat-skins, or low huts roofed with branches and stifling with smoke. These poeple are Mahometans only nominally, and their women do not veil. There are hundreds of their small village encampments scattered through Asia Minor, their place in the centre and north-east being taken by Turcomans, who are rather more disposed to a settled life, and not unfrequently cultivate the soil and live in permanent villages. All these have many sheep and goats, and frequently breed camels.

**Turkish agriculturists.**

The true Turks are in the main agriculturists, with brownish complexions, black eyes, dark hair, and slightly prominent cheeks. They are rather a coarse-looking race, physically strong, but neither very adaptable nor skilful, slow and deliberate, and encumbered by heavy clothing. Unlike the official or the European Turk, they are naturally honest and truth-telling, for which they are ridiculed by their Greek and Armenian neighbours. They are both kind and hospitable, welcoming and assisting strangers, and treating them as honoured visitors, placing everything at their disposal. They are also for the most part much more tolerant as to religious matters than the Christians of various sects and nationalities by whom they are surrounded.

**Hospitality and tolerance.**

TARTAR GIRL IN EAST ARMENIA.

Their diet is simple, rarely including meat; bread, eggs, and milk are the staple foods, and even vegetables and fruit are little used. Coffee, freshly roasted and pounded,

ARMENIAN WOMEN OF PONTUS COAST.

is as universal as tobacco-smoking; with these the Mahometan Turk is content, and desires no alcohol.

As a rule, the Asiatic Turks have but one wife, some whole cities not including a case of polygamy. In the country, however, the Turk often has a second wife, "to have another servant," he says; but family peace and fidelity are the rule. Wives are well treated; children brought up with kindness and equal rights. Animals, too, are for the most part very well treated. The stork perches on the roof of the Turk, and avoids that of the Greek.

**Wives.**

Not being such keen business men as the Greeks and Armenians, the Anatolian peasants are often cheated, and pay high interest for money to the rascally money-lenders. Not being skilled at concealing any wealth they may acquire, they are fleeced by the officials more successfully than the Greeks and Armenians. In fact, what with conscription, billeting, and purveying for officials, the Anatolian Turk suffers pitiably, and may well be dejected and depressed; it is needless to say that he rarely receives his proper pay as a soldier. Fatalism and resignation make the Anatolians not resist; and they are gradually being crushed. Yet they receive numerous reinforcements from people of other nationalities, brought into Asia in Turkish armies, and as exiles or voluntary immigrants. Among these are Albanians, Bosniaks, and Mahometan Bulgarians and Nogai Tartars. Turks also, says Reclus, are the officials, sons of Georgian or Circassian women, and descended from all the nations which have contributed to the harems. Among the Osmanli also are classed the descendants of Arabs and of negroes from every quarter of Africa, brought by the slave-trade. In many cities of Asia Minor a great proportion of the population is evidently crossed with negroes.

**Sufferings and patience of Anatolians.**

**Mixed population.**

The Greeks of Asia Minor, abounding in all the coast districts, occupy the Ionian coast and islands almost exclusively. They are for the most part the descendants of the old Ionians, but can scarcely be considered a pure race. It is by their religious profession and practices that they are most clearly distinguishable. Instead of Greeks being expelled by the Turks, as was formerly so often the case, the Greeks are gaining ground on the Turks, by their unscrupulousness

**The Greeks of Asia Minor.**

and keenness in money matters and trickery. It cannot be denied that the Greek shows himself much more capable—more of an all-round man of business; and that, taking up every learned as well as mercantile profession, he manages to get hold of the best things for himself. His schools are an absorbing care. The Turk was a warrior developed out of a predatory nomad; ceasing to be a warrior, he seems to lack the

Success in business.

ARMENIAN HOME SCENE.

power of becoming much else, and is declining. Many Greeks by descent, however, use the Turkish language; but, thanks partly to their religion, the Asiatic Greeks are all imbued with the sentiment of patriotism, and feel themselves one with the inhabitants of Greece. Some time there may yet be a Greek empire which shall include Asia Minor.

Greek populations, scarcely changed in the course of

two thousand years, may still be found, not only in the Greek Archipelago, but also in the islands of Carpathos (Scarpanto), Rhodes, and the neighbouring islands, and in some valleys on the coast of Caria. In many of the islands still linger survivals of very primitive times. In the interior of Cos and Mitylene daughters alone inherit, and make proposals of marriage; and when

**Primitive communities.**

IN A TARTAR HOUSE, ARMENIA.

the eldest daughter has chosen her husband, the father gives up his home to her.

At the other end of Asia Minor, near Armenia, there remain communities of Greeks speaking their old Greek dialect with little modification. Thus, at Pharazeh, on the border of Cappadocia and Cilicia, the Greeks are proud of their language, as being purer than the modern (Romaic)

Greek, and keep up the tradition of their having come from the Peloponnesus. On the other hand, if these stick to the old paths, many of other races join the growing nationality of the Greeks; many Bulgarians, Wallachians, Circassians, and even Cossacks, learn Greek, and as far as possible become one with them.

For centuries there was established, in the ports and

ARMENIAN GIRLS FROM ANTI-TAURUS.

mercantile towns of the Levant, a class of traders known as Levantines, who were mostly Italians by race, and Roman Catholics, who carried on the greater part of the trade. There had grown up with their traffic a sort of "lingua Franca" of words without inflexion, chiefly Italian, but also including Spanish, Provençal, French, Greek, Turkish, and other terms; in fact, one might call it a counterpart of "pigeon English" as spoken at Hong Kong; but this is giving way, as indeed the Levantines themselves are,

**Levantines.**

**Lingua Franca.**

before the advance of the Greeks; but French is becoming largely used in commercial intercourse. Of the numerous Jews, Circassians, Abkasians, gipsies, etc., of Asia Minor, no particular mention need here be made.

**The Armenians.**

What the Greeks are to Western Asia Minor, the Armenians are to the rest, being especially congregated in Armenia proper. These people, distributed though they are between three powers, preserve still their national character and feeling, and are perhaps as skilful in drawing attention to their grievances and making the most of them as they are in doing business.

KURDISH WOMEN.

It is certain that they are not more oppressed than the Anatolian Turks. They call themselves "Haïk," attributing the name to their descent from Haïk, a great-grandson of Japhet.

**Language.**

The Armenian language is undoubtedly connected more or less closely with the Iranian group. It has 38 letters, and is written from left to right. Its character is rough and consonantal, and it is accented on the last syllable. There are no gender signs, gender being denoted by the words for man or woman being prefixed to a word. The nouns have seven cases. In syntax Armenian approaches classical Greek. The extant Armenian literature was developed by the adoption of Christianity, and at first consisted largely of translations from other languages. The Armenian version of the Scriptures was made early in the fifth century, and is of considerable value on account of its antiquity, and its representing Hebrew and Greek texts which are not now extant. Numerous other works have been preserved in Armenian, the originals of which had been lost; such as the Chronicle of Eusebius and some of the works of Philo, the great Alexandrian philosopher. Besides the fifth century, the twelfth and thirteenth centuries were notable periods in Armenian literature, and produced numerous histories and theological works. The last century witnessed a revival of Armenian letters, which still continues; and numerous magazines and newspapers are published in Armenian. Much of this may be attributed to the interest which Western, and especially American, Christians have taken in the Armenian Church, one of the most ancient now existing; but it is also attributable to the keen intellect of the Armenians, which, if associated with a more honest national character, may yet have a great future.

**Christianity.**

**Armenian Scriptures.**

The Armenian Church is almost identical in doctrine with the Greek Church. The seven sacraments are administered, and prayers for the pardon of the dead are used; but purgatory and indulgences are denied. The Church has four patriarchs (their seats being at Constantinople, Jerusalem, Sis, and Etchmiadzin), archbishops, bishops, doctors of theology, and black and white clergy, the former being monks (alone eligible for the higher offices), and the latter parish priests. The priests may marry before ordination, but not after. The priesthood is hereditary, and, although a priest's heir may follow a secular calling, he must give it up and become a priest when his father dies.

**Armenian Church.**

Though outwardly very servile to their rulers, the Armenians really despise them. They are not at all warlike, and rather timid and silent. Their women are kept seriously at work, and not treated by their husbands as equals. The Armenians are much attached to their country and their home, and have no desire to be absorbed by the Russians. **Character of people.**

The Armenians are a fine-looking people, with large eyes and mouths, long, somewhat hooked, noses, and dark-olive complexions. "The expressive and swimming black eyes of the women," says Mr. Creagh, "always shaded behind lashes of unusual length and thickness, lend their clear olive complexions a peculiar charm, heightened perhaps by a certain diffidence or timidity which leaves them when they talk. Although inclined, even when still young, to obesity, their waists are small, their arms rounded, their throats firm, and the thorax largely developed. Waddling about the streets, the greatest Armenian beauties look just like animated bundles of rags. In their own homes, and in a loose undress, the girls present a very different appearance. Their ordinary costume, when they are not disfigured by what they call ornamenting themselves for company, and when they loll about on cushions, consists of a pair of very loose, bright-coloured trousers, secured tightly over the ankle, so as to expose the naked foot; a chemise, laying bare the throat, fastened tightly round the waist with a gold, silver, or velvet belt, and reaching down outside the pantaloons no further than the knee; together with a kind of embroidered waistcoat, cut square, very open in front, and secured with a string just below the bosom; but beyond these three garments they wear nothing else. Their hair, usually silky and of exuberant growth, falls down the back in a great thick plait, tied up at the end with bunches of ribbons." When going out, they cover themselves with a bright-coloured gown, and this with another thickly-wadded garment, the head and shoulders being enveloped in a thin white shawl, which is tightly drawn round their faces (all but the eyes) at the approach of men. **Features of women.** **Women's dress.**

Marriages are largely arranged by mothers or by go-betweens. Polygamy is forbidden, although divorce is not uncommon. There is a good deal of love-making, and many marriages are truly love matches. In the rural parts, and where there are few Turks, the women go about quite unveiled and bareheaded, and simple virtues abound.

**Marriage.**

The Armenians of the present day scarcely number two millions, about half of whom are Turkish subjects (in Europe and Asia), and three-quarters of a million Russian subjects; the remainder being in Persia and other countries.

**The Kurds.**

The Kurds are, like the Armenians, distributed between the Turkish, Russian, and Persian empires, inhabiting largely the Kurdistan highlands forming the Turkish governments of Van and Diarbekir. They are scarcely so distinct a race as the Armenians, being largely crossed in some districts with Turcomans, Armenians, and Persians. But they may be regarded as predominantly Iranian. Some of them are of a coarse and ugly type, while others are among the most handsome and haughty of Eastern populations. Many have receding foreheads, wide eyebrows, long eyelashes, large mouths, aquiline noses, and prominent chins. The women are unveiled, and have usually regular features, large eyes, long and black hair, and robust figures. Many wear a ring through the nostril. They are even known to bear arms in case of need, and show great courage. Their children are good-looking and very attractive.

**Costume.**

The Kurd is above all things picturesque and self-decorative. He loves bright colours, rich stuffs, lofty head-dresses and hats, heavy girdles loaded with pistols and knives, and fine decorated spears. These are of course most generally possessed by the upper class, or nobles, who, as a rule, are of a heavier type, though fine-looking, than the lower caste, or Gurans. Their dialects are varied, but are in the main Iranian. Many are Sunnite Mahometans; but in the heart of the mountains are settlements of tribes known as Kizil-bashis, etc., still almost heathen, mingling some reverence for Mahomet-

**Religion.**

KURDISH AMAZON (KARA FATMA).

anism with regard for some supposed living incarnation of the Deity.

On the whole, the Kurd in his haughtiness has a bad time of it, and a worse reputation. Neither Turks nor Persians like him, and they will believe any evil of him. He is certainly given to plundering expeditions, and to attacking and maltreating Christians in particular. Yet within their own borders the Kurds are true and hospitable, and only shed blood in family feuds. Their women are well treated, and have more freedom than among Turks and Persians. It appears, however, that the Kurds are diminishing, and will gradually become absorbed in the surrounding peoples.

**Character.**

The modern Nestorians are a people who claim to represent the ancient Chaldeans, and the early Christians of Mesopotamia, and speak a dialect of Syriac, having spread from Syria eastward in the fifth century, after the banishment of Nestorius from the Roman empire. Nestorius, patriarch of Constantinople from 428 to 431, had protested against the use of the title "Mother of God" for the Virgin Mary. Some of these people repudiate the name Nestorians and the implied connection with the followers of Nestorius. They inhabit eastern Kurdistan, and are also found on Persian territory west of Lake Urmia. Early in the last century the Church of Rome instituted missions from Aleppo to the Chaldeans of Mesopotamia, and has made many converts, who conform more or less strictly to the Roman rites.

**The Nestorians.**

The Nestorians of the Kurdistan highlands long maintained their independence in their inaccessible homes, and even in some parts held the Kurds in subjection. But in 1843 the Mahometan Kurds, encouraged by the Turkish rulers, attacked them in force, massacred ten thousand men, sold the women into slavery, and compelled the boys to become Mahometans. Among those who remain, stock-breeding is the principal occupation. Their dwellings are very plain, of one room, sometimes underground; and they make their own utensils. Some of them are skilful basket-makers and spinners, but most are very poor; yet they will share any food they have with a stranger. Their clergy are extremely ignorant, but are much revered, like their creed and their churches. The people also submit to hereditary village chiefs, called meliks or "kings."

# CHAPTER XIX.

## The Inhabitants of Turkey in Asia.—II.

A WOMAN OF GERMAN COLONY: SYRIA.

**The Accadians—Assyrian empire—Babylonian empire—Vast ruins—Physical character of Assyrians—Food and drink—Assyrian bas-reliefs—Cuneiform writing—Early literature—Early traditions of creation, flood, etc.—Astronomy and astrology—Historical records—Physical character of Babylonians—Early Syrians—The Romans and Arabs—The inhabitants of Palestine—Subjection to foreign nations—Dispersion of the Jews—Asiatic Jews—The Beni Israel—The Aramaic languages—The Phœnicians—Phœnicia conquered—Phœnician religion—Arabs—Syrians—Syrian Christians—The Cypriotes.**

SYRIA, Palestine, Mesopotamia,—scenes of past life that still lives, that is still being unravelled,—are certainly more interesting by reason of their history than of their present condition. Early civilisation, mighty empires, intercourse between diverse peoples, intermixture, spread of languages, religions, and arts—all these combine to make the southern portion of the Turkish empire in Asia of deep interest.

Babylon is the Greek form of Babel, the gate of the

gods. It was preceded in predominance over Babylonia and Assyria by several cities, the first of which we have any account being Ur. But still earlier the plain of Mesopotamia was peopled by the Accad or Accadians, (that is, highlanders,) who descended from the hill-country lying to the north, and were almost certainly a Mongoloid people allied to the Finno-Ugrian group. The earliest sovereign of whom we have any account reigned at Ur, on the right bank of the Euphrates, over all Babylonia, and built many vast brick temples to the moon, to the sun, to Bel, and Ishtar. At this early date brick-making had assumed vast proportions, bitumen being used instead of mortar. Many architectural devices testify to the skill of these Accadian people; but they also originated the cuneiform system of writing, which, in an imperfect form, they brought with them from the North, and they had considerable artistic skill in carving signet rings. Later, various cities gained temporary supremacy in Babylonia, and meanwhile the Semitic element from Arabia and Syria had been gaining more and more predominance, and the Semitic language was adopted by the State.

**The Accadians.**

Without attempting to estimate how long civilised rulers had existed in Babylon, we may say that certainly the kingdom of Assyria had become powerful in the fourteenth century B.C., and that frequent wars arose between Assyria and Babylon. Tiglath-Pileser I., who became king of Assyria about B.C. 1120, took Babylon and extended his empire to the Mediterranean, the Caspian, and the Persian Gulf. But his conquests did not last, and it was not till three centuries later that Assyria again grew powerful. Assur-nasir-pal and Shalmaneser were then conspicuous conquerors; and the latter, in B.C. 854, defeated Benhadad, king of Syria, and Ahab, king of Israel. Tiglath-pileser II., a usurper (B.C. 744), raised Assyria to an unrivalled position, Babylon becoming a mere province of the empire; he destroyed the kingdoms of Damascus and Hamath, and reduced Israel to vassalage. Sargon, his successor, attacked and defeated the Egyptians. Under Sennacherib (B.C. 705), Esar-

**Assyrian empire.**

haddon, and Assur-bani-pal (Sardanapalus), the Assyrian empire rose to unrivalled power, conquering Egypt, Media, much of Asia Minor, and extending almost to India; but, as so often happens, the greatest success was the prelude to complete ruin. Towards the end of the seventh century B.C., Nabopolassar, viceroy of Babylonia, made himself independent, and his son Nebuchadnezzar (B.C. 604–561) raised Babylon to the height which Assyria had previously held. But this empire was not as long-lived as that of Assyria. It fell before the prowess of Cyrus, king of Persia, B.C. 539; and now, and for many centuries, Mesopotamia has been little better than a heap of ruins.

**Babylonian empire.**

How great these ruins are, we yet realise but imperfectly; and only a small proportion of the treasures of art and information they contain has yet been recovered. The Babylonians were perhaps the greatest builders in brick the world has ever seen. Vast and lofty temples of brick, stage upon stage, surmounted by a shrine and observatory, attest the religious zeal of Babylon; while in less religious Assyria the wide courts of less lofty palaces of stone rise not more than two stories high. The clay coffins of Babylon astonish us by their number, while Assyria has left us no tombs.

**Vast ruins.**

The ancient Assyrians, as depicted in their sculptures, are purely Semitic, having straight, full foreheads, large almond-shaped eyes, aquiline noses, rather thick lips, strong chins, and abundant curly black hair and beard. They were at the same time very muscular and large limbed. Their cruelty, treachery, and arrogance, as well as their courage, are evident from the scenes depicted by them. They wore plain short-sleeved tunics, reaching to the knees, and girdled at the waist; and it does not appear that they covered their abundant hair. Tunics and cloaks of ornamental character were worn by the powerful, and on special occasions. Simple wheaten or barley cakes, with fruit, formed the staple diet of the poor; but the soldiery fed on meat. Wine was drunk abundantly at feasts, and music was a favourite accompaniment—

**Physical character of Assyrians.**

**Food and drink.**

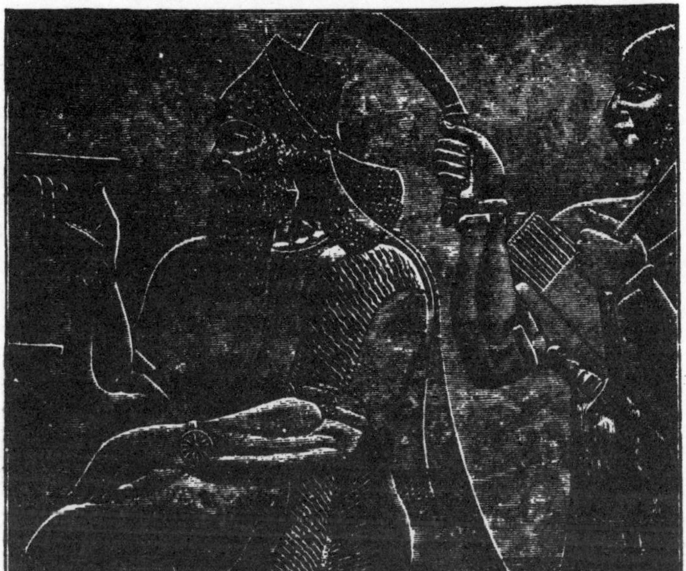

ASSUR-NASIR-PAL, KING OF ASSYRIA, ON HIS THRONE, 885–860, B.C.
*(From a Bas-relief in the British Museum.)*

wind, string, and percussion instruments being varied and numerous.

The chief monuments of art left by the Assyrians are bas-reliefs, of which many are now at the British Museum.

**Assyrian bas-reliefs.** They are singularly heavy in style, and for the most part represent everything in profile; their value is extreme in conveying to us ideas of the men and animals of nearly three thousand years ago. Animals, especially lions and horses, are very well delineated. Their religion was polytheistic, Assur being the father and supreme god, while Ishtar was the chief goddess. Many other deities were borrowed from Babylon. Spirits, or genii, chiefly malicious, were also held in reverence. The images of the gods were worshipped.

It is possible that much of our Western civilisation may be really traced back to the Accadians the early

**Cuneiform writing.** conquerors of Mesopotamia. Whether the Accadians were the original inventors of writing it is impossible to say; but they practised it in an extremely simple hieroglyphic form by representing the objects themselves; later they used symbols, or ideographs, and combined two or more to express complex ideas. Later, these signs were connected with certain sounds, and words were formed by combining them. Whether or not leather was the first writing-tablet, clay tablets or bricks, written upon when wet, and afterwards burnt to make them permanent, superseded them, and constitute

**Early literature.** the extant Accadian, Assyrian, and Babylonian literature. From it we learn that the Accadians had the germs of Greek arts and sciences, philosophy and mythology. As far as literary invention went, the Assyrians and Babylonians were but imitators of the Accadians. They took their writing and modified it into the regular cuneiform or wedge-form, since writing on stiff clay made anything but wedges and straight lines difficult to write. A vast number of the Ninevite books are but translations of Accadian ones into the Semitic language; and in some cases the two are given side by side. Large numbers of books belonging to the library of Assur-bani-pal at Nineveh, formed about B.C. 670 (discovered in 1850), have been brought to England, and are in the British Museum. The library contained historical and mythological, religious, legal, geographical, astronomical, poetical, zoological and commercial works, besides royal proclamations and petitions to the king. Among them are narratives of the Creation, of the Deluge, of the solar hero Izdubar, with his twelve adventures representing the months, and many others, which evidently are earlier forms of the more fully-developed Hebrew and Greek traditions. From the early spirit-religion, which deified every object or force of nature, the Accadians progressed to the worship of the sun and moon and sky; and their poets expressed a consciousness of sin and need of a redeemer, in language very much akin to that of the Psalms. Their religious poems were formed into a kind of prayer-book for use in religious services; and the Assyrian and Babylonian priests long afterwards repeated these hymns in the ancient Accadian language.

**Early traditions of creation, flood, etc.**

The surprising knowledge of astronomical facts by the ancient Babylonians is well known; but they were led by fanciful interpretations into creating a system of astrology which became famous, though valueless. Nevertheless, many of their observations have their value even now. Among other valuable records we have chronologies drawn up with the utmost exactitude, and "contract tablets," which give details of all kinds of mercantile transactions, and show that the ancient Semite, like the modern Jew, was bent on trade, and successful in it.

**Astronomy and astrology.**

Both Assyrian and Babylonian kings were accustomed to have historical records made upon prisms, often called cylinders, inscribed upon six or ten sides, and bury one in each corner of their new palaces; and many of these have been disinterred. One of Assur-bani-pal's, in the British Museum, has no fewer than 1500 lines upon it.

**Historical records.**

"In stature," says Mr. E. A. Budge ("Babylonian Life and History"), "the Babylonians were short and thick-set; they had the characteristic Semitic nose, thick lips, and 'oblique eyes.' Their hair was thick and curly, and of course black. They wore dyed raiment, probably of a brilliant colour, girdles round their waist, and sandals on their feet." Thus we must conclude the few details we can find space for, of the mighty peoples who studied the stars and ruled vast empires long before our land contained any but rude tribes.

**Physical character of Babylonians.**

The word Syria is really an abbreviation of Assyria; but after the fall of the Assyrian empire the term became limited to the country west of the Euphrates, although the people west of the Tigris continued to be called Syrians. The modern Semitic people occupying Syria are most accurately termed Aramæans. When we first hear of the inhabitants of Syria, they were divided into small tribes around towns or cities. But there is much doubt as to the origin, character, and achievements of the people known from Egyptian records as "Cheta," who had a powerful kingdom or confederation extending far beyond Syria, with a capital called Carchemish—and who have been identified in modern times with the Hittites. Many believe them to have been a Semitic people dominated by a Manchu or Tartar race, represented on monuments, wearing a pigtail. We must not here dwell on the varying fortunes of the kingdom of Damascus, or other small States in Syria. The dominant fact is, that Syria, lying between Asia and Egypt, was a battle-field and subject of contest of most of the great empires of the East. Antioch, founded about 300 B.C., became the seat of the Seleucid kingdom. Pompey added Syria to the Roman dominions in 64 B.C., and Antioch grew still greater as the seat of the provincial government. In the seventh century, Syria was conquered by the Mahometan Arabs, and Damascus became the capital of the first Ommyad caliph. In 750, however, the capital was transferred to Bagdad. After partial possession by the Crusaders, the Mongols, and the Mamelukes, Syria fell under the Ottoman Turks in 1516, and they have ever since held it.

**Early Syrians.**

**The Romans and Arabs.**

Palestine, like Syria, appears to have been inhabited

by non-Semitic people at a very early time; but when historical records begin, it was already occupied by Semitic tribes—some commercial, on the coast, some agricultural, some nomadic and pastoral. When the Israelites settled in Palestine, they partly assimilated, partly drove out or slew the previous in- **The inhabitants of Palestine.**

JEWESS OF PALESTINE.

habitants. Under Moses, who had brought them out of Egypt, they enlarged and intensified their belief in Jehovah as the one God of Israel, the God of righteousness, who cared for and led His people and gave them laws. At first, the nomadic patriarchal government of families and clans continued; later, the priesthood of Jehovah became the resource for determining important questions, and a series of warlike leaders gained authority as judges over portions of the land. Meanwhile, the Israelites yielded to a considerable extent to the Canaanite worship

JEW OF PALESTINE.

of Baal as the giver of corn, wine, and oil. The subsequent growth and conquests of the Philistines led to the selection of a king as national leader; and David, the second king, established his capital at Jerusalem, and besides subduing the Philistines, extended his rule over several peoples to the east of the river Jordan. But not long after the death of his son Solomon, who had built the Temple at Jerusalem as the centre of national religious life, the young kingdom was broken into two, the Northern being seated at Samaria. Numerous conflicts between the two weakened them, and they became a prey to Assyrian and Egyptian alliances or attacks, being ultimately reduced to a state of abject subjection to Assyria and Babylon. The Northern kingdom suffered first, and most completely. The Southern people retained in captivity so much of the essence of their religion that they formed a sufficient community to return and revive their ancient system with further developments. In the main, these depended on ceremonial observances, which have always been so powerful with the Jews; and the true Israelite kept proudly aloof from the Semitic peoples who had occupied the land in their absence. A complicated system of traditional observances grew up around the Temple; and the upper-class Jews at the time of Christ enforced a highly artificial and pedantic ceremonial. Persia, Alexander, the Seleucid monarchs of Syria, Egypt, Rome, in succession dominated Palestine; and the latter finally crushed its life by the destruction of Jerusalem in A.D. 70. Since then, Palestine has been a comparatively insignificant portion of Syria, only becoming more conspicuous when the Crusaders endeavoured to wrest it from the Saracens.

**Subjection to foreign nations.**

Before the Christian era, the dispersion of the Jews had commenced with the various captivities which they had undergone. Alexander the Great's successors encouraged the settlement of Jews in Asia Minor, Syria, and Egypt. Intercourse with the Greeks profoundly influenced Jewish life and thought; and in many cases they adapted themselves greatly to their surroundings, retaining their meetings for worship as a secret bond of national union. The Greek language became generally used by them, instead of the Aramæan, which had come into use after the disuse of old Hebrew. The trading instinct of the Jews led them to follow the Roman arms wherever they penetrated.

**Dispersion of the Jews.**

At present Asiatic Turkey does not contain more than 100,000 to 130,000 Jews, a large proportion of whom live in Smyrna, Bagdad, and Aleppo. Fifteen thousand Jews still live in Jerusalem, most of them engaged in studying the Talmud, or collection of Jewish traditional learning, being supported by contributions from Jews all over the world. The Polish and German Jews in Jerusalem keep themselves distinct from the Spanish and Portuguese Jews, the latter adopting an Oriental style of dress.

**Asiatic Jews.**

We may here briefly refer to the other Jews of Asia. There are settlements of Jews in Kurdistan, and in the plain of Urmia, speaking an Aramaic dialect, which they write in Hebrew characters. Altogether, there are about 10,000 Jews in Persia. It is said that they all wear charms as safeguards against the evil eye, diseases, and enemies. Turkestan contains many Jews; and small colonies, long settled, are found in China, quite distinct from the recently-settled European Jews. There are about 15,000 Jews in Arabia.

In Bombay there is the remarkable settlement of the Beni Israel, 5,000 in number, chiefly artisans. They say that they were shipwrecked on the coast more than a thousand years ago. Their vernacular is Marathi, but their features and their observance of Jewish rites prove their descent, though their precise history cannot now be ascertained.

**The Beni Israel.**

A word or two must be devoted to the Aramaic languages. They are named from Aram, which originally meant the same as Syria, including Mesopotamia, but excluding Palestine. So the Aramaic languages are those Semitic forms of speech which were spoken in these countries. They had few vowels, and very few forms of declension by internal changes, so characteristic of Hebrew. Chaldee and Syriac are the two main Aramaic languages, that known as Chaldee having been adopted by the Jews in the Babylonian captivity, and being the language of the Book of Daniel; and from that time there was a gradual substitution of this dialect for old Hebrew in Palestine itself. Syriac

**The Aramaic languages.**

had a much greater literary development, having been first placed on a sound basis by the Peshito translation of the Bible, and subsequently becoming the vehicle for much religious as well as philosophical literature from the ourth to the tenth century. It adopted many Greek words and forms of thought. After the tenth and eleventh centuries it was superseded by Arabic, as also was the Samaritan dialect of Aramaic (in which we have a version of the Pentateuch).

The coastland of Southern Syria and Northern Palestine has become known as Phœnicia, through the commercial and colonising enterprise of the Phœnicians, who, whether Semitic by race or not, spoke a Semitic language, and showed many resemblances to the Semitic peoples. The name Phœnician was given them by the Greeks; they called themselves Canaanites. Tyre and Sidon were already great cities in the time of Solomon, while the Homeric poems represent them as trading in Greek cities. Their great industries were glass-making, embroidery, and purple dyeing. All these they were formerly believed to have invented; but this is now considered doubtful. They certainly perfected them, and spread their knowledge widely, as well as that of writing and the alphabet. We cannot here follow the spread and settlements of the Phœnicians, which had so profound an influence on the ancient world; but we may note that they procured gold and silver from Spain, tin from Britain, and amber from Northern Europe, and founded colonies in Sicily, Spain, North and West Africa; and they appear to have circumnavigated Africa about 600 B.C.; but at this time Phœnicia was already declining.

The Phœnicians.

Phœnicia was at various times attacked by the Assyrians, and frequently had to pay tribute to them. About 720 B.C. the Assyrians took Tyre; and from that time Phœnicia grew continually weaker, and during the same period many of the Phœnician colonies were subdued by their enemies. Nebuchadnezzar took Tyre, after a siege of thirteen years, in B.C. 574, and in 538 the Persians succeeded to the Babylonians as rulers of Phœnicia. Finally, Alexander the Great took Tyre

Phœnicia conquered.

in B.C. 332, and sold 30,000 of the inhabitants as slaves. Thenceforward Phœnicia ceased to have a distinct existence although Tyre and Sidon remained wealthy and important towns.

**Phœnician religion.** The Phœnician religion may be briefly described as an idolatry of the sun, moon, and earth, and of rivers (as sacred to gods), trees (sacred to goddesses), and mountains. Baal, the sun god, and Astarte, the moon-goddess, are well known to us through the Old Testament, as having tempted the Israelites to idolatry. The Phœnicians set up symbolic stone pillars, or fantastic images, and sacrificed oxen and male animals, sometimes even resorting to human sacrifices.

**Arabs.** The majority of the present inhabitants of the southern portion of Asiatic Turkey, as dealt with in this chapter, are Arabs and Mahometans, a great proportion of them being Bedouins, or nomad tribes; but there are many settled Arabs in the towns and their neighbourhood. Arab life and character will be dealt with in the next chapter. It need only be said that the Arabs form a very difficult element for the Turks to manage, that they act very independently of government, and that many of them exact a good deal of blackmail from the settled population.

**Syrians.** It is a disputed point how far the present population of Syria includes elements derived from the early inhabitants. They are rather a blend of very many races, predominantly Semitic; but it is certain that the Syrians who are not clearly Arabs may be distinguished by a general community of type, having regular features, a well-formed nose, fine almond-shaped eyes, and very expressive countenances. They are very intelligent and have much resource, being nearly as clever bargainers and liars as the Armenians or Greeks of the Levant. Added to this, they are extremely vain. Arabic is spoken almost everywhere.

The Syrian Christians are very numerous, and have been favourably spoken of by many writers, not only for their intelligence, but for their moral character. Many Christian missions have been established in various localities. The Lebanon Christians are known as Maronites, the name being derived from Maron, a celebrated recluse of the fourth century. They have a sort of connection with the Roman Church, but retain married priests and many other peculiarities. The district is governed by a Christian pasha. The Druses, the hereditary enemies of the Maronites, profess a sort of Unitarianism which Mussulmans do not recognise; but they have many half-pagan beliefs and practices. Many of them have become converts to Christianity.

**Syrian Christians.**

The Island of Cyprus, leased and controlled in 1878 by Great Britain, has had a chequered history, was early colonised from Phœnicia, from Greece, and from Egypt, and has always had a very mixed population. The vicissitudes of its history are too numerous to enter upon. The Turks in 1570-71, took it from the Venetians, and retained it till they handed it over to Great Britain.

The population of Cyprus largely consists of Greeks of the Greek Church, speaking a special Cypriot dialect of Greek. Many of the Mahometans, whether Turks, Syrians, or Arabs, also speak Greek. The inhabitants are more simple-mannered, less passionate, less fiery than the Cretans. Poverty and want of enterprise have become acclimatised among them under the rule of the Turks.

**The Cypriotes.**

"The dress of the peasants," says Mrs. Scott-Stevenson ("Our Home in Cyprus"), "is picturesque, and certainly becoming to young people; yellow or crimson shoes, short white socks, loose white trousers fastened at the ankle, a skirt of light cotton, and a richly embroidered bodice (generally in velvet), cut in a low square on the bosom, which is covered with a transparent piece of worked muslin. Innumerable glass bangles on the arms complete the costume. On their heads they wear a silk handkerchief tightly fastened across the top, and holding back two long plaits of hair. Bunches of jessamine and sweet-scented geranium-leaves are fastened on one side, and on the other a half-wreath of worsted and silk flowers on wire."

# CHAPTER XX.

## The Arabs.

ARABIAN EMIR'S WIFE.

**Origin—Early history—The Koreysh—Mahomet—The Holy War—Removal of the Caliphate—The Wahhabees—Wars of conquest—Mehemet Ali—Present states—The Bedouins—The Sheikhs—Mode of life—Physical characters—Manners—Clothing—Arab horses and other animals—The settled Arabs—Slaves—Hospitality—Clothing—Arab towns—Modern influence—Holy places.**

Origin.

MR. W. G. PALGRAVE, in his masterly article on Arabia in the Encyclopædia Britannica, is inclined to assign to the pure Arabs a community of origin with the Hamitic races of north-eastern Africa. The term "Himyar," or dusky, applied, now to the ruling class, now to the entire nation, supports this view. The Mustareb Arabs of the North have evidently mixed much with Asiatic peoples, both Semitic and Mongoloid. But the Arab as a whole, is, perhaps, as pure an example of a special race of mankind as we can find; and this may be accounted for by the character of his physical surroundings, having impressed themselves upon his physique, and selected those fitted for the wild desert life.

Before the rise of Mahometanism, Arabia was peopled by the present Arab races, the monarchs of Yemen having ruled over the southern half of the peninsula for many centuries. Other lesser monarchies were dotted over the vast country; but the central parts

Early history.

ARABS.

were peopled by wilder, more energetic "Mustareb" tribes, nomadic and pastoral, much akin to the Hebrews. In the fifth century there appeared among them a leader of great ability, Koleyb, who, about 500 A.D., slew the agent sent from Sana, the capital of Yemen, to collect tribute, and endeavoured to form a confederacy of Arabs under his leadership. The sixth century was occupied in conflicts by which these tribes were widening their rule and developing a national feeling. Early in the seventh century, the clan of Koreysh, settled

The Koreysh.

near Mecca, gained the control of the ancient temple or shrine, the Kaaba, of Mecca, which even then was the resort of pilgrims, thus gaining the possession of the accumulated offerings of ages, engaging in Red Sea commerce at the port of Jeddah, and holding a predominant position at the great national fair of Okad, near Mecca.

Then came the marvellous successes of Mahomet, who by no means invented the idea of Allah as the one supreme

BEDOUIN FAMILY.

**Mahomet.** God, but developed what he already found growing among a few thinkers with whom he came in contact. In the few years between his flight to Medina in A.D. 622, and his death in 632, he had established his supremacy, and that of the religion known by his name, over all Arabia, except some portions which remained subject to Persia and to the Byzantine Greeks. When he died, he had inaugurated a Holy War against the surrounding countries, which was to be the keynote of Mahometanism, consolidating it at home by giving the Arabs a common object offering rich booty. They comparatively easily conquered the lands occupied by the Semitic peoples; but Persia and Egypt, offering more resistance, still further aided the strengthening of Mahometanism, until the Arabs and their subjects seemed about to gain a world-wide dominion.

**The Holy War.**

TYPES OF ARAB WOMEN.

At first Arabia prospered during the successes of the Caliphs, but after the Ommyads fell, A.D. 750, the country suffered greatly, for the new Abbaside Caliphs relied most on their non-Arab subjects, and the capital of the Moslem empire was removed from Damascus, close to Arabia, to Hashimeyah, on the Euphrates, and later to Bagdad. In the tenth century the Arabians generally revolted from the Caliphate. In 929 Mecca was stormed and the Kaaba ruined by Suleiman, the leader of

**Removal of the caliphate.**

the Karmathian Arabs, and Arabia relapsed almost into barbarism. No outside power has since then waged a war of conquest with Arabia, but the north-eastern corner, Oman, with the adjacent coast bordering on the Persian Gulf, became a semi-elective monarchy, the head of which takes the title of Imam. Yemen, the southern corner, was split up into a number of tribes like the central and eastern regions; while the Red Sea coast strip (the Hejaz), with the sacred territory of Mecca, under the headship of the shereefs or nobles, the descendants of the Koreysh, acknowledged more or less completely the headship of the Caliph of Bagdad, and later the Fatimite Caliphs who reigned in Egypt, and their successors in power, the Ottoman Sultans.

The most important movement of modern times in which the Arabs have been concerned has been that of the Wahhabees, so named from Abd-el-Wahhab (1691–1787), a great reformer, who opposed the invocation of saints, honouring the shrines of the dead, wearing silver and gold, using intoxicating drinks and tobacco, and roused the Arabs to animosity against the Turks and other foreigners whom he regarded as not true followers of Mahomet. Extending his influence, partly by persuasion, partly by force, Abd-el-Wahhab at his death saw his doctrines prevailing from the Persian Gulf to Mocha and Aden. Nejd had become united into one government, and the ruler took the titles of Imam and Sultan. Provinces south of Mecca and on the frontier of Yemen having been added to the Wahhabee dominions, the Shereef or governor of Mecca took alarm and obtained an army of Turks to attack the Wahhabee capital of Hasa (Hofhoof), on the Persian Gulf, which proved a futile expedition. The Wahhabees in turn took the offensive and stormed Kerbela, in the territory of Bagdad, in 1801, took Mecca in 1803, and Medina in 1804, and dictated to the Mahometan world the terms on which alone they could obtain access to the sacred places. In 1811 the Porte entrusted Mehemet Ali, the viceroy of Egypt, with the subjugation of the Wahhabees, which he accomplished after much diffi-

*Margin notes:* The Wahhabees. — Wars of conquest. — Mehemet Ali.

culty and with great cruelty. In 1812 Medina was taken, in 1818 Mecca was occupied, and in 1818 Arabia lay at the mercy of the conquerors. But a reaction ensued against the oppressive treatment of the Turks, and the Wahhabees have recovered their rule over a great part of Arabia, the exceptions being the following: the eastern kingdom of Oman, seated at Muscat, and the Hejaz (a large part of the Red Sea coast, Yemen (partially), and El-hasa, on the Persian Gulf, under Turkish rule. The Wahhabee kingdom itself is now split up, in consequence of the rise of the kingdom of Shammar, in the north and west of the Nejd.

**Present States.**

The Arabs of the present day are best divided into the Bedouins, or "dwellers in the open land," and the dwellers in towns and settled localities. The Bedouins live in tents in the vast extent of country between the coast districts and the central plateau, and are essentially shepherds and herdsmen, who migrate from spot to spot according to the abundance of grass and water for their flocks. Thus the disputes about the possession of wells, narrated in the Bible, still continue, leading to plunder in some cases, to want in others. Far removed from crowded haunts of men and control of regular authority, many peculiarities of behaviour and of government characterise the Bedouins.

**The Bedouins.**

In every clan, the sheikh, or elder, is paramount, and to him all disputes are referred. This position is not given for descent, age, or wealth, but for some more evident quality of leadership. Under the actual conditions of life, this mode of government suffices. "Much has been said and written," says Mr. Palgrave, "of the independence of the Bedouins, and of their having never submitted themselves to a foreign yoke; and prophecy has been called on to explain a fact which a little reflection would have shown to imply nothing marvellous or exceptional whatever, but to be merely the natural result of condition and circumstances. A nomad population, thinly scattered over a large and open space of meagre pasture-land, will always be unconquerable, because it offers next to nothing to conquer.

**The sheikhs.**

**Mode of life.**

When in camp, a Bedouin's tent consists of a few coverings of the coarsest goat-hair, dyed black, and spread over two or more small poles, in height from eight to nine feet, gipsy fashion. If it be the tent of a sheikh, or man of consequence, its total length may be from thirty to forty feet; if of an ordinary person, it will oftener fall short of twenty. Sometimes a partition separates the quarters allotted to the women and children; sometimes they are housed under a lower and narrower covering. A piece of rough carpet or an old mat may or may not be spread on the sandy floor; while camel-saddles, ropes, halters, and the like, constitute the entire furniture of the dwelling; ornament there is none. To the list two or three cauldrons for cooking, one or two platters, and a wooden drinking-bowl, must be added; and with these, including the master's arms in one side of the tent, and his spear stuck in the ground at the door, the household valuables are complete. When the time comes for moving, all these several articles are easily fastened in bundles on the backs of one or more camels; the men mount their saddles, the women their litters, and in an hour the blackened stones that served for a cooking hearth remain as almost the only sign where the encampment has been." See also Doughty's "Travels in Arabia Deserta," 1888.

Both men and women are rather undersized and slender, with dark complexions, in the south approaching that of the negro. The hair is abundant, coarse, and black, the beard less abundant, the nose aquiline; the eyes are dark, the features well formed. The Bedouins age rapidly, their skin becomes early wrinkled, and at forty the beard is grey, which accounts for the grey beard associated with the idea of a sheikh. But though not very muscular, the Bedouin, owing to his open-air life, is singularly healthy. In all the ordinary relations of life the Bedouin may be described as gentle, kind, affectionate, and sensible, with passions well under control, a lively imagination, and much unstudied eloquence, often expended in soliciting backsheesh when they come in contact with Europeans. They, however, are by no means generally truthful, are

**Physical characters.**

**Manners.**

restless and uncertain, envious, and not a little sensual.

The men wear long cotton shirts, open above, and frequently a girdle. Neither trousers nor turban are essentials of their costume, a mere handkerchief covering the head. A long wooden wand in his hand, and frequently sandals on the feet, complete the Bedouin's dress, except when a hair cloak is thrown over the shoulders. The women have somewhat similar garments, but are covered with a great mantle or wrapper from head to foot, which is almost closed over the face when strangers approach. Rings and bangles of glass, copper, or iron, sometimes of more precious metals, bead necklaces, rarely ear-rings and nose rings, form their personal adornment; but dress for purposes of attraction can scarcely be said to exist among the Arab women.

**Clothing.**

The nomads are guiltless of literature or writing, and hence know little of the Koran except by oral teaching; and many of them are only nominal Mahometans, and are little prone to go on pilgrimage. Even sun-worship and tree-worship still exist among the wilder tribes. Ordinary morality is not high among them. Marriage is a matter of purchase, settled by go-betweens; and divorce is not uncommon. His horse is more valued than his wife by the Arab; and the pure breed of the Nejd is still kept up, and almost entirely restricted to the central plateau. Although not of great size, nor of racing speed, "for perfection of form, symmetry of limb, cleanness of muscle, beauty of appearance for endurance of fatigue, for docility, and for speed maintained to distances so long as to appear incredible, the Nejdee horse has no equal" (Palgrave). The best horses are almost the exclusive property of the chiefs, and are used principally for war or parade. The camel is far more useful to the Arab, though less highly esteemed; and, in addition to services as a beast of burden, supplies the most frequent meat diet, as well as milk, and wool for articles of clothing. Sheep, goats, oxen, and asses form the remaining "stock" animals of Arabia.

**Arab horses and other animals.**

The settled Arabs have this much in contrast to the

nomads, whom they far outnumber, that they are attached to localities, and their clans have a strict relation to place. The descendants of the Koreysh, it is true, are widely spread, and rank everywhere as a nobility, with the title of shereef, and often act as governors. Sheiks exist in every village; emirs predominate over considerable districts; while the title of sultan is assumed by the rulers of Nejd, Oman, and some other tracts. Owing to much intermixture of population, the Northern Arabs and Eastern Arabs show considerable affinities to Persians and Hindus, the southern to the African negroes. Slaves are very common, and sheikhs often marry negro slaves. Very many slaves are emancipated at the end of seven years, if they adopt Mahometanism; and, once free, there is no prejudice against their rising to almost any position of which they are capable—sheikh, kadi, or judge, or even emir.

**The settled Arabs.**

**Slaves.**

The unruffled demeanour and serious behaviour of the Arabs have always excited remark. It is noteworthy how slight a hold games or playfulness of any kind have on them. Politeness is truly natural to them, but it often cloaks an extortionate and passionate spirit. Very great variety of complexion prevails among them, from nearly black, or mulatto in many parts, to a merely Italian swarthiness in the mountains of Yemen. The majority are a good deal taller than the Bedouins, and better made, although ophthalmia, due to the heat and the sandy soil, is frequent. From their abstemious habits they often reach extreme old age in good health.

Hospitality is a general virtue, though the central regions excel the coast provinces. Coffee, always roasted, pounded, and boiled freshly on each occasion, is invariably offered to a visitor in the settled parts, and indeed is drunk very frequently in the day, without milk or sugar. Wine is rare, but tobacco-smoking is universal, except where the Wahhabees rule. Arab cookery is very simple, the women not having much skill as cooks. Boiled meat (a luxury), millet-cakes, thin wheaten cakes, dates, and fruits are the chief foods. Washing after meals is always practised, and indeed the

**Hospitality.**

ARAB LADY OF BAGDAD.

settled Arabs are very cleanly, observing the ablutions prescribed by their religion with scrupulous care.

**Clothing.** Dress varies considerably. Drawers or trousers are not often worn, and the simplicity of dress of the Bedouins is frequent. In Hejaz and Yemen, under Turkish rule, trousers are worn, and a great sash round the waist; and the full turban is frequent, as also in Oman. Women in these provinces wear loose drawers or trousers, and some wear veils. Ornaments of gold and silver are abundant, and the hair is plaited in a long plait hanging down behind.

**Arab towns.** Arab towns and villages are always walled round, if only by a rampart of dried earth. The streets are irregular and tortuous, the houses seldom of more than two storeys, with flat mud roofs and little ornament. Shops are few and drainage does not exist, though the dryness of the air makes this less injurious than in other climates.

**Modern influence.** Whether the Arabs can regain their former wide influence may be doubted. Their philosophy and science were hardly their own product, having been mostly the work of others than natives of Arabia. At the present time they are producing important effects among the negro and Hamitic populations of Africa. Extreme fanaticism and fierce courage, jealous watchfulness of their trade-routes, and resolute maintenance of the slave trade, are the chief features of their dealings with other races.

**Holy places.** Mecca, with its great mosque, enclosing the Kaaba, or "Holy House," containing the meteorite fabled to have been given by God to Abraham, and Medina with the tomb of Mahomet, are the objects of multitudes of pilgrimages of believers, all others being jealously excluded. Sana, the capital of Yemen, Haïl, of the Shammar State, Riad, of the Wahhabee State, Muscat, of Oman, are all considerable towns; but Aden, occupied since 1838 by the English, is far more important commercially and politically.

# CHAPTER XXI.

## Distribution of Asiatic Races.

THE largest portion of Asia is inhabited by people of the Mongoloid race, as will be seen by the accompanying map, marked to show the localities inhabited by the principal races. The Malay Archipelago, inhabited chiefly by Malays, is included for convenience in this map. The Arabic numerals signify the following nations or peoples:—1. Ostiaks; 2. Kirghiz; 3. Koriaks; 4. Tungusians; 5. Kalmucks; 6. Usbegs; 7. Japanese; 8. Georgians; 9. Kurds; 10. Armenians; 11. Circassians; 12. Persians; 13. Hindus; 14. Dravidians; 15. Chinese; 16. Malays; 17. Negritos; 18. Arabs; 19. Turcomans; 20. Tibetans; 21. Siamese, etc.; 22. Dyaks.

The following table shows approximately the distribution of races in Asia:—

*THE CAUCASIANS,*

Or fair type of mankind, are largely represented in their principal groups.

ARYANS (ALSO TERMED INDO-EUROPEANS).

| | | |
|---|---|---|
| HINDUS:—The predominant race in India, though much mixed in some parts with Aboriginal (Dravidian) tribes, and partly also with Mongols. The majority profess Hinduism, but many are Mahometans. | Hindi (Central & North-western Provinces, Oudh, &c.) . . . | 100,000,000 |
| | Bengali (Bengal chiefly) . . | 40,000,000 |
| | Punjabi (Punjab, &c.) . . . | 17,000,000 |
| | Other Indian sections . . . | 34,000,000 |

| | | |
|---|---|---|
| AFGHANS:—Divided into numerous tribes, who are Mahometans in religion. | Including Pathans of N.W. India | 3,300,000 |

**ASIA.**

(The numbers on the Map indicate the regions inhabited by the different races and peoples.)

| | | |
|---|---|---|
| GREEKS:— | Asiatic Turkey and the Levant . . | 2,000,000 |
| SLAVS:—Modern immigrants and political exiles from Russia. | Russians and Poles (Siberia and Russian Turkestan) . | 6,500,000 |

| | | |
|---|---|---|
| TEUTONS:— | Settlers in India, China, &c., including Eurasians or half breeds with Hindus | 500,000 |
| | *Total* | 203,300,000 |

### IRANIANS.

Tall, bold, handsome people of South-west Asia; many of them formerly fire-worshippers, now mostly Mahometans.

| | |
|---|---|
| PERSIANS AND TAJIKS:—In Afghanistan and neighbouring countries . . . . . . | 6,300,000 |
| KURDS:—Kurdistan, Persia, &c., partly subject to Persia and Turkey . . . . . | 3,000,000 |
| BALUCHIS:—Baluchistan . . . . . . . . . | 300,000 |
| GALCHAS:—Afghanistan, Oxus Valley, and Hindoo Koosh Mountains . . . . | 500,000 |
| ARMENIANS:—Partly under Russia, mostly under Turkey, professing Christianity . | 4,000,000 |
| *Total* | 14,100,000 |

### CIRCASSIANS.

A group of many races with different languages and dialects, inhabitants of the Caucasus Provinces and Georgia.

| | |
|---|---|
| GEORGIANS, MINGRELIANS, AND CIRCASSIANS . . . . | 1,500,000 |
| LESGHIANS (Daghestan) . . . . . . . . . . | 500,000 |
| Other Groups . . . . . . . . . . . . | 300,000 |
| *Total* | 2,300,000 |

### SEMITES.

| | |
|---|---|
| ARAMÆANS:—Modern Syrians, including inhabitants of Holy Land and parts of Asia Minor | 2,250,000 |
| JEWS:—Widely distributed . . . . . . . | 200,000 |
| ARABS:—Arabia, Palestine, Asia Minor, Persia, India . | 8,000,000 |
| *Total* | 10,450,000 |

Asia is the great stronghold of the—

### *MONGOLOIDS.*

| | |
|---|---|
| CHINESE . . . . . . . . . . . . . | 390,000,000 |
| COREANS . . . . . . . . . . . . . | 10,500,000 |

| | | |
|---|---|---|
| **Japanese** | | 38,000,000 |
| **Annamese**:—Tonkin, Cochin China | | 20,000,000 |
| **Siamese**:—The Tai group, including the Laos (Buddhists) of Siam and the Shans of Burmah, &c. | | 5,000,000 |
| **Tibetans** (Buddhists) | | 4,000,000 |
| **Tibeto-Burmese**:—Including many aboriginal tribes of the Himalayas, Assam, and Burmah | | 8,700,000 |
| **Turki Group** (mostly Mahometans):— | Anatolian Turks—Asia Minor, &c. | 11,500,000 |
| | Usbegs—Bokhara, &c. | 2,000,000 |
| | Kirghiz—Independent Tartary & Russian Tartary | 3,000,000 |
| | Turcomans, &c.—Turkestan & Russian Empire | 3,000,000 |
| | Yakuts—Siberia (river Lena) | 200,000 |
| **Manchu Tartars** (Manchuria and China) | | 8,000,000 |
| **Kashgarians** (Kashgar, Central Asia) | | 750,000 |
| **Mongolians** (Central Asia) | | 3,000,000 |
| **Malays** (Malacca, &c.) | | 1,000,000 |
| **Buriats** and **Tunguses** (Siberia) | | 350,000 |
| **Finns** (**Samoyedes**, **Ostiaks**, &c.) | | 50,000 |
| | *Total* | 509,050,000 |

## THE AUSTRALOIDS,

A not very well defined group, include—

| | | |
|---|---|---|
| **Dravidians** (Southern India):—The Indian Coolies, very dark brown in complexion: mixed more or less with Aryan Hindus, but speaking distinct languages. | Tamil (Carnatic, Travancore, Mysore, North Ceylon) | 20,000,000 |
| | Telugu (Hyderabad, Mysore) | 16,000,000 |
| | Canarese (Mysore, Canara) | 10,000,000 |
| | Malayalim (Malabar) | 4,000,000 |
| | Others, including Hill Tribes | 3,000,000 |
| **Kolarians**:—Aboriginal Hill Tribes of India, chiefly in Central Provinces and Orissa, speaking a distinct group of languages. | Santhals (Orissa, Bengal)<br>Bhils (Vindhya Mountains)<br>Kol (Chota Nagpore) | 4,000,000 |
| | *Total* | 57,000,000 |

In addition to the above are the Ainos, the aboriginal hairy people of Japan, some of the Kurile Isles and part of the adjacent mainland, the Kamchadales, inhabiting Kamtschatka, the Koriaks and Tchukchi of Siberia, etc., which may perhaps all belong to a group of Palæ-Asiatics or primitive Asiatics, who have been driven North and East by the more successful Mongols, and now are but few in number. There are also a few thousand Negritos in the peninsula of Malacca.

Thus, of the nearly eight hundred millions of estimated inhabitants of Asia, one half are Chinese, and another hundred millions belong to closely related stocks. The races more akin to Europeans do not number 250 millions, and they include nearly all the main subdivisions of the Caucasians, or fair and dark whites. The precise relationship of the darker peoples in India who have descended from the aboriginal inhabitants has not yet been determined, and if we term them Australoids, that must only be taken as a provisional name. Some are of opinion that they are the mixed product of Negritos and lark whites.

THE END.